10 |06

THE WHISKEY REBELLION

George Washington, Alexander Hamilton,
and the Frontier Rebels Who Challenged
America's Newfound Sovereignty

WILLIAM HOGELAND

A LISA DREW BOOK

SCRIBNER
New York   London   Toronto   Sydney

A LISA DREW BOOK/SCRIBNER
1230 Avenue of the Americas
New York, NY 10020

SCRIBNER and design are trademarks of Macmillan Library Reference USA, Inc.,
used under license by Simon & Schuster, the publisher of this work.

A LISA DREW BOOK is a trademark of Simon & Schuster, Inc.

DESIGNED BY ERICH HOBBING

Text set in Adobe Caslon

Manufactured in the United States of America

ISBN-13: 978-0-7432-5490-8
ISBN-10: 0-7432-5490-2

to Gail

CONTENTS

Prologue: The President, the West, and the Rebellion   1

1. Over the Mountains   11
2. The Curse of Pulp   27
3. Spirits Distilled Within the United States   51
4. Herman Husband   71
5. The Neville Connection   97
6. Tom the Tinker   117
7. The Hills Give Light to the Vales   133
8. A New Sodom   161
9. Talking   185
10. The General Goes West   207
11. That So-Called Whiskey Rebellion   237

Notes   245
Sources   279
Acknowledgments   287
Index   291

FORKS of the OHIO
1794

N

ALLEGHENY R.

OHIO R.

PITTSBURGH
BRADDOCK'S FIELD

CHARTIERS CR.

MILLER HOUSE

BOWER HILL

COUCH'S FORT

TURTLE CR.

BRUSH CR.

FINDLEY'S HOUSE

PENNSYLVANIA

YOUGHIOGHENY R.

MINGO CHURCH

PARKINSON'S FERRY

B. PARKINSON HOUSE

TOWN OF WASHINGTON

PIGEON CR.

JACOB'S CR.

WELLS HOUSE

REDSTONE CR.

BROWNSVILLE

MONONGAHELA R.

UNIONTOWN

GALLATIN HOUSE

HUSBAND'S HOUSE

BEDFORD

ALLEGHENY MTNS.

TO CARLISLE AND PHILADELPHIA

MARYLAND

VIRGINIA

TO KENTUCKY

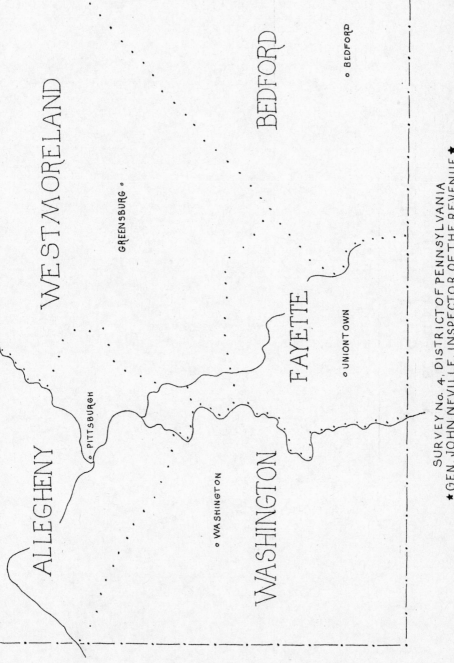

SURVEY No. 4, DISTRICT OF PENNSYLVANIA
★ GEN. JOHN NEVILLE, INSPECTOR OF THE REVENUE ★

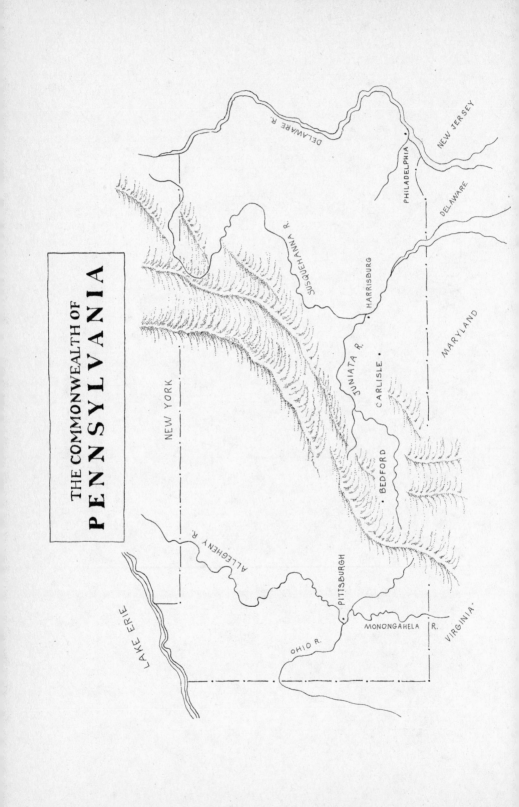

THE COMMONWEALTH OF
PENNSYLVANIA

LAKE ERIE

NEW YORK

ALLEGHENY R.

OHIO R.

PITTSBURGH

MONONGAHELA R.

VIRGINIA

BEDFORD

CARLISLE

JUNIATA R.

HARRISBURG

SUSQUEHANNA R.

MARYLAND

DELAWARE

PHILADELPHIA

NEW JERSEY

DELAWARE R.

THE WHISKEY REBELLION

The President, the West, and the Rebellion

President Washington was traveling home to Virginia in June of 1794 when he got hurt. He was sixteen months into his second term. He'd hoped to avoid serving it: at sixty-two, he had begun to feel irretrievably old. He kept catching low-grade, lingering fevers. His inflamed gums endured the pressure of tusk and hinged steel. Rifling through papers, he looked for proof of things people claimed he'd said, waving off polite reminders from subordinates who, the president could see, were shaken by pinholes in his memory.

He'd been embodying republican judgment for so long that what might have been oppressive requirements of office—audiences, dinners, dances, teas—seemed to come naturally. In black velvet or purple satin, his huge frame, still magnificently straight, could endow any occasion with serenity and seriousness, with grace. Yet what George Washington really had to do all day was apply his enormous capacity for administrative thoroughness to a pile of awful problems that grew more numerous all the time. They were problems of mere survival. The Royal Navy was seizing U.S. ships. The British Army declined to evacuate forts on U.S. soil. Indian wars brought terrible carnage and no progress. Washington had been harried, throughout his first term, by battles within his own cabinet: Secretary of State Thomas Jefferson and Secretary of the Treasury Alexander Hamilton undermined each other and, inevitably, Washington's efforts. Yet both men had been essential to him. Now Jefferson had quit to lead the nation's first opposition party. Hamilton, still in the cabinet, ever more essential, led the party in power. Of all dangers to the new nation, Washington was sure that party politics would be the deadliest.

So he was relieved to be able to get home at all this spring. The trip would be so brief that Mrs. Washington had remained in Philadelphia, and when traveling without her, Washington liked to push the pace, keeping the journey to five days. Yet the weather was hot, the horses out of shape, and presidential travel a production. The president's light, long-distance coach went bouncing over ruts, holes, and rocks. Up top sat the driver and a postilion, both in livery. Riding alongside was a secretary; on the other side a friend might ride as bodyguard. Some ways behind, the baggage wagon lumbered; behind the wagon stepped the president's saddle horse, led by a mounted slave. Overnight stops meant dinners, tours of friends' properties, ride-alongs, and side trips. And there was frequent communication with the office.

Washington didn't want rest. What he wanted, the only reason for taking this quick break, was to be working on Mount Vernon, his five farms on eight thousand acres. He'd been trying for most of his life to make Mount Vernon both a self-sufficient manor in the ancient Roman style and a source of wealth through the sale of produce. Such an estate would normally be ancestral home to a dynasty, but while his wife had borne her first husband four children, George Washington had none. On soil made almost barren by tobacco cultivation before he'd inherited it, he experimented with common crops like wheat and corn and with exotics like treebox, grapes, horse chestnuts, clover, and gourds. He'd planted five kinds of fruit trees. He'd spent years fighting the encroachment of waste by sprinkling plaster on soil, sowing oats and peas, searching in manure for what he called the first transmutation toward gold: fertility. He bred cattle, mules, hogs, sheep, and horses. Support came from smithies, charcoal burners, carpentry shops, mills, looms, cobblers, breweries, creameries, and a fishery. Voluminous accounts were kept separately for each farm, and more than three hundred people managed—most enslaved, many indentured, some free. At the foot of Mount Vernon's lawns, the product of all this hard-won fecundity was loaded from wharves onto boats in the Potomac.

Yet Washington always had great difficulty keeping the place on a paying basis. Each week in Philadelphia he sat at a desk and wrote his farm manager page after page of instructions, caveats, reminders, neatly hand-drawn crop-rotation tables and charts; each week he required an equally detailed report in response. He was sure his managers were incompetent, his workers selling butter on the side, his slaves lazy and poorly managed. Finally he couldn't stand it any longer. With the end of the congressional session, he pushed the cabinet to close executive business, snatched a few weeks from the nation, and started south to give Mount Vernon the personal attention it desperately needed.

After too many days on the road, almost home now, he decided on a quick side trip. He wanted to inspect the construction zone on tidal marshes known as the Great Columbian Federal City; one day it would bear his name. Touring the site, he could see the congressional building and the president's house, separated by bleak woods, still scaffolded, under construction. Those two buildings were all that suggested potential for civilization. Washington had been trying to whip up interest in land sales that were supposed to be funding the venture, but buyers were few, and it wasn't hard to understand why. The mall existed only on paper and included an open sluice for sewage. Most people saw this site as wet, buggy scrub.

What George Washington saw was a city that didn't struggle upward from necessity and convenience. Purpose-built, it would be a neoclassical commercial and political center, surrounded by manorial farms like his own, organizing agrarian bounty and financial savvy, the north and the south, Hamiltonians and Jeffersonians, in the wisdom and strength of central government. The city would serve as an embarkation point for products of the rich, fresh soil of the interior, barely tapped, yet already owned and controlled in massive tracts by George Washington, his fellow tidewater planters, and northern speculators. The western produce would tumble, one day, out of the mountains, ride down the Potomac, and be dispatched into the Chesapeake Bay and across the Atlantic for the markets of Europe. When that happened, both the Federal City and the president's huge landholdings in the west would assume enormous value.

There was an obstacle to realizing this dream, something he needed to look at, again, on this side trip. The Potomac, spreading as an estuary alongside the future capital city, then quietly passing Mount Vernon's lawns, seemed hospitably southern here near the bay. Follow it upstream, though—Washington had done so for the first time more than forty years earlier—and even before leaving civilization you came to white cataracts, sluices, drop-offs, rocky twists and turns; the river narrowed and became unnavigable. Above the fall line it leveled for a shallow stretch, then steepened again, regaining speed and fight. Arriving many days later at the highest springs, a good surveyor would be disappointed to note that in the western mountains the river simply petered out. Moving western produce eastward called for a road to the shore. The Potomac wasn't it.

The president knew the Potomac, and he knew the west. Near the crest of the Appalachians, where other streams rise, Washington the redhead colonial had panted his way up the most forbidding passes in the country. Among ice chunks in the raging Allegheny he'd swum for his life. He'd hauled chains and tripods; he'd led snooty superiors to places where, of white men, only he and his rough scouts had been before. He'd followed the streams that flowed down the other way and converged at the headwaters of the Ohio River, which cut southwest and poured at last into the Mississippi; he'd floated the Ohio looking for good land. What Washington had been puzzling over since his teens was how to make the tricky, east-flowing Potomac somehow navigable, then connect it—and thus connect Mount Vernon, and now his Federal City—by a high, wide road across the mountains, to the west-flowing Ohio, thence with the Mississippi, at last with the gulf. He was weaving a mental network that might pull divergent watersheds together, gathering up a continent's opposing forces, tilting the American west toward the eastern shore.

Yet lately he'd grown discouraged. After a lifetime of purchasing western tracts and attempting development, he found his far-off property still squatted on, his rents uncollected. Law in the west was disastrously incompetent. Mills needed constant repair yet never produced enough to make expenditures worthwhile. His land agents were passive. He'd started exploring the possibility of selling off his western lands.

It was a dream that would die hard. After taking a look at his Federal City-in-progress, the president, mounted now, turned not downstream toward home but upstream for a quick inspection of his most exciting east–west project, the canal works at the Potomac's lower falls. The young man's imaginings had long since been put busily into practice: he'd been made president of the Potomac Company long before becoming president of the United States. Here at the fall line, engineers were taking a standard approach. They diverted flow into trenches dug beside the river; wood-gated, stone-walled locks would float boats up steps. It was above the falls, in the second phase, where the great vision was projected. Washington and his business partners planned to avoid cutting waterways beside the river. They'd dig out the banks instead, take the fight out of the currents by widening the river, dispense with locks; they'd make a new Potomac, an interstate highway, level and calm, pursuing it into the mountains till defeated by the river's narrowing. Then phase three: the overland mountain road, which they imagined congested, someday, with wagons portaging goods eastward from the Ohio River.

The president's horse lurched. It lurched again. From the rocks above the lower falls, he'd been viewing the construction; the horse's feet were tender, the ground was hard, and suddenly the horse couldn't stop running and bucking. Washington was giving all he had to staying in the saddle and keeping himself and the horse from hurtling down the rocks into rushing water. When he succeeded at last in pulling the horse to a panting halt, his back was in such excruciating pain that he couldn't stay mounted.

He got down with difficulty, joined by his anxious party. Virginia gentry saw themselves as horse-tamers out of Homer. Washington was deemed the greatest rider of his age. Now he couldn't hoist himself into the saddle. With help, he did at last mount up, but the pain was paralyzing and getting worse. At Mount Vernon at last, but unable to stand, he lay around the house. Hands-on management required day-long gallops over miles of country. He was used to dismounting, taking off his coat, joining in the work. In battle, flying lead had torn holes in his clothes while men fell screaming around him, and when dysentery swept through the ranks, it had killed dozens while making him temporarily miserable. An often-told story placed him in the sights of a crack British rifleman, overwhelmed by the nobility of the target, who couldn't bring himself to shoot. It was amazing but true: never before, in a long and persistently dangerous career, had George Washington been injured. This damage to his back, he was told, would be with him the rest of his life.

Furious, he left Mount Vernon, having done nothing, riding back toward Philadelphia in a coach on what he'd been advised was the smoothest road. The road wasn't smooth. He sat rigid with pain, day after day, as the carriage bounced and swayed. Rain started falling, then pouring. The entourage slowed in the mud. He caught a bad cold. After seven days of misery he arrived at Philadelphia, planning to go straight to bed, but a party of Chickasaws, he was told, had arrived days earlier and patiently awaited a meeting with the president.

Washington went to dinner. He had world-famous posture; in the presence of Indians there was no question of reclining or even slouching. He sat up straight, smoking the peace pipe and exchanging polite remarks. He badly wanted to make another trip to Mount Vernon, somehow, as soon as possible.

What the president didn't know, as he forced himself upright for one more diplomatic dinner: attempts at federal law enforcement, over the mountains in his old Ohio River stomping grounds, had run into a kind of trouble the United States hadn't yet faced. He wouldn't return to Mount Vernon soon. The old general, with his wrenched and faulty back, would be leading troops again, making his last trip west.

The national crisis that came to be known as the Whiskey Rebellion, a scene of climactic moments in the lives of famous founders like George Washington and Alexander Hamilton, and in those of equally determined and idiosyncratic Americans whose names have been forgotten, began in the fall of 1791, when gangs on the western frontier started attacking collectors of the first federal tax on an American product, hard liquor. The attacks took lurid and, to contemporaries, familiar form. The attackers' faces were blackened; the victims were tortured and humiliated. Sometimes the gangs dressed as their own worst nightmare. Stripped to deerskin breeches, they streaked their chests and faces with herb-dyed clay and stuck feathers in their hair, imitating a native raiding party. Or they borrowed their wives' dresses. Black faces framed by white caps, they kicked the awkward skirts while confronting human prey.

Those attacks would develop, over the course of more than two years, into something far more frightening to eastern authorities than freakish rioting: a regional movement, centered at the headwaters of the Ohio in western Pennsylvania, dedicated to resisting federal authority west of the Alleghenies. In the fall of 1794, the rebellion would climax when President Washington raised thirteen thousand federal troops—more than had beaten the British at Yorktown—and led them over the Appalachians, where armed Americans were no longer petitioning for redress, or carrying out grotesque attacks on officers, but leading a secessionist insurgency against the United States of America.

The perpetrators were the toughest and hardest of westerners: farmers, laborers, hunters, and Indian fighters; most were disillusioned war veterans. Expert woodsmen and marksmen, adept not only in musket drill but also in rifle sharpshooting, they were organized in disciplined militias and comfortable with danger. The president's decision to suppress the rebellion, in which he deployed the first federal force of any significant size—and led it as commander in chief—became a test of the fragile new nation's viability, the biggest news of the day. Triggered by the tax on domestic whiskey, with which the prodigiously energetic Alexander Hamilton was realizing his visions of high finance and commercial empire, the rebellion brought to a climax an ongoing struggle not over taxation but over the meaning and purpose of the American Revolution itself.

That struggle had financial, political, and spiritual aspects. In the most literal sense it was about paying the revolution's debt. The whiskey rebels weren't against taxes. They were against what they called unequal taxation, which redistributed wealth to a few holders of federal bonds and kept small farms and businesses commercially paralyzed. Farmers and artisans, facing daily anxiety over debt foreclosure and tax imprisonment, feared becoming landless laborers, their businesses bought cheaply by the very men in whose mills and factories they would then be forced to toil. They saw resisting the whiskey tax as a last, desperate hope for justice in a decades-long fight over economic inequality. Alexander Hamilton and his allies, meanwhile, whose dreams had long been obstructed by ordinary people's tactics—crude, violent, sometimes effective—for influencing public finance policy, saw enforcing the whiskey tax as a way of resolving that fight in favor of a moneyed class with the power to spur industrial progress.

Problems facing rural people everywhere were amplified west of the Appalachians, and the whiskey tax, wreaking a special kind of havoc on westerners' lives, helped shape the national concept of the American west. Some of the whiskey rebels envisioned stranding the seaboard cities, vile pits of unrestrained greed, on the far side of the Appalachian ridge and leaving the coast a vestige. Some imagined a new west, spiritually redeemed, with perfect democratic and economic justice: small farmers, artisans, and laborers would thrive, while bankers, big landowners, and lawyers would be closely regulated, even suppressed. Believing they could wrest their country back from frontier merchants and creditors, their own neighbors, some rebels wanted to banish big businessmen as traitors to the region even while fending off the distant federal government in all its growing might.

The rebellion thus became a primal national drama that pitted President Washington and other eastern founders, along with their well-heeled frontier protégés and allies—all recent revolutionaries themselves—against western laborers with a radical vision of the American future. The rebellion also troubled the inner circle of the president's administration. Alexander Hamilton and George Washington brought to suppressing the rebellion a long-standing tension and a peculiar closeness, whose background was in the ambiguous wartime politics of the revolution. Edmund Randolph, the new secretary of state, urged the president to avoid the drastic, irreversible step of bringing military force against American citizens; he became the isolated cabinet moderate. Within the insurgency were moderates too, accused by the government of leading insurrection, yet in fact dissenting from their neighbors' extreme radicalism. Committed to peaceful petitioning, yet unable to control or direct the fury of their neighbors, western moderates faced danger from all sides as the rebellion and its suppression turned into outright conflict. By the time federal forces marched west, the Whiskey Rebellion was bathing all of its actors—founders and terrorists, extremists and moderates—in the stark light, not of an argument between genteel parties in Congress, but of a guerrilla war on the country's ragged margin, our first war for the American soul.

CHAPTER ONE

Over the Mountains

Hugh Henry Brackenridge was the most cultivated man in Pittsburgh, the village at the headwaters of the Ohio where he practiced law and worked on the great American novel. He'd trained for the ministry at the most advanced college in the colonies and immersed himself in the Enlightenment; he'd served in Pennsylvania's assembly, when it called a convention to ratify the United States Constitution, of which Mr. Brackenridge was a dedicated admirer. Though he enjoyed great local prominence—he'd helped found Pittsburgh's college and newspaper and lived, amid log buildings, in the biggest of the town's few brick mansions—a kind of relentless realism made him do and say things that disturbed his neighbors. Mr. Brackenridge's eyes, gazing with reserve while popping like a bird's, could make him look at once terrified and amused. And he was. The foolishness with which every class of neighbor confronted him every day could drive him, against his democratic will, to despair of human nature. The same realism could make him see his own despair as, in the end, nothing but comic. When in the early 1790s terror began to grip the countryside, comedy and realism began jostling so terribly within him that he feared, in the end, not only for his life but also for his reason.

He'd arrived at this strange attempt at a town in 1781, riding in from the east at the breakpoint age of thirty-three, saddlebags stuffed with law books. About four hundred people lived in Pittsburgh then, mostly in log houses nastily redolent of the dying flour and fur trades; the outlying country had a history of remoteness, almost a complete cutting-off from rolling hills, flat barrens, and seaboard cities back east across the Alleghenies. Ten years after Mr. Brackenridge's arrival, there were about a thousand residents—plus a quarry, mills, a boatyard, a pottery, and other industries—yet wildness still seemed to press against the town. Log and brick buildings lined earthen streets, often muddy, on the low point of land where the two rivers, pinching a point's tip, converged to become the Ohio and flow west. Along the south side ran the mud-floored Monongahela, up from Virginia in wide bends, seemingly lazy yet treacherous, recurrently flooding the point where a colonial fort had once inspired the first settlement. Across that river, a forested ridge swept up from the bank to look back on the village from a startling height. The ridge darkened the water with a greenish-brown reflection, a permanent shadow, tracking Monongahela mud ahead of the point into the Ohio. Green in summer, stark in winter, at night the ridge became a looming wall under the stars.

Turning away from the Monongahela, a few minutes' stroll across the village brought you to the Allegheny, a northern river flowing blue and crisp over granite from New York. Across the Allegheny was no forbidding barrier: hummocks and green hills rolled and flattened toward lakes Ontario and Erie. But all of that was Indian country, by tenuous treaty with the Six Nations of the Iroquois. It was from the south, and from behind that high ridge across the Monongahela, that white people came to town. They farmed the hollows and slopes of steep, wooded areas marked out by the Monongahela; its small tributaries, the Mingo and the Pigeon; a big tributary called the Youghiogheny—which the settlers called the "Yock"—and the Youghiogheny's own tributaries, the Sewickley, the Turtle, the Jacobs, and the Brush. Those rivers, which pooled through woods and dropped over granite, had made chaotically ridged and tilting land with deep, narrow valleys. Sweeping down from heights and up from the south and becoming, at Pittsburgh, the flat Ohio, the creeks and rivers were also, by the 1790s, powering ironworks, brickworks, and commercial mills.

There was new business to do, and when people came to Pittsburgh to do it, they arrived on the high ridge and were presented with a bird's-eye vista. The Ohio, segmented in flashing glints by rows of hazily violet hills, curled northward before making its big southwestern turn. People rode down the steep slope to the waterfront, busy in the 1790s with flatboats and keelboats, to ford or be ferried to the little town on the point.

Despite the remoteness, and because of it, white people had been attracted to the region for a long time. They'd violated royal proclamations preserving this land for Indians. They'd disregarded rules of the provinces of Pennsylvania and Virginia. They'd raided and been raided by Delaware and Shawnee, who were resettled in the area by the Six Nations empire, which also maintained here its own emissaries and governors. Building a town at the Ohio headwaters was never in anyone's official plans. The Six Nations had thought of the area as a reserve for hunting, fur trading, military adventures with armies of European allies, and resettlement of native peoples conquered and depopulated elsewhere—emphatically not a good place for white people to be digging into and settling down on. As late as the 1750s, the only whites legitimately in the region, which became known as the Forks of the Ohio, were traders, who didn't build. Traders, considered reprobate by the competing companies and governments—French, British, and provincial—who invested in them, moved through, buying pelts from and selling European goods to Indians. For years Indian market centers boomed while the only structures of whites were storehouses and camps.

When Virginia and Britain began sponsoring settlement companies at the Forks of the Ohio, the young Virginia militia commander George Washington killed a French emissary just south of the Forks and was forced to surrender and apologize. The Seven Years' War began. That near-global conflict among imperial powers of Europe involved the natives too. The earliest white authority at the Forks wasn't a province, state, or other civic entity. The far-flung British Army, stationed at a wilderness outpost they called Fort Pitt, commanded the strategic point where the Monongahela and the

Allegheny met. When the British started building the fort, the French took it; trying to retake the area, most of a force led by British General Braddock and his young colonial sidekick Washington were slaughtered by French and Shawnee forces. After the British did take back the point in 1758, the officers tolerated and tried in vain to regulate a scrubby set of huts, legally part of no town or province, clinging to Fort Pitt's walls as a kind of supply-and-support system for imperial soldiers. This poorly defined set of relationships would become Pittsburgh.

Even to British officers and men, the settlers seemed shockingly tough and bold. When the army adopted a policy of selling arms to Indians, a local militia turned fearlessly on the army. Men blackened their faces and dressed like Indians, ambushing drovers who moved arms and supplies on lonely tracks; the "blacks," as they were known, stole army rum, whiskey, and arms and set supplies on fire. They captured officers, forcing them to resign and imposing local rules to keep witnesses from testifying and juries from convicting. When suspects were scheduled to be taken out of the area for trial—trying suspects outside their neighborhoods was considered, in common law, the most heinous abuse of power—the blacks made dashing rescues. There were calmer times too. Bored troops made sorties to clear out illegal settlements, which kept springing up amid what eastern visitors perceived as the horror and gloom of the forest primeval.

In 1763, the king drew, by royal proclamation, a line at the crest of the Appalachians, reserving lands to its west for Indians, prohibiting new white settlements there, and ending existing ones. Whites stayed anyway. Leading defiant, subsistence lives, they were considered as savage as Indians by soldiers at Fort Pitt and by authorities in the east and in England. Where General Braddock had been defeated, children played around his soldiers' bloated, half-eaten bodies and bones, thickly piled on the field and growing over with grass. Commanders at the desolate river outpost kept trying to control the squatters, trappers, legal and illegal fur traders, and hangers-on who surrounded their fort, but a town subject to no civic authority was growing; outlying villages on rivers and streams were growing too.

When a treaty authorized a purchase of the Forks area from the Indians, for the province of Pennsylvania, the region theoretically became subject to provincial, not just military, authority. But people went on living as they'd always lived, in part because Pennsylvania and Virginia both claimed the region. New settlers were coming from the south and the east, many known as Scots-Irish, as indeed earlier settlers had also been: these were the notably tough descendants of Protestant Scots peasantry, who had resettled in Ulster and then been forced, by exorbitant rents and English taxes, to migrate to North America. Absentee speculators too started registering claims and buying large acreages. Pennsylvania erected counties; Virginia opened land offices for the same area, undercutting Pennsylvania's prices, asymmetrically laying its own counties over Pennsylvania's. The area had recently been barely governed and officially unsettled. Suddenly comparatively crowded, it was now being subjected to the authorities of two governments, which tried to collect taxes and issued competing titles to former squatters and absentee speculators at once. Having two governments was tantamount to having none. Some people did feel loyalty to one province or the other: Virginia and Pennsylvania militias fought skirmishes that verged on outright war. But many people were eager to remain oblivious to the supposed requirements of either province. The very idea of authority seemed, to some settlers at the Forks, merely annoying. The British soldiers meanwhile marched away. Fort Pitt, though used in the border war, deteriorated.

When the revolution came, it meant long service far from home for people at the Forks, as well as the devastation of their settlements by British-allied Indians and militias from Canada: Towns were burned, prisoners taken, people killed; often whole neighborhoods abandoned homes and sheltered in stockades. The idea of independence had long had special meaning to Forks settlers. As early as 1771, formal associations of squatters were escorting Pennsylvania's provincial deputies out of the area with orders never to come west again. In 1776, with the breakdown of all royal and provincial authority, a regional independence movement began to flourish not only among people at the Forks but also among settlers all along the frontier. Watauga, a settlement high in the western mountains claimed by North Carolina, heard rumors of conflicts between the colonies and Great Britain, declared independence, and asked to be legitimized as part of North Carolina, which already had title to the area and didn't want people living there. Denied representation in North Carolina, the Wataugans named the three western counties of North Carolina the independent state of Franklin, which drew up a constitution and applied to the Congress as a separate state, to no avail. Franklin would soon look to the Spanish across the Ohio for help. Vermont—which also named itself, declared its independence, and drew up a constitution—petitioned Congress for statehood; rejected, it considered an alliance with Great Britain. And at the Forks of the Ohio, still fought over by Pennsylvania and Virginia, some people started calling the place Westsylvania.

By the time Mr. Brackenridge arrived in Pittsburgh in 1781, the Westsylvanians had a constitution too; they planned to secede from Pennsylvania. They were organizing marksmen. If Congress rejected them, there was talk of going to Britain or Spain.

Mr. Brackenridge's first project was to put a stop to new-state and secessionist talk. He was that rare thing, both a western sympathizer and a nationalist. When he arrived in Pittsburgh, he hoped for a national government, but he was no stranger to the high regard for regional independence held by westward migrants. In the 1750s, when he was five, the Brackenridges fled rural poverty in Scotland and arrived on the busy Philadelphia docks. They started walking west, through settled farmlands and rolling hills. The dirt road became a track through dark, high thickets. Arriving at the small plot they'd bought, in a Scots settlement in the barrens of York County, then on the western edge of the province's white settlement, they began to cut the huge hardwoods and vines and break into tough, poor soil.

The growing boy never liked hard labor. He'd plow all day, then read by the firelight. Once a cow made him distraught by chewing up his copy of Horace.

Yet he wasn't considered unduly effete. Scots immigrants in the York barrens respected Greek, Latin, and learning. He got his classical education by studying with a local scholar. His mother delightedly envisioned him a Presbyterian minister of the gospel, and at the College of New Jersey at Princeton, he did train for the ministry, but like so many Princetonians of his day, he also came under the influence of Dr. Witherspoon, the college president, who was introducing his charges to modern French and Scottish philosophers. Visions of an enlightened classical republic fired members of the self-styled Whig Literary Club, ambitious young-sters like Brackenridge and James Madison, who wrote and declaimed broad, self-congratulatory satires in a manner that, they thought, combined the best of Cervantes, Swift, and Lucian.

In 1779, with war far from over, the British abandoned Philadel-phia, and Mr. Brackenridge went there to live. His plan was to start a newspaper for the United States. Though he'd been ordained a minister, he'd long since taken up the rationalism of the philosophers and wits, and when revolution came, he had written a verse drama to celebrate the Battle of Bunker Hill, then gained a post in the army of General Washington himself. The post was as chaplain. Mr. Brackenridge's preaching consisted solely of independence agitprop. He wanted his Philadelphia paper to extend that spirit. The defin-ing cultural organ for an emerging nation, it would blast Tories and glorify both independence and rationalism, in the process founding a distinctively American literature and earning Mr. Brackenridge honor and a good living as that literature's chief author.

But wartime Philadelphia was already crowded with intellect and politics. Three years earlier, independence had been declared there; now the Congress was coming back, and some of those men were giants. In Philadelphia, Hugh Henry Brackenridge was hardly the most cultivated man, or even the most ambitious.

He may have been the most realistic. After only a year, his paper a failure, he assessed his position and came to the conclusion that he had no chance of becoming anything in Philadelphia. He was disappointed in the quality of the American mind, which had failed to respond to his paper; he needed to make his name elsewhere, he decided, and then come back. The western frontier had moved since his hard childhood in the barrens. Across the Allegheny watershed, he reasoned, he might distinguish himself.

He turned out to be right about that. Hugh Henry Brackenridge's ideas about western development, like his ideas about most things, struck people in his new home in Pittsburgh as odd. He was like them mainly in not being able to stand Indians. Romantics back in Philadelphia, full of ideas cribbed from Rousseau, went on and on about natives' natural nobility, but Mr. Brackenridge enjoyed telling of a philosophical botanist, visiting from France, who made impassioned pro-savage speeches and ended up scalped. Mr. Brackenridge had interviewed survivors of an ingenious, slow-burning murder practiced by the Shawnee, whose naked victims, bound to the stake, begged to be shot; as a boy in York he'd lived with the night terrors of the French and Indian War, when babies' limbs were sliced off while their mothers were forced to watch, the babies' brains dashed out, the mothers then scalped and killed. Most absurd to him was the idea that natives' prior occupation of the land gave them a current right to it. Why couldn't the buffalo make the same claim against the Indians, since they were here before the Indians, and whatever was here before the buffalo against the buffalo, and so forth? Indians didn't improve land, and right to land, for Mr. Brackenridge, came from improvement. He wasn't in favor of slaughtering Indians. He wanted Indians permanently subdued, then absorbed, to whatever extent possible, in the new American culture.

His neighbors agreed with him about Indians' savagery. So his taking the case of an Indian accused of murdering a white man seemed nothing but perfect contrariness. Mr. Brackenridge's usual description of Indians as murderous drunks couldn't have been better embodied than by his client, Mamachtaga, charged with killing a white man *while* drunk, a charge that the defendant couldn't and didn't deny. Mr. Brackenridge's view was that if the savages were ever to be converted to civilized ways, their legal rights had to be protected. There were mitigating circumstances in Mamachtaga's case, and the lawyer was fascinated, during trial, by Mamachtaga's declining to take refuge in them.

The lawyer lost the case. His client, refusing an easy chance to escape, was hanged. Aside from the beaver furs in which he was paid, Mr. Brackenridge gained only the bewilderment of the people at the Forks of the Ohio. Yet he continued to puzzle over Mamachtaga. The name translated as "trees blown around by a storm." The Indian was at once too depraved and too honest, Mr. Brackenridge concluded, to live in either white or savage society. He'd been shunned even by his own tribe.

While shocking both rich and poor by defending an Indian, Mr. Brackenridge was selectively annoying the rich with another specialty: defending squatters. Tiny illegal farms—a log shack or two, some skinny livestock, and stumpy fields—might be surrounded by miles of timber, standing and fallen on slopes barely penetrable for vines and laurel thicket. Squatters' farms were hard to find, yet when land agents sent word to eastern speculators that their property was being used at will, the landlords sent sheriffs into the woods, and sometimes squatters were rounded up and evicted. Mr. Brackenridge's view was that eastern speculators were just like Indians— indolent, unimproving. Most owners hadn't set eyes on their lands. They rented lots cheaply to tenants, who did the hard work of clearing. Owners hoped, once lands were cleared and Indian problems straightened out, to raise rents sharply or sell at huge profits to later speculators. Mr. Brackenridge insisted that it was good policy to encourage not idle people from far away but hard workers who lived at the Forks. He lost a lot of squatters' cases too.

The maddening irony was that these small-scale farmers he kept touting as the future of the west thought of him as an Indian lover, and he might have done better with the farmers if he hadn't also sometimes taken the cases of rich landlords, who needed his legal services too, but regarded him as a crank. Mr. Brackenridge kept professing belief in republican democracy, in what his college friend James Madison famously called the genius of the people. Genius, meaning creative spirit, was something the whole people might indeed possess. Yet individual people, rich and poor alike, kept forcing on Mr. Brackenridge the impression that they'd never be repositories of wisdom. He always found it at once awful and hilarious that for all his education and prominence, which nobody ever denied, nobody ever got the point of what he was doing or saying.

One night in early September of 1791, Robert Johnson, recently appointed collector of the federal revenue for Washington and Allegheny counties in far western Pennsylvania, was riding through a lonely part of the forest near a tributary of the Monongahela called Pigeon Creek, when he found his way blocked by men who forced him to dismount. The gang numbered fifteen to twenty, armed with muskets, rifles, and clubs. They were blackfaced. Many wore women's dresses.

Johnson was amiable but dim. A sharper person might not have been surprised to be confronted, in an isolated part of the forest, by these all-round hunters, militiamen, woodsmen, and laborers, flamboyantly disguised and as hard as men can be. The tax that Johnson had been hired to collect was on distilled liquor, the first tax ever levied by the United States on a domestic product. Only two weeks earlier, a meeting in the nearby town of Washington had adopted a resolution spelling out what ought to be done with people like Johnson, and the resolution had been published in the *Pittsburgh Gazette*. The tax, the Washington committee complained, advancing a radical social idea, didn't operate in proportion to property. So as far as the committee was concerned, federal tax officers were to be considered not just silly lowlifes (tax collectors were assumed to be that) but also public enemies. All decent people should refuse these officers aid and cooperation and treat them with contempt.

Tonight the gang in dresses set about treating Robert Johnson with contempt. Their procedure, for all the whiskey drinking and hilarity that usually attended such an adventure, was far from improvised. When the object was ritual humiliation, not torture, a gentler version was favored, in which a victim was left clothed, but that wasn't the idea tonight. Soon Robert Johnson was naked. With sharp blades the men cut his hair to bare his skull. On flesh, hot tar not only inflicts pain but also can sear. Pores close, and skin, orifices, and genitals can suffer permanent injury.

Johnson may have been stupid, but despite abject terror, flickering firelight, and crazy disguise, he was noting the identities of some of his attackers. Collectors weren't emissaries from the east but local hires; the job paid a percentage of what collectors took from their neighbors. He saw that one of his attackers was Daniel Hamilton, a memorably tough member of the large, generally well-regarded Hamilton family. Loose-knit, both closely and distantly interconnected, with generations that overlapped in age, and roots in Pennsylvania's Scots settlement back in York, the Hamiltons now lived around Mingo Creek, not far from the town of Washington. The most prominent among them was probably John Hamilton, commander of a regiment of state militia and soon to be the county's high sheriff. John Hamilton enjoyed the kind of success, as a self-made, well-to-do farmer and businessman, that many people in the area were finding it harder and harder to achieve. He was here too, Johnson noted.

Daniel Hamilton hadn't done so well. At forty, he was charismatic and risk-seeking, with combat experience in the revolution and a strong sense of his own power to intimidate. His life had been going wrong. People like Daniel, when asked where they lived or how to get somewhere, tended to orient and identify themselves by creeks and rivers. The Mingo Creek area was a four-county hub: The rivers divided the area in discrete sections; along the rivers were strung boatworks, mills, tanneries, iron furnaces, and artisan shops. Eastern visitors, overawed by mountain outcroppings and virgin timber, could mistake this area for howling wilderness and miss the fact that it was also a complex of neighborhoods and industries. Daniel Hamilton and the other gang members were farmers and hunters, mainly for subsistence and seasonally for barter, sometimes for cash: they grew corn, wheat, barley, rye, ginseng, hemp, flax, and vegetables. Famous sharpshooters, they used muskets and rifles to kill rabbits, bears, deer, squirrels, and birds. But they had industrial skills too: tanning hides, working iron, sawing wood, milling grain, and making bricks, saddles, hats, nails, and boats. Many had the talent, ambition, and skill to make money, by moving and distributing their food and wares, selling them to the army and to buyers across the mountains to the east. If their federal government could get them access to the Spanish-controlled Mississippi, there were huge, untapped markets in the other direction too.

Yet many of these river industries were no longer owned and operated by the settlers themselves. Men labored more and more often in the mills and yards of rich entrepreneurs and merchants. An ironworks could employ dozens of men while its owner bought up thousands of foreclosed acres recently owned by his laborers. The rivers had become roads for moving products into the Ohio to supply Indian-country forts downriver. Hired men loaded keelboats with milled grain, fodder, ammunition, tar, and horseshoes and steered the boats through tricky Ohio currents, then applied unrelenting muscle to poling and hauling the boats back up to town. Even many who engaged in farmwork no longer owned their own land; they'd become tenants of large landowners and hired hands of commercial farmers.

Daniel Hamilton had once owned 240 acres. Soon he'd own only 100, and in a few years all of his land would be gone. That these losses were being sustained by a disappointed war veteran made Daniel no different from many others at this tar and feathering; older settlers had even served under harsh British officers in the Seven Years' War. The War of Independence had meant hard marches to faraway places, leaving families unprotected from hideous torture and slaughter by British-allied Indians. When the war ended at last, these men had mustered out of the army virtually unpaid.

Daniel was typical; still he stood out. To moments like this tar and feathering he brought a degree of enthusiasm that people remembered. There was a chilling edge of delight in his rendition of the Indian war whoop. He had no compunction about putting his hands on weaker men and seeing them shake, and he could rattle off terrifying descriptions of what his victims would soon be suffering. Made incandescent by loss and betrayal, Daniel Hamilton was focusing his enthusiasm for violence on a belief, shared with his fellows, that wrongdoing could be overawed by terrifying displays of physical punishment.

As Daniel and the gang applied hot, noxiously fuming tar to the shaved pate and nude body of Robert Johnson, the sludge's oiliness was absorbed by Johnson's skin, and a scalding crust grabbed hair, holes, and pores and clung everywhere. When Johnson was sufficiently sticky the gang applied poultry feathers, which, when shaken over a freshly tarred victim, or when he was made to lie down and roll in them, bonded with the slowly hardening blackness and could be removed only with time and effort. The triumphant gang took Johnson's horse and fled. Anguished by the scorn due all public enemies, the taxman was left alone in the dark forest.

The next day, Mr. Brackenridge attended a meeting in Pittsburgh. It was September 7, 1791, the second day of a three-day conference at the Sign of the Green Tree, a tavern on the Monongahela waterfront. The conference had been called to discuss local feeling against the federal whiskey tax and other policies of the new federal government. Angry talk by men like Daniel Hamilton and his cohort, at militia musters, taverns, and impromptu meetings, had inspired a self-appointed committee of prominent men to meet during the summer at a town called Brownsville, down the Monongahela. The Brownsville meeting had proposed that each township in the four western counties—Fayette, Westmoreland, Allegheny, and Washington—formally elect delegates for county conventions, which in turn would send county representatives to this meeting at the Sign of the Green Tree.

The meeting's agenda wasn't to attack anyone. These men were leaders at the Forks; many had experience in and hopes for elective office in the state and federal governments. Now they had a message from their constituents: the previous night's treatment of Robert Johnson. He'd been left clothed tightly in nothing but pitch and feathers. He had no transportation. Praying for a quick death was the only alternative to an immediate, unforgiving need: start walking your naked, disfigured body along the track. Your goal would be to present your awful condition to someone. You'd have to be seen in this sorriest of states, and that's what would make the operation a success. Johnson did somehow make it home. A scouring mixture of grease, soap, and sand finally removed tar and feathers. He would soon swear out a complaint, in which he would bring the names of Daniel Hamilton and others he'd recognized to the attention of the federal government.

What most of the prominent men at the Sign of the Green Tree wanted to do was send a petition, explaining the negative local effects of the whiskey tax, to the Pennsylvania assembly at the statehouse in Philadelphia and to the U.S. House of Representatives, also in Philadelphia. Not all of these men were so moderate, however. One was John Hamilton, the prominent and well-off Hamilton, colonel of a regiment of Mingo Creek militia and a tar-and-featherer of Johnson the night before. Many attendees didn't know one another; no love was lost among some who did. David Bradford, a rich man from the town of Washington, had successfully invaded Mr. Brackenridge's law practice, partly by suggesting, to Mr. Brackenridge's indignation, that the Pittsburgher had no natural sympathy with common people. Bradford had the fanciest house in the town of Washington, but he'd attended the radical Washington County meeting, and for all his wealth he'd long been engaging in populist actions. At the other extreme was an even bitterer professional enemy of Mr. Brackenridge, the lawyer John Woods, a member of the little Pittsburgh elite that scorned Mr. Brackenridge for defending squatters and was sewing up army trade and monopolizing land and business throughout the area. Woods's friends favored federal policies, including taxes; Woods was clearly here as a spy.

Mr. Brackenridge had been asked to bring an opening address.

He'd also brought some resolutions for debate. He planned to make the speech, introduce the resolutions, then stay aloof. As he rose to speak to the Green Tree meeting, he made his first move in what would become, as events outran his ability to repair them, a persistent, ultimately impossible task: imposing reason on the unreason that seemed to proliferate on every side.

Though he could not now imagine the madness toward which the next three years would drive him, Mr. Brackenridge had been given a glimpse of things to come when, on his first journey to his new home over the mountains, he'd stopped for the night with an old man who lived above an Allegheny valley known as the Glades. The man was white-haired and disheveled. He lived in a small house on a farm that he and his grown sons had cleared more than a decade earlier, when no other white people had settled in these mountains.

This was Herman Husband, also known as the Philosopher of the Allegheny, as the Quaker, as Hutrim Hutrim, and as Tuscape Death. Looking at him, Mr. Brackenridge might not have guessed that Husband had been raised the pampered scion of colonial tidewater gentility, had made a fortune in business, and was an autodidact of profound if spotty learning. The lawyer did know that Husband had come into these mountains as a fugitive wanted by the royal governor of North Carolina for violent agitation on behalf of farmers against provincial authorities. Husband had also been elected to the revolutionary Pennsylvania assembly. Mr. Brackenridge's main impression was of a loony old man.

The impression was confirmed when Husband, pleased to have educated company, showed Mr. Brackenridge some maps of the area that Husband had drawn up himself. Apparently he'd spent many hours—years, really—bushwhacking the almost impassable ridges and the deepest valleys, and he'd come to believe that the Alleghenies were one of the walls of the New Jerusalem of biblical prophecy. Husband was a draftsman. As he showed his guest the maps, beautifully detailed and plotted to scale, with neat notes, symbols, and keys, he pointed out connections between the geological features of the mountains and passages in the books of Daniel and Ezekiel.

Listening, Mr. Brackenridge achieved the command of himself that he often tried for but could so rarely sustain. He gave a perfect imitation of a man struck with fascination by the brilliance of what he was hearing. His certainty, now, that he was in the presence of a madman he concealed by asking pertinent questions that showed depths of understanding. Husband was moved. Nobody other than Mrs. Husband, he told Mr. Brackenridge, had understood what he was saying about these things. While nodding sympathetically at the insensitivity of the world, Mr. Brackenridge made a mental note that Husband's church, like many others, was made up of two classes of people, the lying—Mr. Brackenridge himself—and the stupid, which Husband had just proven his wife to be. Then he went on drawing Husband out.

That night, when he was thirty-three, Hugh Henry Brackenridge hadn't yet seen the town that would become the home he'd love and deride. He couldn't imagine that one day he'd be a wanted man, named with this Herman Husband, stalked by soldiers as ringleader of a rebellion against a United States of America that, as they talked in the firelight of the visions of Daniel, did not yet exist, and for whose founding Mr. Brackenridge only hoped. If he could have imagined what lay ahead, his eyes might have relayed their characteristic blend of terror and humor. He might have laughed outright, and he might have turned back for a life of obscurity in Philadelphia.

CHAPTER TWO

The Curse of Pulp

The law that both the blackfaced gang in dresses and the politicians at the Sign of the Green Tree wanted repealed, or at least adjusted, was entitled "An Act Repealing, after the Last Day of June Next, the Duties Heretofore Laid upon Distilled Spirits Imported from Abroad, and Laying Others in their Stead, and Also upon Spirits Distilled within the United States and for Appropriating the Same." Passed by the first Congress of the United States in March of 1791, part of that cumbersomely named act—"and Also upon Spirits Distilled within the United States"—heralded something new, the first federal tax on an American product.

Excises, as such duties—laid not on imports but on domestic products—were commonly called, had long caused lamentation where rights and liberties sacred to Englishmen were worshiped. Because excises had traditionally been attended by summary arrests and denial of jury trials, aristocratic literature condemned all excises as nasty attempts by crown and ministry to shift the economy from its only legitimate basis, land, associated by landowners with aboriginal English freedoms, to grubby ones like manufacture and slimy ones like finance, associated by landowners with decadence and tyranny. It was an irony of English politics that this rhetorical abomination of excise had long enabled alliances between landowners and merchants, groups whose real interests were often at odds. Colonial Americans had forged just such an alliance, drawing on familiar antiexcise themes and condemning the Stamp Act as an arbitrary internal tax. With independence won, a U.S. Congress's imposing hated excise would seem, to some, the ultimate in ideological betrayal.

Others saw things differently. American merchants and financiers might employ the poetry of English rights when resisting England, but they preferred a critique of power and law when it came to making policies for their own nation. A tax might represent good or bad policy, or benefit one interest or another, but how can a fundamental evil arise from a tax's operating internally, not externally? It was easy to see a federal excise on whiskey as an innocuous luxury tax, easily passed on by distillers to drinkers, surely nothing to tar and feather anyone over.

What people in the western backcountry recognized, and most Congressmen lacked the expertise to understand, were mechanisms embedded in the tax for keeping wealth in the hands of a few while denying western laborers and small farmers their last, slim chances for economic opportunity. The Daniel Hamilton gang that attacked Robert Johnson was less concerned that the whiskey tax could be classified an excise, so offensive to genteel libertarians, than that it worked on laboring people at the Forks of the Ohio in a particular way. Those whom the tax disabled, as well as its author Alexander Hamilton, knew that in getting the act passed, Hamilton was dropping a very smart bomb on a target he'd been softening for years. The secretary of the treasury was celebrating a victory, which some at the Forks had every intention of cutting short, in a long struggle over nothing less than the power of money in the lives of the American people.

Alexander Hamilton had first taken up that struggle at twenty-seven, when, having completed active service in the Continental Army, he came to the confederation Congress late in 1782 as a delegate appointed by the New York legislature. Though dauntlessly self-creating and experimental, Hamilton liked ledgers, balances, and order. Born on a Caribbean island, abandoned by his drunken Scottish father, soon bereaved of his beautiful, French-speaking mother, he'd started clerking in an office on the St. Croix docks before he was fifteen. When his boss went to New York, Hamilton, barely seventeen, took command of the office and bore down on those who owed the company money. Wishing for war, the youth was also writing poetry and reading widely, a romantic who longed to distinguish himself in combat and love. He was charismatic and obviously brilliant and people took him up. He was helped to emigrate to New York and matriculate at Columbia, where he made up for his lack of education by digesting classical and modern authors, pacing beside the Hudson to memorize Latin and Greek and compose his essays. The war he'd longed for came on cue. Still in his teens, he published impassioned attacks on British oppression and rationales for American independence. He so distinguished himself as an artillery captain on Harlem Heights, where he took charge of building an earthworks, and then in battles in New Jersey, that he was invited to join General Washington's staff, of which he quickly became de facto chief.

For all his obduracy in business, war, and politics, verbal fluidity gave Hamilton startling charm, almost a kind of femininity. He was small and stylish, proud of the notable length of his nose and the penetration of his intellect; he had violet eyes and striking physical grace. Long renowned as a dashing ladies' man, he married into the patrician Schuyler family of New York. As war neared its end, he led a light-infantry battalion that acquitted itself with distinction at the climactic battle of Yorktown. He went to Congress a self-taught student of finance who knew more about the subject than almost anyone else in government. He brought from the military a love of hierarchy and combat.

As a delegate, Hamilton discovered a new kind of combat that engaged his highest yearnings. It devolved on a repository of hopes and anxieties known as the war debt. Some of the debt was owed to foreign countries, but the debt to American investors, which lay at the heart of the drama, and to which Hamilton would one day dedicate the whiskey tax, took the form of a welter of notes, interest-bearing and otherwise, issued on chaotically overlapping bases by the Congress and various state legislatures to raise cash for the war.

The most exciting notes—beautifully engraved federal certificates paying 6 percent interest—were held by a small group of money-men, the sort who had embraced young Hamilton in New York's first families.

Those creditors kept reminding Congress that their investment in the war had been patriotic and should be rewarded as such. But their patriotism had a special relationship to their investing, which gave Hamilton a real-life crucible in which to test his book knowledge of the purposes and mechanics of taxation. Back in '76, when Washington's army was being butchered in Brooklyn, and the Congress had first floated bonds to raise cash for supplying wet, hungry men, those same financiers had yawned. Congress had been offering a paltry 4 percent interest. Congress dangled 6 percent. Still nothing. Then Congress offered to pay the 6 percent in a far more attractive medium than the paper currency it was issuing. Paper wasn't money; though often issued by various colonies, because cash was often scarce, it had value only in a generally depreciating relation to silver and gold coin from England, Spain, and Mexico. There were two tricks to keeping paper currency's value somewhat stable against metal, which the confederation Congress, when it began issuing paper, couldn't perform. One was to strictly limit the number of bills in circulation. The other was to retire them, scheduling taxes payable in the paper itself, taking back the bills and burning them. Some provincial paper currencies had maintained strong value against coin.

The Congress, however, couldn't tax to withdraw its bills: a meeting of delegates representing sovereign states, it had no power to tax anyone. Every state was therefore supposed to levy taxes to retire a proportionate amount of Continental paper. But the colonies had been suffering a thirty-year economic slide, which war was now making full-on depression. People in the countryside were desperate. States couldn't collect taxes and were already failing to make agreed-upon requisitions of funds to Congress; they also issued their own paper currencies and offered their own interest-paying war bonds. So Congress printed more and more of its poorly supported paper—war expenses were out of hand—violating the cardinal rule of strictly limiting supply. As early as '76, everybody knew Continental paper would depreciate deeply, and by 1780 the Congress had to stop printing it. The bills soon traded at a rate of $125 in paper to $1 in coin. After passing out of circulation, they sold to long-shot gamblers at five hundred to one.

So potential investors in Congress's war bonds would hardly want to be paid interest in paper. To attract the biggest investors, Robert Morris, the leading merchant in Congress, began to play a role from which Alexander Hamilton, a Morris protégé even before arriving in Congress, took much. Congress announced it would pay investors the 6 percent interest not in Continental paper but in bills of exchange—certificates issued by merchant firms and European governments and banking houses, backed by firms' coin reserves, payable in cash on set dates. Bills of exchange traded at the real price of metal. Still, creditors wondered how Congress could reliably fund such bills.

Robert Morris showed them how. He was fat; his financial presence was fatter. He owned ships and warehouses and ran his own network of trading partners, connecting Philadelphia to New Orleans, Europe, and the West Indies; soon he'd be investing in the China trade. He hadn't favored American independence, but given a fait accompli, Morris would find opportunities. Exploiting the potential of a war economy, he hoped to unleash high finance, turn America into a commercial empire, and make the merchant class fabulously rich. On behalf of the Congress, Morris helped make a deal with France for a large cash loan dedicated to paying bondholders their interest in bills of exchange, as good as gold.

Well backed, the bonds now sold to a small group: mainly Robert Morris's partners, associates, and clients, who knew about the bonds' unexpected reliability. The sweetest part was that Congress accepted, in selling bonds, the same Continental paper that investors scorned to be paid interest in. That paper had already started depreciating, yet Congress took it back at face value for bonds. When $1,000 in Continental paper was worth only $200 in trade, you could dump that $200 and pick up a thousand-dollar bond drawing 6 percent interest, in metal, on its face value. Four interest payments alone would bring in more than the real purchase price—and you still had a thousand-dollar bond, whose value would hold up well: The offer's brevity (the deal ended in March of 1778) made the certificates so special that they depreciated slowly.

Thus did the founding $2.5 million of what became the domestic war debt of the United States, the preferred, blue-chip tier, backed by French coin and paying cash interest, come to be held by a network dominated by the man his cronies called Bob Morris. Congress got in exchange a lot of its own bad paper. This and similar feats would give Bob Morris his place in history as financier of the revolution. He also became the richest American merchant. It was just the mercantile code. Every day, in capitals and outposts of European empires, agents and brokers in coffeehouses, taverns, and dockside warehouses made deals for their principals in the absence of any institutional structure. Bob Morris was making a national art of the self-dealing and inside communication that had long been industry standard in large-scale buying and selling. In Congress, Morris used public funds for dozens of personal speculations and awarded his own and his partners' firms and middlemen millions in congressional contracts, commissions, and outright disbursements. Morris and the revolution financed each other.

The mercantile code wasn't everybody's code. Landed men with a country-gentry philosophy, deeming the whole enterprise of buying, selling, and investing a sewer of corruption, disdained to learn anything about how it worked. When they exposed Morris's scams, they could do little but be scandalized. And they needed him. Early in the war, the British were winning; the economy was crashing. State legislatures stopped collecting or even imposing taxes for requisitions to Congress. Instead of throwing Morris in jail, Congress made him superintendent of finance. He expressed reluctance, so they let him name his terms. When Alexander Hamilton came to Congress, Bob Morris was explicitly permitted to conduct his own and the Congress's business with no carping about conflicts of interest. Committees became departments commanded by individuals with executive power, and Morris's people headed not only Finance but also Foreign Affairs and War. The financier controlled all real power in Congress, as well as the Continental Army.

The philosopher David Hume had argued that key to a nation's economic prosperity is concentrating wealth in the hands of the few people who can use it to finance ambitious projects. Alexander Hamilton, devouring books on finance, found in Bob Morris an embodiment—to the perspicacious Hamilton, perhaps a somewhat primitive one—of Hume's ideal. But despite the power he wielded, things were not, as far as Morris was concerned, going well, and he enlisted young Hamilton, whom he found more than promising as a financier, in a full-scale project to get the war effort focused on what Morris saw as its main purpose: paying interest to the bondholding class. Tight cash forced choices between paying soldiers and paying creditors. Creditors came first: Morris officially suspended army pay, already shaky enough, and he prohibited legislatures from paying their own soldiers, insisting states send all money to Congress, to be distributed as he saw fit.

Yet state assemblies kept finding ways to avoid sending full requisitions to Congress, and the main problem, in Morris's view, was that they weren't collecting the necessary taxes from the mass of ordinary people. He therefore became intent on imposing on all the people, throughout the states, direct federal taxes, payable by the people to Congress—in coin. These taxes would be collected not by weak state governments but by a powerful cadre of federal officers.

Here was the origin of Hamilton's whiskey tax of 1791. Here too was the origin of a resistance movement—typified by the tar-and-featherer Daniel Hamilton—that would treat the whiskey tax as the last, intolerable stroke in a long flogging. The conflict that Alexander Hamilton was taking up in the confederation Congress, and which he would pursue with increasing intensity to its climax in the 1790s, was really a conflict between creditors and debtors.

What was frustrating the creditors, led by Robert Morris, was a third American political philosophy, less articulate than that of either the mercantile or landed party, inchoate, spasmodic—the philosophy of a people's movement. Recently liberated by the revolution, the people's movement had strong opinions about democracy and economic fairness. Its gnarled roots were in fables of Oliver Cromwell's English revolutions of the 1600s, when the Puritans challenged royal privilege, rejected established religion, and decapitated the king. Some groups had then called for "leveling," or broad democracy that would more evenly distribute economic opportunity. Others had revolted against Cromwell in hopes of bringing on the Christian millennium. Some unemployed laborers and landless peasants, so-called diggers, planted crops on common land and tried to inspire widespread spiritual communism. In America, the people's movement drew energy from the Great Awakening, whose spiritual radicalism had gripped the colonies in the 1730s and '40s. By the 1770s, the movement wanted laws to dictate fair and equal distribution of wealth and credit. It wanted to limit the profits that a few moneyed men could reap from what it saw as the suffering and degradation of entire communities. To achieve those goals, it wanted democratic access to the political process.

Denied that, the people's movement had long employed tactics that were extralegal, often illegal, as well as ancient, local, and direct, drawn in part from communal forms of regulation in English villages, where wife-beaters, husband-scolders, and other irritating neighbors could be hauled from their homes by dancing gangs who shook pebbles in cups, banged shovels on stone, shrieked horribly, and shouted obscene improvised rhymes. When new laws had abridged old common-law rights to hunt deer in Windsor Forest, blackfaced gangs had instantly appeared to attack officials; England's notorious Black Act responded by making it a capital crime merely to blacken your face. In the colonies, Fort Pitt commanders had learned in the 1760s that disguised gangs might waylay officials and attack soldiers, with juries refusing to convict perpetrators. Teams spent days of hard labor felling trees and stacking them high across roads, keeping officialdom out. People made no-buy covenants, boycotting sheriffs' auctions of foreclosed farms, and they enforced those covenants by making transgressors ride poles in tar and feathers. Judges in remote areas refrained from hearing government suits against tax felons. Crowds in crazy garb closed courts and opened jails to free people imprisoned for debt.

Paper was the people's finance. For long periods, gold and silver were rarely seen by ordinary people, and paper currency in small denominations gave the mass of cashless citizens a medium, allowing them to avoid borrowing from merchants like Bob Morris. Possessors of those rarest of things, cash and credit, merchants issued bills of exchange backed by their own coin, cashed their bills and other firms' for a cut, and, most significantly for the conflict that Morris and Hamilton were pursuing in Congress, loaned money to small farmers, small businesspeople, and lesser merchants with no coin of their own. Interest rates sometimes ran as high as 10 to 12 percent per month, but ordinary people, paralyzed and reduced to barter, had to borrow. When high payments became a further source of desperation, and retiring a debt was out of sight, creditors came in effect to own debtors' labor and property. Farmers overworked their soil in hopes of success and only failed more rapidly. When they couldn't pay, their farms and businesses were seized. The colonial era had seen pandemics of loss, with families sent in droves from their farms and shops to prisons or poorhouses, their land, livestock, and furniture auctioned off, sometimes to the very creditors who had foreclosed and were now picking up, at bargain prices, the debtors' lands, mills, and tools.

The people's movement wanted that cycle stopped by law and had often used rowdy and sadistic tactics to frighten legislatures into providing relief. Provinces had issued paper currency and passed legal-tender laws that required creditors to accept that paper for payments on loans. Paper depreciated; Morris and other creditors, forced by governments to accept bills whose real value was less than the interest owed, castigated paper as rotten, pulp, a curse, and legal tender as confiscatory, mobbish, and leveling, the legalized pillage of the rich. Legislatures also established public lending institutions, known as land banks, which issued low-interest government mortgages secured by land, providing farmers with small amounts of cash on easy terms and robbing creditors of their markets for high-interest loans. Land-bank mortgage notes, passed around in trade, entered the economy as another form of paper currency that sometimes gave even landless people a circulating medium.

To Robert Morris, the revolution had aggravated the curse of pulp, especially in his own state of Pennsylvania, where upscale revolutionaries had been forced to ally themselves with the mob. In Philadelphia in 1776, Thomas Paine's long pamphlet *Common Sense* had set out the popular movement's goal for its participation in the revolution: broad democracy to ensure economic fairness. That same year, to the disgust of Bob Morris and friends, Pennsylvania adopted a constitution that, unlike those of Massachusetts and Virginia, fulfilled Paine's prescriptions. Pennsylvania's executive branch was now a committee, its members elected by county, its head chosen by a legislative branch with only one chamber; free of checks from an upper house, the legislature was elected, in an especially radical change, in proportion to population. The thing that truly dismayed the Morris circle was the Pennsylvania property requirement for voting: virtually none. Nor was there one for officeholding. The poor could not only vote in Pennsylvania but also hold office. The Pennsylvania assembly passed legal-tender laws and antimonopoly regulations. The Massachusetts revolutionary John Adams, when he read the Pennsylvania constitution, predicted that Pennsylvanians would soon want King George back.

Hence the program in which Morris began enlisting Hamilton and other congressional nationalists in 1782. Pennsylvania only epitomized, by legalizing, a problem of all the states, which, as far as Morris was concerned, had habitually robbed private creditors by pandering to the people's movement and paper finance. Now states were robbing those same investors, in their function as public creditors, by failing to collect cash taxes for requisitions to Congress, with which Morris wanted to fund bonds.

Morris's plans for repairing the situation involved such things as a central bank, privately financed by Morris and his friends, and the issuing of large-denomination notes backed by his own credit, "Mr. Morris's notes." He insisted on states' paying their requisitions not in what they had—state paper and actual army supplies—but in the bank's notes, or in Mr. Morris's notes, or in coin.

But his main goal was to get Congress to lay a 5 percent tax, called an impost, on all imports countrywide. And the impost was only a wedge. Once people were inured to direct federal taxation, Morris told Hamilton and other followers, cash poll taxes, cash land taxes, and cash excises would soon follow. To ensure payment to the creditors, Morris intended to open, as he put it, the purses of the people. That those purses were almost always empty of the metal he wanted did not faze him.

He faced stiff opposition to a national tax. Taxing power was sovereign power. Although Morris, Hamilton, and the nationalists hoped to slip the federal impost through Congress as just one more revenue bill—it took only nine states to ratify such measures—the state legislatures recognized the tax bill as a fundamental amendment to the Articles of Confederation by which the Congress had been formed. Amendments required the unanimous approval of the member states. Morris deployed his team to seek support in the states for revising the Articles. Hamilton went home to New York; the governor called a special session of the assembly at Poughkeepsie, and Hamilton's father-in-law, Philip Schuyler, introduced resolutions that Hamilton had written. When the legislature passed those resolutions, Hamilton distinguished himself for the first time as a nationalist politician. Soon Congress seemed on the verge of amending its Articles and creating the impost.

Morris and his team kept the pressure on. Another part of the Morris plan, critical to enabling Hamilton's later projects, was to swell the federal debt to massive proportions. A sufficiently huge debt, Morris believed, would force the Congress to pass federal taxes, and while the best thing would have been for the central government to assume responsibility for the states' bonds and paper as well, Morris could calculate Congress's debt alone at an astronomical number. Another $8.5 million in bonds had been offered for sale, far less appealing than the first tier, because interest was paid in Continental paper. When its currency finally collapsed, Congress started issuing these bonds in lieu of payment to merchants and big army suppliers. The bonds depreciated more slowly than currency, and to induce their acceptance as payment, Congress and army agents overpaid in them. A class of speculator lower than Morris's friends, yet ultimately crucial to his plans, bought and traded this type of bond.

Morris also had his eye on a controversial, incalculably large chunk of debt, scattered in slivers and shards: IOUs from Congress and the army to small farmers and artisans who supplied army goods. There had been no refusing to sell to armed troops: People who readily complied got more chits; those who argued got few or none. States passed laws to seize crops deemed excessive of the needs of families, and who was issuing a chit, the state or the army, wasn't always clear to a coerced seller. In face value, ordinary citizens of Pennsylvania held perhaps $20 million in forced loans, with similar amounts in New York and New Jersey. As the war moved south, Virginians complained of being ravaged by impressment. The total may have reached $95 million. But face value seemed meaningless: nobody expected Congress to pay on these things. Pockets were stuffed with them. After 1780, some states accepted them for taxes, but their purchasing power was pennies on the dollar.

Morris wanted Congress to call in all of those chits and exchange them—at face, not the low market value—for interest-bearing bonds. Speculators would buy the chits in bulk, at the market rate of pennies on the dollar, from desperate people ignorant of the deal. Exchanging chits at face value for bonds, speculators would create huge profits for themselves and a massive addition to the national debt. To pay it, Congress would have to collect a federal tax, in coin, from the very people who had been forced by the army to take paper IOUs, and had then sold them, at an extraordinary discount, to people with inside information. Proceeds would be earmarked for making tax-free interest payments to bondholders.

With debate on the impost raging in Congress, Morris applied maximum pressure, using a counterintuitive tactic: he suspended interest payments on the first tier of bonds, those mainly owned by his friends and associates. If Congress wouldn't raise the money through a federal tax, top bondholders wouldn't get paid. Morris rightly predicted clamor. Influential creditors came to his office; he told them his hands were tied. Talk to Congress, he advised. Get the Articles revised to allow the impost; demand federal laws prohibiting states' populist legal-tender laws, price-control regulations, antimonopoly rules. Do it high-mindedly, he coached them: invoke widows, orphans, patriotism. Bondholders followed his advice, but they started pressuring their state legislatures too for payment, and the states threatened to start paying off their own citizens' federal debts. This was a problem for Morris. Such a system, which could only be accomplished with fancy bookkeeping and yet more paper, would defeat his plan to concentrate all public finance under federal control. Alexander Hamilton went back to New York. At a bondholder meeting in Albany, with Schuyler presiding, Hamilton urged the lobby not to seek redress from states. The prime directive was to demand federal taxes. Bondholders' sights must remain trained on Congress.

As a result of Hamilton's and others' efforts, a congressional committee did finally agree in principle not just to the impost but also to federal poll taxes, land taxes, and an excise. The nationalists felt crushed, therefore, when Rhode Island's delegate to Congress decried the impost, railing against loss of state sovereignty and painting a picture of the states chained together like prisoners under a tyrant. The Rhode Island legislature voted not to relinquish its sole right to tax its citizens. Virginia learned of Rhode Island's refusal and pulled out too. Morris and the nationalists veered toward despair. The worst thing was that peace was in the air. The end of war would remove Congress's incentive to control the states at all. A tide of rotten state paper would wash away the financiers' investments, placing the debt effectively in default.

So Morris now began defining the purpose of the war as sustaining the war debt. Only extending the military conflict, he said, could hold the country together long enough for the government to grow strong and the people resigned to paying national taxes. He wrote to General Washington, who was near exhaustion and hoping for a permanent vacation, to suggest that more fighting would be better than peace for producing necessary funds and increasing the authority of Congress. For all his commitment to nationalism, Washington chose to ignore that suggestion. He had more immediate problems to deal with.

As if by providence, Washington's biggest problem gave Bob Morris, Alexander Hamilton, and the nationalist coalition an opportunity to swell and strengthen the bondholding class by adding to it a new lobby that seemed, literally, irresistible: the army. In the winter and spring of 1783, through a series of events that came to be known as the Newburgh crisis, Morris brought his career as superintendent of finance to a climax and Hamilton dove with immense brio, for the first but by no means the last time, into the riskiest kind of power politics. The nationalists would emerge from the Newburgh crisis with matters arranged to enable what would one day become Hamilton's whiskey tax. In the process, Hamilton and Washington discovered new elements in their relationship that would, in the 1790s, influence their response to tax resistance at the Forks of the Ohio.

Mutiny was what Washington most feared. War was effectively won, and in late 1782 his army, anything but happy and relaxed, was arrayed about the rolling hills on the Hudson River near Newburgh, New York, in a large winter cantonment. The past seven years had been a slog through cold, starvation, at times near-nakedness, along with the daily horrors of slaughter. The oppression continued in Newburgh. Neither officers nor men had been paid in years. Washington himself was near bankruptcy. He blamed Congress. Uncertainty about pay was haunting—and uniting—a large, angry force, 550 officers and around 10,000 enlisted men, who might refuse to be sent home impoverished and in debt.

Throughout the fall of 1782, officers at Newburgh pumped themselves up over what they could do if they wanted to. A group led by Washington's enemy, General Horatio Gates, who thought he should be commander in chief, plotted mutiny and takeover of Congress. Loyal officers were angry too, and Washington worked with them, persuading them to put their grievances in a petition to Congress.

Henry Knox, Washington's irreproachably loyal artillery general, wrote the petition and sent a letter to the Congress's secretary of war to prepare him for its arrival. The way the petition arrived, in January of 1783, made clear how serious it was. A major general and two colonels delivered it and then settled into Philadelphia to wait for the only response they seemed prepared to accept.

The great opportunity for Bob Morris and the nationalists in Congress came with the officers' main demand, which had to do with pensions. Congress had tried to make up for lost salaries with a promise that when the war was over, officers would receive half pay for life. With the army now about to disband, and no money in Congress, officers couldn't see how the promise would be honored. The officer emissaries from Newburgh were therefore demanding that Congress commute lifetime half pay into a lump sum of cash, payable right now. They'd accept it either from the Congress or from the officers' individual states.

Within a day of their arrival in Philadelphia, Morris met with the three officers unofficially and hailed them as fellow creditors. He urged them not to look to the states for payment: the only solution was to demand federal taxes to pay not just officers but all creditors. The officer class, unlike the nationalists in Congress, was armed. Morris advised the officers to refuse to lay down their arms unless the states agreed to federal taxes.

When the officers met with Congress they did mention mutiny as the probable outcome of demands not being met. They also wrote to Knox at Newburgh, urging him to take the lead in an outright refusal to disband unless states agreed to federal taxes. Knox didn't reply. Bob Morris, his assistant and fellow financier Gouverneur Morris (who was no relation), and Alexander Hamilton now determined to build the situation into a genuine crisis. That the crisis really might end in coup and military government was a risk they had to take. They even considered the potential benefits to their national agenda of the success of such a coup. But their main idea was merely to frighten the states with the threat of military takeover.

The Morrises and Hamilton reached out to the generals up at Newburgh. Gouverneur Morris wrote to say that if the army stuck with its insistence on a national tax, the states would have no choice but to agree to it, and he wrote again to Knox to urge him to lead: if the generals, so to speak, took the hill, Gouverneur assured Knox, the nationalists in the Congress would, so to speak, supply them. Robert Morris had a connection with the mutinous cabal led by General Gates: the two men most deeply in personal debt to Morris were Charles Lee, another enemy of Washington, and Gates himself. While it would have been safer for the conspirators to rely on Knox, they kept Gates, a more dangerous tool, whom Hamilton especially disliked and disrespected, at the ready.

The risks Hamilton was taking, at this early and critical moment in his career, called for immense daring and agility. Nobody despised Gates more than Hamilton's father-in-law and mentor Schuyler, whose shock and disgust, should he ever learn of Hamilton's collaboration in sedition, would be catastrophic. The trickiest part for Hamilton lay in his main assignment: to work on General Washington, whom the conspirators wanted either leading the threat of military coup or somehow neutralized. Approaching Washington, finesse would be everything. Hamilton and Washington had already caused each other difficulties.

At twenty-two Hamilton had more or less appointed himself chief of the general's staff, and Washington had come to rely on the brash, almost preternaturally accomplished young man, and had given him, under the pressure of the British invasion of Philadelphia, the job of requisitioning supplies from terrified citizens, which Hamilton had brought off with striking tact. The two had worked late, side by side, preparing dispatches and orders. Hamilton referred to headquarters, where he was called Hammy, as home; Washington called his staff a family. There were parties and outings and Martha Washington named her tomcat Hamilton to tease the young staffer about his success with women. Some had felt that the youth exercised too great an influence on the commander in chief. Hamilton, for his part, was eager for exploit and battlefield command; he saw opportunities for fame dissolving while he did desk work, but Washington needed him too much to let him go. Hamilton also suffered with ordinary staffers Washington's displays of frustration. The general couldn't expose his temper beyond the family and took it out on subordinates behind closed doors.

One day at headquarters Washington and his chief of staff passed on the stairs. Washington said he needed to speak to Hamilton. Hamilton continued downstairs and delivered a note. Then he spoke with the Marquis de Lafayette. When Hamilton did go up, Washington met him at the top of the stairs, furiously accusing him of disrespect. Hamilton said that if Washington felt that way, they must part; Washington acquiesced in what he called Hamilton's choice; the two men stalked off. An hour later, the general sent a message apologizing for ill temper and asking Hamilton to come speak to him. Hamilton sent a message back. He saw no purpose in a conversation, he said. His mind was made up about leaving; if Washington insisted, of course Hamilton would speak to him, but he preferred not to.

This high-handedness stunned everybody, not least Schuyler. But Hamilton told people privately that for all the incense the world burned for the great man, working for him was hell. The general had always wanted greater closeness between them, according to Hamilton; he'd been forced, he said, to rebuff Washington's advances and keep their relationship military and professional. Washington's generalship too, Hamilton confided, wasn't all it should be. Still, the general's popularity, he conceded, had been essential to the country and might still be useful.

After leaving the staff, Hamilton didn't shrink from bugging Washington repeatedly, in letters, for the high command he felt he was owed. Finally, with the war nearly over, Washington gave Hamilton command of a battalion, and at Yorktown, after much pleading from Hamilton, the general made the young man's dream come true. He sent Hamilton's light infantry on a classic charge. The brigade emerged all at once from a trench, guns unloaded and bayonets fixed, and ran, screaming horribly, through flying lead, handily capturing a critical position. Hamilton had daydreamed about such an achievement since his days on the St. Croix docks.

Now, to bring off the Newburgh crisis, Hamilton surprised his former boss—they hadn't been closely in touch—with a friendly letter of unsolicited advice, subtly inviting Washington into the conspiracy. Congress was out of money, Hamilton reported. There would be no army payments; sadly, troops would be justified in staying armed. The general's admirable integrity, Hamilton said, and delicacy about exploiting a powerful position, might be viewed by some—Washington's own officers, Hamilton hinted—as obstructing progress toward getting paid. Mutiny was in the air. How much better if Washington, instead of discouraging attempts at redress—Hamilton stage-whispered by underlining—*took direction of them?*

When Washington responded, his tone was remote, disturbed, full of good judgment. He fully endorsed the goal of national taxation and a strong federal government, without which everything he and the country had gone through would be for nothing. Yet he wouldn't, he said, give in to fear of mutiny. He knew all about Gates, but he hoped instead for better elements in the army to prevail. Things were calm at Newburgh, he reported.

Calm at Newburgh wasn't what the conspirators wanted. Hamilton continued a delicate correspondence with Washington; the

Morrises finally sent a personal emissary to Knox, who did speak at last. No, Knox said. The army's threatening the states with refusal to disband would be highly improper. With no support from a legitimate leader, the conspirators turned to General Gates, sending him word that the financier and the creditor class would support whatever he decided to do.

Gates's people began circulating anonymous memos among officers in the Newburgh camps, attacking Washington's moderation on the pay issue and calling an unofficial meeting to discuss officer grievances. At that meeting, Gates and his crew expected to take over the army.

In Congress, meanwhile, James Madison, a nationalist not included in the scheme, noted the positive effect that fear of coup was having on tax debate. Hamilton again and again addressed the body to rule out compromises. He opposed a motion to levy the impost only for paying officers: all bondholders must be included. Excitement, Madison noted, led Hamilton to expose the real agenda, depicting for Congress the glories of a United States woven together by a system of tax collectors. Meanwhile, General Arthur St. Clair, a Morris ally and debtor, was working on the officer emissaries, urging them to consider taking commuted half pay in interest-bearing bonds. This would fully cement the officers' might to the bondholders' goals. Should the officers refuse to accept payment in bonds, Robert Morris threatened them through St. Clair, they might get nothing.

Then, in the middle of debate in Congress, Morris dramatically resigned his office. He wrote to Congress to say that if funds for every kind of public debt were not permanently secured, his own integrity would be baseless. With the Gates cabal at Newburgh moving, on the pledge of Morris's support, to unite the officers in mutiny against Washington and Congress, Morris published his threatened resignation, creating maximum anxiety about pay even among loyal officers at Newburgh.

At last Washington acted. Learning of the mutinous memos circulating in camp, he wrote to Hamilton asking him to explain to

Congress and the states that if the worst should happen, it would be their fault; they hadn't addressed the desperate needs of his army. He sent his officers a memo preempting the unofficial meeting, calling his own meeting, at which he appointed Gates to preside; Washington asked for a full report on what occurred at the meeting. The inference was that he wouldn't attend. When the officers had gathered, in a huge, barnlike structure on a hill, with Gates in the chair and ready to rouse them to mutiny, Washington walked into the room. Gates gave up the chair and could only watch as Washington made a stern and beautiful speech on remaining loyal to the country's promise for civil authority and republican government. The vast majority of officers were already moved when Washington sealed the matter with a gesture that brought some to tears and established his reputation for all time. He started to read aloud a letter from Congress promising attention to officer pay, but finding that he couldn't read it, he reached for his glasses. Apologizing as he settled the glasses on his nose, he remarked that having already gone gray in the service of his country, he now seemed to have gone blind too.

The sensation left Gates unmoored. All he could do was thank the general for his speech as Washington swept out of the room to acclaim, and Knox and other loyal generals, on cue, moved in to propose resolutions, to which the assembled officers enthusiastically assented, abhorring mutiny.

Washington instantly wrote to Congress. He'd barely averted disaster, he said; now Congress should give immediate satisfaction to officer demands. Congress, relieved, did just that, and everything Washington had hoped for, when suggesting that his officers petition Congress—officer payment, no mutiny—was accomplished. Officers were offered five years' full pay. If they preferred to get it from states, officers of any state line could apply by a set deadline—but only collectively—to their legislature; after that, officer payment would be considered part of the federal debt. Just as Morris had hoped, all army obligations thus passed easily to the federal government, adding $5 million to the debt. The officers agreed to take the payoff in interest-bearing bonds, to be funded after final settlement of states' accounts with Congress. Each general received $10,000 worth of bonds (average family income was under $200 per year). The officers formed the Society of the Cincinnati, a hereditary organization with a chapter in each state. Every officer of the Continental Army was a member, and each officer's eldest male descendant, in every future generation, would be a member too. The society unified the families of those who would become the country's most influential men, creating a hereditary interstate lobby with roots in fear of coup. The society's president was General Washington (who took no bonds or pay).

Soldiers got $200 to $300 in bonds at the officers' behest. It was a stopgap side deal; addressing back pay for the men was put off for final settlement among the states, and the soldiers, needing cash, and with no time to wait for interest or payment on debt instruments, sold their bonds to speculators at up to a thirtieth of face value. When Pennsylvania troops rebelled over nonpayment, the officers, now bondholders of high standing, were far from supportive, and the rebellion was put down. In April, peace became official and the soldiers were sent home. They were supposed to be paid three months' salary in Mr. Morris's notes. Morris took his time sending the notes; army contractors gave soldiers goods on credit and took the soldiers' notes, when they did at last arrive, at 40 and 50 percent markdowns. There was no final settlement with the men. Morris said he had no authority to make it, and by the time Congress gave him authority, everybody had gone home. The soldiers hardly got paid at all. The countryside filled up with broke, indebted veterans of a long war.

In Congress, the impost was passed—but only in a diluted version, still dependent on state collection, thus useless. The Morrises' and Hamilton's most extreme efforts failed to get genuine federal taxes passed in the confederation Congress. Yet by 1791, when Hamilton was in a position to fund the debt, its size, and the influential nature of those who held it, helped him pursue the Morris agenda to its conclusion in a new, national context.

For Washington and Hamilton, meanwhile, the crisis had renewed a relationship that became crucial to Hamilton's hopes. Even as the Morrises were giving up on Washington and Knox and risking everything by turning to Gates, Hamilton was making himself the repository for Washington's private thoughts on quelling the mutiny. Praising the wisdom of Washington's decisions—which departed sharply from what he'd at first solicited Washington to do—Hamilton was keeping all avenues open. After the war, as the victorious general, returning to his farm, became more august than ever, Hamilton emerged not as a conspirator in sedition but as one of Washington's important correspondents in the Congress.

They delved remarkably freely into the real sources of the crisis. Washington believed creditors had been manipulating his much abused army and risking a national disaster just to get payments for bondholders. Such was Hamilton's agility that he confessed to a great deal of what Washington suspected him of. Confession invested the correspondence with a new intimacy. When Washington expressed suspicion of Robert Morris, Hamilton defended Morris—but he did confide an opinion that Morris's judgment could sometimes be clouded. When Washington seemed to chide Hamilton, calling an army a dangerous thing to play with, Hamilton wrote a passionate justification, admitting that he and the Morrises had indeed blended creditor and officer interest—he would do it again, he said—but swearing he'd always had the army's interest at heart. Hamilton crossed out an admission that the conspirators had hoped, at least briefly, to create rather than merely benefit from a threat of coup. And revealing the collaboration with Gates would have ended the revived relationship for good. Hamilton left that out altogether.

But before receiving Hamilton's reply, Washington had written again to qualify his remark about playing with the army. He'd been tired, he said; he'd only meant that the army is volatile, that manipulating it might have ended with state sovereignists, not nationalists, winning. Nobody, Washington repeated, more favored national government and federal taxation than he.

So Hamilton might have avoided writing his letter of half confession, so careful yet so intense, and might have gotten away with revealing less. But the letter had the effect of pulling the two men more deeply into a special way of collaborating, to which they would resort with even more complex results in the 1790s, when Hamilton reconnected national finance with domestic military power. Hadn't he courted terrible danger, Hamilton was saying in his post-Newburgh letters—somehow he put it both bluntly and subtly—and admittedly done outright wrong, only to achieve the strong nationhood that Washington wanted too?

CHAPTER THREE

Spirits Distilled Within
the United States

Six years later, authoring the whiskey tax as President Washington's treasury secretary, Hamilton had matured in the practice of law and politics, and the United States of America had become, thanks in part to Hamilton's efforts, a government with direct powers over citizens throughout the states. Opening the purses of the people, in Robert Morris's expression, was possible at last, and Hamilton was in full command of his excitement, impatient with anyone whose imagination lacked the scope of his own. He had a relentless commitment—it was uncanny, given the fertility of his imagination—to the minutiae involved in administering whatever his ambitions demanded. There was no argument he couldn't make impregnable, no argument he couldn't eviscerate.

As when he'd made himself chief of the general's staff, he saw Treasury as top job in the president's cabinet. He'd been recommended for it by Robert Morris, who had turned it down; as an economist Hamilton was ahead of Morris now. Even before he'd gone to the Congress, he'd written the superintendent a letter offering what he called some ideas, which in fact ran to thirty pages of figures and argument, a thoroughgoing analysis of a central bank's ideal charter, with the recommendation that Morris's bank issue smaller, more generally usable bills and pushing for a larger capital than Morris deemed prudent. Since then he'd learned more, and he had reason to see himself as the only person in the country qualified not only to do this job, but also to use it as a lever for moving the executive branch, and the whole government, toward the highest national goals.

It was a busy fall. He had to get loans to cover immediate operating expenses. He had to take over the chaotic process of final settlement—flattening the debts, expenses, and common charges that states had run up against one another under the defunct confederation. The first U.S. Congress had finally passed a real federal impost on foreign goods. He had to comprehend every facet of customs processes, the operation of lighthouses, the cargo typically listed on manifests. He deployed deputies and assistants and got his Broadway office up and running with the robustness and efficiency he loved. He couldn't abide a cluttered desk.

At the end of the month, Congress closed its first session and went home. By October the president and the rest of the cabinet had left town too. New York was Hamilton's home, and as daylight fled, and winds drove waves against the Battery, he kept lamps burning. He was developing a far-reaching plan of finance for the United States. It would realize the old plan of funding the domestic debt, liberating the nation's commercial energy while placing all significant public investment in federal hands, not through the long slate of taxes that Morris had wanted—overkill with a blunt instrument—but by adding to the import duties a single tax, exhaustively calculated to serve precise purposes: the federal excise, soon to be known as the whiskey tax. This time Hamilton meant to give the debtor class no further chance for resistance, no choice but to pay.

That class was both rampant and desperate. Its activism had shifted westward after the war—mountainous regions remained in depression during a postwar recovery of the east—and the radicals had involved themselves in two incidents in the 1780s that inadvertently helped enable Hamilton to impose the federal whiskey tax of 1791. One was traditional in being criminal and violent. The other, even more disconcerting to creditors, was lawful and political.

The violent incident occurred in western Massachusetts, where the failed economy led to insurrection. Belittled by creditors as the Shays Rebellion, as if inspired only by the audacity of one of its leaders, Daniel Shays, the outbreak was the most focused of many violent debtor actions in western and rural parts of many states, frightening creditors throughout the country. The Massachusetts assembly had taken an aggressive approach to consolidating and paying its war debts, benefiting the few who held interest-bearing state notes. The assembly paid interest on notes at their value when issued: if depreciation had made a one-dollar note worth 25 cents when issued, the note would be paid at 25 cents, despite having depreciated, by the late 1780s, to 2 cents. Taxes to raise coin for this payoff to state bondholders were already heavy enough; then the state decided to pay the entire principal of its army debt too—and then to pay the principal of the state notes. Further taxes were levied on the people. Though some were payable in various kinds of paper, they were simply not payable at all by many; mass foreclosures ensued. Protest took the form of petitions and meetings, demanding a revaluation of the debt along realistic lines and the opening of a state land bank for farmers' relief. In 1786 the debtors staged a classic court riot in Northampton. In January of '87 they tried to seize the federal arsenal in Springfield, where they were put down by the state militia and ringleaders were arrested.

But after suppressing the Shays Rebellion, the Massachusetts legislature repealed the crushing tax laws. To nationalists like Hamilton, it was the old story. State assemblies, left to their own devices, would either try to retire state debts overaggressively, or lower taxes and open land banks, thus perpetuating the curse of pulp, or—showing perfect irrationality—do both. In every circumstance, legislatures reacted to the people's violence by passing laws that robbed investors.

The other event in which finance radicals distinguished themselves in the 1780s, at least as frightening to creditors as the Shays Rebellion and Massachusetts's response, occurred in Pennsylvania. There the radical state constitution allowed ordinary people an unusual degree of access to the government. The Pennsylvania assembly became a tense place. Throughout the eighties, power lurched back and forth from the party of creditors and merchants led by Robert Morris—now in the Pennsylvania assembly, having left the confederation Congress—to a populist alliance that was shaky at best. One problem for rural farmers and artisans was that they rarely voted. Western counties were huge. Getting to and from polling places could take days, and incumbents were rich, with machines dedicated to stifling opposition. Still, in the mid-1780s, citizens of Cumberland and Westmoreland counties, organizing to vote in large numbers, had a farmer, Robert Whitehill, and a weaver, William Findley, in the assembly in Philadelphia. Creditors all over the country saw what might happen to investments if democracy got a grip on legitimate politics.

Whitehill and Findley urged their fellow assemblymen to revoke the charter for Bob Morris's bank, which, they argued, served no public function. That the bank might lose its privilege to operate terrified the merchants who relied on it for large-scale funding—including Morris himself and the bank's other directors, who were accustomed to approving massive, poorly secured loans to fund their many speculations. James Wilson, Morris's chief ally in the assembly, had personally borrowed more than $250,000 to speculate in western land. In debate, Whitehill pointed out that strapped farmers and artisans couldn't get loans at Morris's bank; Findley noted that almost a third of the families in his county had been foreclosed. Morris and Wilson waved away widespread depression in the countryside as a figment of radicals' imaginations: any farmer in the state, they said, could of course open an account at the bank—as long as he had good connections in the city and could get someone respectable to endorse his notes. Exasperation prevailed. Whitehill and Findley were also demanding a new land bank, to give ordinary people credit, as well as more liberal paper emissions. If an angel from heaven, Bob Morris said, were to inform Robert Whitehill that the central bank was a good thing, Whitehill would still deny it. Whitehill declared that any pro-bank angel would be a fallen one.

A remarkable victory for populist lawmaking occurred when

the radicals gained the unlikely support of speculators operating from a lower rung than Morris's and Wilson's; they'd long resented being excluded from the banking clique. The assembly did revoke the bank's charter. In the next session, it refused to reinstate it. Bob Morris accused the assembly of confiscating his bank's property. Not so, Whitehill triumphantly replied: the charter was the property not of Morris but of the people of Pennsylvania.

Emboldened, radicals now proposed a plan for state bonds that would have defeated the purpose of buying them. Morris and other creditors had begun picking up depreciated Pennsylvania bonds, at a fraction of face value, from people in urgent need of cash. Having bought at a deep discount, creditors now hoped to get the state not merely to pay interest on but to actually pay off the debt, at face value, for an overnight creditor bonanza. The radicals proposed instead to depreciate the bonds, by law, to real market value, about one-quarter face value, and make those depreciated certificates a legal tender for paying taxes, state mortgages, public fees of all kinds—never indeed redeeming them in gold and silver. This plan would give people a way to pay taxes and land-bank mortgages in paper. Speculators would still derive value from the bonds, the radicals argued: now a public currency, bonds could be used in trade for goods and services. When all certificates were reabsorbed by the state, the war debt would be paid off, small holders' property stabilized, burdens equalized, and the best goals of the revolution realized.

Whether the plan was unrealistic became academic. The populists' sometime allies, low-rung speculators, held plenty of state bonds themselves; this time the populists could not get a majority. No debate was held, no action taken. In the end, a compromise prevailed, whose most significant feature, for the future of the country, was the dissatisfaction it caused both sides. The weaver William Findley announced that staving off plutocracy and preserving liberty in Pennsylvania had been defeated. Bob Morris savaged the assembly as leveling and confiscatory. Both the creditors and the debtors, having engaged in a direct legislative contest, ended by feeling cheated and weak.

Outbreaks like the Shays Rebellion, as well as the qualified legislative successes of Pennsylvania radicals, inspired some decisive new alliances. By the late eighties, nationalists and creditors everywhere feared that federal bonds would never pay, that the state debt instruments in which they'd invested would be voided by paper schemes, that cash taxes could never be effectively imposed to service public debt. State sovereigntists, for their part, once bitterly opposed to any talk of nationhood, were seeing their states' authority eroding in the mountains and beyond them. The idea of some limited form of collective strength began to take on new appeal in the legislatures.

Disappointed radicals, meanwhile, now mainly from the west, were interested in collective strength too. They were explicitly connecting the debt that kept them paralyzed with two failures, which they blamed equally on the confederation Congress and on state governments in the east: the lack of any agreement with Spain to open the Mississippi River to American trade, and the lack of any effective protection from Indian attacks. The Mississippi problem robbed westerners of chances for the small-scale commercial development through which they longed to free themselves from depression, barter economies, and dependency on landlords and creditors. The east was accessible only by bad roads, at great expense, over a mountain barrier. Westerners looked farther west, in Spanish Louisiana and beyond the Gulf of Mexico, for markets. But George Washington and other land speculators, whose ambitions required keeping west linked to east, hoped to postpone a Mississippi opening until some kind of national cohesiveness could be enforced. The river remained closed.

The Indian problem, ignored by governments in the east, was turning westerners even more urgently to their own devices. An afternoon trip to church or town could become a scene of butchery. At night a cabin could be abruptly filled with whooping warriors, swinging children by their feet to open their skulls, slicing limbs and taking scalps, disappearing into the woods with wailing captives. The imagined fates of kidnapped children made parents long for their own deaths. Survivors' faces carried lifelong maiming by tomahawks. Settlers formed posses, and in some famous massacres turned peaceful Indian settlements into slaughterhouses, lining up innocent men, women, and children by the dozen, aged and newborn alike, for scalping and bludgeoning to death. Members of Congress and state legislatures deplored the westerners' barbarity but didn't create credible policies for security. State taxes seemed earmarked for anything but western defense. Things could be expected to get worse: England was working with the western tribes to amplify native harassment.

The various western new-state movements, spurned by Congress, were becoming a single western defiance movement. The state of Franklin, which had formed itself out of three counties of North Carolina, agreed to swear fealty to the king of Spain—a Roman Catholic!—if that would open the Mississippi to western products. The Pennsylvania movement calling itself Westsylvania had been discouraged by a state law making it a capital crime even to discuss independence. Yet near the Forks of the Ohio, and especially in Washington County, south of Pittsburgh, meetings still went on, making common cause with western Virginians, creating committees of correspondence, sending circulars to other western regions. When Kentuckians called a convention, in response to a circular from the Forks of the Ohio, they amplified the mood of the Shays Rebellion. To the dismay and anxiety of nationalists and state governments alike, Kentucky was urging the whole west to resist the dominance of eastern creditors and politicians.

That was 1787. Only two years later, the Constitution of the United States had been ratified, and the first U.S. Congress was settling into its temporary home in New York City, confirming Alexander Hamilton's appointment to the executive branch of a government with pervasive powers throughout the states. Nationalists had won. State-sovereigntists had won too: They administered their own counties and court systems and passed their own laws; their legislatures appointed U.S. senators and delegates to the state colleges for electing the president. Since both sides had won, both felt they'd lost too much, and dissatisfaction was rampant among both federalists and states-rights proponents. Tensions over the Constitution's meaning would, putting it mildly, persist.

What virtually everybody who pushed for ratification believed, however, was that the Constitution would disable rural populism's political wing in the state assemblies while subjecting its violent wing in the countryside to strong policing. The popular movement had managed to bring together forces that shared almost nothing but a vital interest in suppressing the popular movement. On the Constitutional Convention's first day of business, Edmund Randolph of plantation Virginia—hardly a Morris-style merchant-financier—identified the problem the convention must address and repair. "Insufficient checks against the democracy," Randolph called it, and to demonstrate the incompetence of the confederation, he cited the financiers' two frustrations: Congress's failure to pass a viable impost, and the debilitating effects of the states' paper-finance schemes. To Randolph, the Shays Rebellion and other violent protests pointed to something second only in embarrassment to the lack of a national power to defend against foreign attack: lack of power to suppress insurrection. The federal government must, he said, be given the rights to tax, enforce taxes, and create a peacetime army. At least as important: states must be prevented from issuing currency and bonds.

So when Alexander Hamilton sat in his Broadway office at the end of 1790, working up his finance plan, he had exciting new powers to work with. The U.S. Constitution, Article One, section eight, clause one, gave the federal government a right to collect every kind of tax from the whole people of the United States. Even before creating the office of secretary of the treasury, the U.S. Congress had exercised that power, imposing the long-stymied country-wide duty on foreign goods, with specific taxes on dozens of items; in a separate act, Congress created and deployed a cadre of federal officers to collect the impost, and the officers' powers, which included search and seizure, were unhampered by state lines or state laws. Just as Hamilton had predicted to the confederation Congress in 1782, the nation was being unified by tax officers. Furthermore, sections fifteen and sixteen empowered the federal government to call out the state militias to enforce federal laws, to organize and control those militias when so engaged, and to prescribe militias' training at all times.

Perhaps the most thoroughgoing continental renovation came with section ten, clause one. It pried loose the paper-finance movement's grip on legitimate politics, always weak, by prohibiting states from printing paper money, issuing bonds, and making anything but gold and silver a legal tender for paying public or private debts.

Even creditors in radical Pennsylvania got their dearest wish. In 1790 a convention met to review the radical state constitution. The land speculator and financier James Wilson, Bob Morris's associate in the assembly, rewrote the document almost single-handedly. There was an upper house in the legislature. A single executive was elected independently of the legislature. District judges were no longer elected in the counties they served but were appointed by the executive in the capital. The power that the people had been given in 1776 was taken away.

Hamilton wanted more. He knew what he'd known in the eighties: the federal impost wasn't enough. Though he took a more nuanced approach than Robert Morris's, his goal for the domestic debt remained making reliable payments to creditors and inspiring confidence in federal bonds as articles of investment and trade. Funding the debt would spring-feed a pool of capital, from which, if managed carefully—with each creation of debt accompanied by a fund dedicated to retiring it over decades—the federal government could draw, and draw again, in nurturing a growing nation. Wealth would be concentrated in the hands of moneyed investors. Their ambitions would fund the nation's ambitions.

The impost taxed merchant importers, the very people who held bonds. To make bonds truly wealth-creating, revenues for paying interest on them would have to be raised from the mass of ordinary citizens who didn't hold them. That called for a tax not on imports but on a domestic product.

In January of 1790, Congress came back to New York, and Hamilton filed his proposed finance plan, the Report on Public Credit. It was a stunning document—almost literally. The reading of its fifty-one pages to the sixty members of the House was followed only by ambient room noise. Nobody could take it all in. To some it seemed an impenetrable monolith, to others a blizzard of infinitesimal detail. With its multiple tables, charts, schedules, and row after row of figures, in schedules A through K, listing every imaginable expenditure and revenue source of government, the plan did not invite input. Such was Hamilton's enthusiasm that he disdained to reel Congress, jerk by jerk, toward potentially distressing elements in the plan: everything the secretary wanted to do, in all its ambition and controversy, was right there in plain arithmetic.

The report urged a three-part program, familiar from the Morris period: paying interest on, rather than paying off or voiding, the federal domestic debt; hugely expanding that debt by absorbing in it all the states' debts; and raising revenues for interest payments on the expanded debt by adding to the customs laws new duties on imported wine and spirits, and imposing an excise on domestically distilled spirits.

But so important was the tax portion of the proposal that Hamilton appended a fully detailed revenue bill—the only aspect for which he included a sample law. Far from waiting to reveal what might have seemed the most controversial element, Hamilton wanted creditors to see exactly how his revenue-raising measures would work.

He was made to wait to sell the beauties of a whiskey tax. The House turned instead to the most palatable part of the report, the funding of the federal debt, which the House chose to debate as a discrete entity, despite the report's insistence on funding, assumption, and revenue as interdependent elements of a unified whole.

Hamilton was nervous. He took intense meetings with his allies and supporters, hung around outside the chamber hoping to snag people, paced outside. The ubiquitous presence of this charismatic, demanding member of the executive branch offended states-rights and separation-of-powers congressmen. (Hamilton had wanted to read the report to Congress himself; he'd been barred.) The plan was making New York the center of a national excitement that further aroused the landed class's inveterate scorn for speculators. The value of all securities was soaring, in nervous anticipation of the government's commitment to funding them, possibly at face value, and finding credible ways to secure revenues for payment. Hamilton was proposing to pay full 6 percent interest on the face value of the federal certificates. You'd be able to take your interest in two attractive ways: combine tracts of federally owned western land with 4 percent in coin, or take no land and get the full 6 percent. Some federal stocks would wait ten years to start drawing cash interest; others would start drawing right away. If you'd bet on full payment, you might already have won.

The House passed a funding bill and sent it to the Senate. But the next phase of the program, assumption of state debts, became a problem that also threatened the whiskey tax. Assumption would add about $25 million to the federal debt, and speculators now gambled daily, in an anguish of hope and fear, on how Congress might treat the state bonds they'd started buying when federal bonds had become scarce. Financial firms like Morris's had dozens of agents rummaging attics and old coat pockets from the Carolinas to Maine, buying devalued state paper cheap in hopes of full federal payoff supported by taxes. Coffeehouses, taverns, and offices became impromptu exchanges for trading. The ethos now was ruin-or-fortune. Everybody was working the margin, borrowing to speculate, hoping to finance one big strike on a major slice of debt. Ships left the New York docks on the mere hint that a cache of state paper had been seen somewhere up or down the coast.

Yet the concept of assumption seemed to confound the House. Hamilton tried to explain it. If accounting was practiced correctly, no state could lose or gain anything from assumption, which he intended to subordinate to the final settlement anyway. In May, Hamilton's ally in Congress, Fisher Ames, argued passionately and at length not only for assuming state debts but also for funding them and the existing federal bonds through a whiskey excise. In June, anti-Hamilton forces responded with a version of the revenue bill that removed the whiskey excise entirely; Hamilton's allies were forced to vote down that toothless version. Then assumption itself was defeated. Some speculators holding state securities—trading had continued to be frantic; prices had gone wild—faced ruin.

In the end, though, deals for assumption were made. James Madison had taken to contesting everything his former nationalist collaborator Hamilton proposed, but he did agree to restrain opposition to assumption and the whiskey tax, if the national capital could be located on the Potomac. Robert Morris helped: he dealt away Philadelphia as a permanent national capital. Hamilton let go of any hope for a capital in New York. When assumption passed the House, the Senate combined funding with assumption in a near-final bill, lowering payments and stripping out some payoff options. Summer ended with two parts of the plan enshrined as law. The only thing missing, despite its obvious centrality, was the tax.

Hamilton stayed cool. In December, he reported to Congress the unsurprising fact that the federal government, in taking on a legal obligation to fund a debt that included all state obligations, had run up a deficit of about $830,000. Fortunately, he reported, the new import duties and the excise on spirits—the revenue bill, that is, proposed in the report of almost a year earlier—would raise $975,000, more than enough to cover the deficit.

He was becoming a mature politician. With the congressmen primed at last, he gave them cover. There was, he said, no alternative to excise, but this excise, he assured them, unlike classic excises that infringed liberties, would give no summary powers to its officers: people accused of failing to pay the tax would be entitled to jury trials. Alternatives like land taxes, he suggested, should be reserved for emergency situations, a thought that couldn't fail to please the crowd that liked to abominate excise on principle but would actually have been hurt by taxes on land. Further import duties, another seeming alternative, would be too burdensome for the merchants who had to pay such duties. Hamilton took a moment to hymn the merchant class. He didn't ask the congress-men to consider that merchants were the very people who held the federal bonds and would thus directly benefit from proceeds of the whiskey tax. He did call it bad policy to contradict anything the group most committed to federal authority deemed proper.

The product Hamilton proposed to tax, distilled spirits, was not, he said, a necessity but a luxury item consumed by those who could afford, by definition, to pay the tax. Throughout debate, his allies had invited the House to see a whiskey tax as a public-health effort; now Hamilton presented a letter from the Philadelphia College of Physicians, who said that domestic distilled spirits, the cheap drink of the laboring classes, had become a ravaging plague requiring immediate treatment.

But what Hamilton especially wanted the congressmen to appre-ciate drew him back to his dreams of the confederation period. This law would be a good thing for the country, he told Congress, because it made collection of public revenue dependent not on the goodwill of the taxed, as state revenue laws always had, but on the vigilance of federal officers. The people's movement had always made itself arbiter of whether taxes could be collected. States hadn't been lazy, Hamilton said, or weak; they'd been scared. Federal officers, he promised, wouldn't be. This tax would be collected everywhere. The means to do it existed. He evinced no reluctance to use force.

He could have gone on piling up arguments and inducements. He didn't have to. The finance plan had given the United States a legal obligation that it couldn't meet without either imposing an excise or resorting to far-out measures like a land tax, or even to something truly wild, a tax on income, or on wealth itself. Hamilton did overplay slightly. Some Congressmen sputtered over being patronized by a bunch of doctors. But after a lot of back-and-forth among House, Senate, and Treasury, with frequent interruptions for debating Hamilton's next big program, a central bank for the United States, which he was losing no time in pushing through, a revenue bill almost identical to the version submitted more than a year earlier passed both houses of Congress, and as the session ended in March of 1791, the whiskey tax became law.

Exactly how an excise on whiskey would open the purses of the people wasn't something Hamilton described to the congressmen. Nor did they ask. The people on whom the tax operated would get little help from Hamilton's opponents in Congress, the representatives of the landed. The law's operation was in fact somewhat obscure; understanding it took a grasp of finance that few in the congressional opposition wanted to have.

Many in the western country did have that grasp. You wouldn't have to be a distiller, or even a drinker (though most in both country and the city were that), to feel the tax on whiskey singling you out for punishment. The tax redistributed wealth by working itself deeply into rural people's peculiar economic relationship with whiskey. Many of Hamilton's congressional opponents wouldn't have understood that relationship. Hamilton did.

Nothing like whiskey occurs naturally. Its origins are alchemical, as implied by the term used in the whiskey-tax law: "spirits." The word "whiskey" anglicizes and abbreviates the Gaelic *"uisce beatha,"* or "water of life"; romance languages used *"aqua vitae"* and *"eau de vie."* All refer to a beverage that comes in many styles and whose production is simple if counterintuitive. Beer and wine would exist (or something like them would) without human intervention. Wet grain will become rank beer; wet flour, sourdough; old juice, bad wine. When controlled and treated right, good things come from what would otherwise be rot.

Nature produces alcohol—but also limits it. Yeast dies, ending the process. Increasing the potency of a fermented beverage, unlike concentrating flavors, can't be accomplished by boiling it down. Alcohol boils before water and dissipates instantly as steam.

Hence distilling, in which the steam rising from a boiling fermentation is made to cool into a dew. The boiled wine or beer, robbed of its spirit, can be thrown away as dross or served to animals. What remains, proportionally small by volume, is huge in kick and heat. Do it again, boiling the distillate, condensing its steam, and you'll have even less of something even more astoundingly strong, at once liquid and fume, the power of wine and beer magnified and trapped for all time. Fermentation makes a virtue of spoilage, but whiskey won't spoil.

Eighteenth-century Americans distilled whiskey just as their ancestors had, using a pot still. A kettle of fermented liquid known as wash—the wash was usually made from rye or corn mash; the best kettles were copper—bubbled over a hardwood fire. A pipe channeled the wash's steam through a tight lid on the kettle and then in coils, known as a worm, through a nearby bucket of water continuously replenished from a stream, and finally out through the side of the bucket. The steam was now a fluid, dripping into a receptacle. Known as low wines, this first run had more alcohol per volume than the original wash but not enough for whiskey. So low wines in turn were boiled, sometimes in a second, smaller still, and on this pass, when ejaculate emerged, it had to be divided. First came the foreshots, poisonous and smelly, not to be drunk by anyone valuing sanity. Then the heads, potable whiskey mixed with the last of the foreshots; using some of the heads lowered quality but added volume. Then the run, purest whiskey; and at the end, feints, weak and funky, also diminishing quality if mixed in excess with the run. Knowing by smell, taste, or hydrometer when the foreshots were ending, recognizing heads and the run, selecting the moment to make the cut, removing the run before overdiluting it with feints—these were among the skills of whiskey-makers.

The good product was clear. Inhaling it would water the eyes and rustle nose hairs. Swallowed, it made a hard impact, then a glowing heat; in the end, the feeling was surprisingly smooth, and soon after recovery, another shot might seem to be in order. Barrel storage darkened the drink and brought out redolent grain, woodsmoke, sugar. Drunk raw or aging, whiskey abruptly made the drinker and the world different.

Americans drank alcoholic beverages in huge quantities. Distilling went on in home stillhouses, at community stills, and in large-scale commercial operations. The Philadelphia elite, downing alcohol with most meals and between them, favored imported wines but also liked French brandy, a whiskey made from wine. Rum—cane whiskey, imported from the Caribbean or distilled domestically from imported molasses—was for a time the country's favorite drink, and army rations routinely included rum, until grain whiskey came in vogue early in the eighteenth century with the influx of Scots-Irish settlers, who brought expertise in domestic distilling. By the time of the revolution, domestic whiskey was gaining popularity; soon it would replace rum as the country's drink.

Many small farmers distilled seasonally. Whiskey was consumed by men, women, and children at all times of day and every sort of gathering: muster, church, election, work, dance, and fight. Often a community distiller kept pot stills going through the harvest, and farmers brought in their grain and took away the whiskey, paying the distiller in a portion of product. The Philadelphia College of Physicians had correctly identified domestic whiskey as the cheap drink of the laboring classes, but people in other classes enjoyed whiskey too, and by the 1790s, even as the west was making itself the home of radical agitation and defiant independence, the best whiskey was known to come from there, especially from the Forks of the Ohio, whose "Monongahela rye" possessed consistent strength and purity. The region achieved brand recognition. Its whiskey was known by name in Philadelphia and in New Orleans.

Easterners lampooned the people of the western mountains as habitual drunks. Yet it was popularity in the east that made whiskey unusual, among the products of small and subsistence farmers, for being a cash crop, with eager markets both within the regions that produced it, where a gallon might sell for 25 cents, and in regions east of the mountains, where high-quality rye whiskey could bring from 50 cents to a dollar. To haul twenty-four bushels of milled rye over the Alleghenies to eastern markets would have taken three pack animals. Six dollars might result from such effort; costs would outrun revenues. Reducing those bushels to two eight-gallon kegs of whiskey reduced transport requirements to a single animal, and while income from such a venture varied with middlemen and rake-offs, it could approach $16.

With a value nearing the absolute—it might vary by region but given countrywide appetites couldn't depreciate—whiskey became currency in places where coin wasn't seen. Barter paralyzed local economies, but whiskey was a true medium, always exchangeable for cash somewhere down the line, thus maintaining value against metal. A liquid commodity both literally and figuratively, the drink democratized local economies, offering even tenants and sharecropping laborers a benefit. Tenants often wanted to pay rent, and laborers often got paid, in a portion of the grain they harvested. Community stills transformed, for a cut, such cumbersome forms of payment into something fungible. And while landlords often refused in-kind crops, or demanded them in extravagant quantities, they'd take whiskey for rent. The product connected popular-finance theories with the small-scale commercial development that, though marginal, had potential to free rural people of debt and dependency.

So a federal tax on whiskey was hardly, to the small distillers who made up the majority that would pay it, the mere luxury-tax-with-concomitant-health-benefit that Hamilton had described to a Congress eager to be swayed. The poorest people, hired hands paid in kind, experienced the whiskey excise as a tax on income: if community distillers had to pay the tax, they'd have to compensate themselves by taking a larger share of whiskey—that is, currency—from people who brought their grain salaries in for conversion. Growers too felt the pain. There was no tax on grain, but westerners who raised grain were forced, in part by federal policies that kept the Mississippi closed, to convert grain to whiskey in order to transport it eastward. The tax thus imposed a federal tax on western farmers while leaving farmers in more convenient and prosperous places untaxed.

The tax had the further potential not merely to crimp but to shut off profits entirely. The duty would be collected by federal officers, in coin, at the point of production, often a log stillhouse on a small farm. It wasn't clear where cash for the payment would come from, and failure to pay would make the product unconveyable. Not registering a still was punishable by a cash fine, set first at $150, soon at $250; either number was higher than the cash equivalent of most people's annual income. Assets—the whiskey and the still itself—could be seized as well.

But even coming up with coin wasn't the worst difficulty the tax would give small farmers and laborers. Hamilton explained the tax as one on drinkers; producers, he said, simply passed the tax along in the price. That fact had an effect he didn't describe. Nobody could work up a subject like Hamilton, and he'd studied distilling: the draft excise bill was replete with knowledgeable calculations regarding proof, heads, and low wines. His inspiration was a success of the British Empire, where distilling and government had a long history together. From as early as the seventeenth century, large distillers had actually favored whiskey excises—had even contributed expertise to helping the government write excise laws. In 1785, an act of Parliament gave a tax rebate to big distillers, and later acts went all the way, placing an outright ban on small stills, making it actually criminal in England to distill on anything but the largest scale. Even as the U.S. Congress was passing its whiskey tax in 1791, Parliament was banning stills of less than five-hundred-gallon capacity.

The goal was industry consolidation. Hamilton had learned from the English that commercial agriculture and large industry, when publicly chartered, given tax breaks, and financed by large loans, might turn the United States into an industrial empire to compete with England's. The labor power dissipated on small family farms and in artisan shops could be gathered up, deployed at factories and diversified commercial farms, and boosted through efficient organization. Big distilling had the potential, given American drinking habits, to be highly profitable—yet small, seasonal producers, especially in the west, competed with industrial distillers and kept revenues scattered, engines weak. Hamilton's whiskey tax didn't merely redistribute wealth from the many to the few, subdue rural economies, and pound the restless, defiant west. It also served as one of the heavier cogs in a machine for restructuring all of American life.

Not that Hamilton was offering an explicit tax break to big distillers, who did pay the tax too. But just as in England, big distillers were all for the excise, and it wasn't hard to see why. Hamilton was giving them overwhelming competitive advantages. He established two modes of paying the tax. Distillers in towns and villages, more readily monitored by tax officials, paid a per-gallon tax on the gallons they actually produced; distillers in what the law defined as the country, where operations were isolated and hard to reach, paid an annual flat fee on the gallon capacities of their stills, defined as the number of gallons of wash held in the pot. Hamilton's arithmetic was informed and precise. He wanted to get 9 cents per gallon produced. To set the rate of the flat, still-capacity tax, he observed that 100 gallons of rye or corn wash yielded about 12 gallons of spirit, and 100-gallon still, running at full capacity, produced about 180 gallons a month. Assuming a four-month distilling season, or 720 gallons, collecting 9 cents per gallon came to a little over $60 per year. If you had a 100-gallon still, that's what you'd pay. Stills with lower capacities paid proportionally lower rates.

But Hamilton's calculation was drawn, not surprisingly, from typical processes of large-scale industrial distillers. Small distillers made whiskey within a much shorter cycle, sometimes a week, rarely longer than two months—and within those cycles they couldn't work stills steadily, at full capacity. They had other things to do; they had few employees or none. Producing many fewer gallons than the number on which the flat fee was calculated, they paid far more per gallon than the 9 cents paid by large distillers. Meanwhile, large distillers, with capital to invest, began seeking ways of producing more than the number of gallons on which the flat rate was based, lowering their taxes substantially.

Producers in towns, whom Hamilton taxed on the actual gallons they produced—these were often the larger distillers—paid their 9-cents-per-gallon tax in cash and received a discount of 2 cents on every ten gallons. If they couldn't pay that way, they posted a bond every quarter to cover the gallons they expected to remove from the still in the ensuing quarter. For the well-capitalized town producer, moving hundreds of gallons, the cash discount was easy to achieve and offered a nice break; bonds too were not hard to post. While most small producers didn't operate in towns, ones who did would have to resort to the punitive bond, which, if it could be posted at all, meant paying a higher tax per gallon than the big producer.

In every configuration, on every level, Hamilton had designed the law to charge small producers who could least afford it a higher tax. And the most significant effect of the higher tax was that it would, as Hamilton said, have to be passed on to consumers. Small producers would have to raise prices. Big producers could lower prices, sharply underselling the small distillers, taking over their customers, ultimately driving small producers out of business. Closing down local whiskey economies, the whiskey tax pushed self-employed farmers and artisans into the factories of their creditors.

More than a fourth of the stills in America were located at the Forks of the Ohio. Even before passage of the tax, meetings had taken place there to redefine, in western independence, the embattled spirit of the popular movement's contribution to the revolution. Men like Daniel Hamilton had fought a war that failed hopes for fairness and democracy. Their state constitution had been altered to restore old, pre-revolutionary relations between the many and the few. Industrial entrepreneurs were engrossing small farms, sewing up trade, and turning Forks settlers into hired laborers. That was bad enough. Then Congress passed the whiskey tax.

CHAPTER FOUR

Herman Husband

Herman Husband still lived in the lonesome farmhouse in the mountains where, almost ten years earlier, he'd shown Mr. Brackenridge maps and discussed Daniel, Ezekiel, and the New Jerusalem. Husband had seemed, to the younger man, old; now Husband was nearly seventy. He'd also seemed mad. In flickering firelight, with disheveled white hair, Husband had been talking about visions. Mr. Brackenridge had visions too, of course: a world-class United States literary culture, the westward expansion of free yeomen. Alexander Hamilton had a vision of an American manufacturing and commercial empire. Herman Husband's visions were qualitatively different from both Hamilton's and Brackenridge's, not only for involving fulfillment, on the North American continent, of Hebrew prophecies and the Christian millennium but also for being not ideas but things.

Husband actually saw his visions. They'd led him from indolence and privilege to this mountainside farm, where he wore loose clothes, went barefoot, and in the early 1790s began preaching an imminent spiritual and political conflagration.

He was born in 1724 and annoyed his family, fifteen years later, by being born again. He wasn't being groomed for religious enthusiasm. The Husbands had risen, in only two generations in America, from laboring in bondage to owning tobacco fields on the Chesapeake Bay, enjoying a second-echelon Anglican plantation lifestyle, and raising a son to reach the first echelon. Herman Husband would spend much of his life trying to smash the system of tenancy and debt that made life impossibly hard for laborers and small farmers. It was a system his grandfather had broken out of, surviving a term as an indentured tobacco worker, marrying a landed widow, obtaining appointments in law enforcement, making shrewd land purchases, planting tobacco, diversifying with a small ironworks. With an inheritance from the former indentured servant, Herman's parents moved east, bought more than 1,700 acres, and built a large brick house on the main road on the east side of the Susquehanna River. They were slave-owning tobacco farmers. The boy grew up in luxury.

The confrontational style that would mark Herman Husband's career became evident at the age of seven, when he was so hard to control that he was sent to live with his maternal grandfather. This grandfather was another hard worker—he kept a tavern, operated a ferry, and grew tobacco—but he was attentive to his own and others' salvation and therefore owned no slaves. He did have indentured laborers, and the boy found himself working alongside them and sleeping in their outbuilding. His grandfather required the workers to recite, before they slept, the Lord's Prayer and the Apostles' Creed. Herman lay in the dark and listened. He took stern correction from his grandfather. When he went home at the age of eight, the grandfather had died, bequeathing the boy strong feelings about dire inner struggles. Still willful and passionate, Herman spent much time alone, seeking salvation. The deep voice of his late grandfather told him that the weekly, polite devotions the Husband family made among other rich Anglicans could do nothing to save each corrupt soul from delighting in the luxury, waste, and greed by which we shut ourselves away from love and forgiveness. Everything the boy saw, as he grew into adolescence and took his part in the gaming, riding, and partying of the Chesapeake planting class—supported, he was more and more agonizingly aware, by the forced labor of thousands of human beings—told him that what his grandfather said was true.

By the time he was fifteen, Herman Husband's willfulness was taking new forms. Hunts, cards, drinking, and house-to-house frolics were the arenas of manly accomplishment in his set, which aped the richest set just above it. He was shy, but his father encouraged him to participate in social life, as did the local Anglican clergyman, who told him that no spiritual degradation could result from taking a rightful place among the cavaliers. A deep inner voice suggested otherwise. The conflict was resolved when George Whitefield came to town.

An English preacher, only twenty-five but already a superstar in Great Britain, Whitefield was making his first major tour of the American colonies. In Philadelphia, where he preached on the courthouse steps, eight thousand people packed the streets around him. He was a skinny youth with a bad squint. What made him riveting were his voice, which carried astoundingly far, somehow wafting every crystalline syllable into the most open parts of listeners' hearts, and his theology. Whitefield was preaching new birth for every person. Individual faith, not received form, was the means of achieving it, and there were no conditions: utter forgiveness of ineradicable sin could be sought with simplicity. Whitefield was unrestrained in arraigning Episcopalian and other established colonial denominations, which, he believed, actively obstructed people's chances for salvation. But hellfire was not his emphasis. Bliss was. Conversion was a feeling, he taught, an unmistakable personal experience not to be achieved by thought or doctrine. Though indescribable, conversion suffused the reborn person with delight in the surpassing loveliness of godhead. It transformed a life.

Shortly after his arrival in the colonies, Whitefield preached in the village of North East, near the Chesapeake, to what was for him a small crowd: publicity had been weak, and only 1,500 people turned out. One of them was Herman Husband, who was hardly the first privileged adolescent in eighteenth-century America to be converted by fervent preaching to a fresh view of himself, his church, and colonial society as a whole. This was the Great Awakening, a movement entering a new phase even as young Husband encountered it. Intense experiences of the kind described by George Whitefield had been inspiring conversions in huge numbers throughout the colonies. As early as the 1720s, certain ministers had stopped worrying specifically about sexual immorality and irreligion and started denouncing all the vagaries and fashions of the modern world. Throughout the thirties, ministers like the famous theologian Jonathan Edwards, of Northampton, Massachusetts, preached less on sensual sin than on ways such sin expresses itself in greed, a sign of general spiritual degradation. People in every denomination and province were challenging practices of established churches, which were coming to be known as "old light" and "old side," in contrast to the "new lights" and "new sides," who broke away from dead churches, flocked to hear preaching in fields, delighted in the immediate presence of godhead, and condemned the acquisitiveness that had long been seen—fatally, new lights believed—as a sign of spiritual virtue.

Not that the first Awakening preachers were mere social reformers. Redemption didn't come, they believed, by tinkering with human institution, inherently flawed, but by grace. Yet they made explicit connections between the transcendent joy of new birth and the general happiness of people in the American colonies. This melding of the redemption of the individual with the redemption of society would determine the course of Herman Husband's life. A half century after he first heard Whitefield preach, Husband would be trying to bring that kind of redemption to the Forks of the Ohio and the entire western country.

During the Great Awakening, every established denomination cracked in two, youth veering new-side, parents clinging to old; unestablished sects like Baptists, known for spontaneity and enthusiasm, gained new members. Yet when the first swell of fervency subsided, the movement became a sustaining force in the lives of urban laborers and artisans and the tenants and smallholders on what, at the time, was frontier: the big Allegheny Valley of Pennsylvania and Virginia, the Carolina mountains, southern New Jersey, western New England's Berkshires. The movement faced opposition from many quarters. Old-light ministers castigated what they saw as the Awakening's preference for hysteria over doctrine. Liberal theologians too, trying to get Enlightenment ideas about human reason into churches, condemned the Awakening's appeal to mere feeling. Bosses were dismayed to find fieldhands and factory laborers dropping work to pray and attend outdoor services.

Evangelical preachers didn't disdain doctrine, reason, or work. They disdained duty imposed from outside and any expression of greed, and they believed that while reason is a particularly beautiful gift (many Evangelicals had a strong interest in natural science), human beings, inherently perverse, will warp reason to rationalization and self-deception: if Anglican liberals believed they could think their way into salvation, they were sadly mistaken. The Awakening confronted bosses and workers, creditors and debtors, landlords and tenants, ministers and worshipers, teachers and students, and men and women with the news that spiritual justification depends not on acts of devotion, nor on passive belief, but on acting, through God, with loving responsibility toward other people.

In 1739, when Herman Husband heard George Whitefield, the movement was undergoing a change. The Awakening began to see itself not as an amazing series of conversions but as the beginning of spiritual renewal for all creation, the impending millennium, prophesied for Christians in the Revelation of Saint John and certain books of the Old Testament. British and American preaching had long turned to interpretation of millennial prophecy, in which, after a period of human degradation, Christ returns unexpectedly with a heaven-splitting shout and conducts a horrible battle, known as Apocalypse, against the beasts and harlots of Satan and their earthly armies. Christ's victory destroys the sinful kingdoms of the world and binds Satan in chains for a thousand years, during which Christ establishes his reign of perfect happiness for believers on earth. That millennium is followed by a brief, easily crushed rebellion by Satan; then Christ makes a last judgment of all souls living and dead and ends history by carrying the saved souls to bliss in heaven.

The story was familiar; it was also confusing. Generations of theologians had devoted much thought and writing to reconciling the internal contradictions in the book of Revelation and discrepancies between that book and the books of Ezekiel and Daniel. Theories about the millennium abounded.

Great Awakening preachers gave the millennium their own twist. A precondition of the thousand-year reign of Christ on earth had long been said to be the horrible Apocalypse, with its destruction of the earthly kingdoms and their unconverted worshipers of luxury and vice. New-light theologians switched the sequence of events. Apocalypse, they suggested, might not come until *after* the thousand years of earthly felicity. This sequence allowed time for the kingdoms of the world to be transformed. Last judgment might not be necessary. All might be brought into God's love, gradually, without fire, flood, and horror. The removal of saints to heaven need not occur either, as the end of history might be accomplished in perfect, eternal happiness of life on earth. Even the Second Coming of Christ took on, in this rendition, new meaning. The Second Coming, while literal, didn't necessarily refer to a personal manifestation of Christ on earth but to the infusion of Christ's redeeming power in all people.

The best news, new-light preachers insisted, was that this universal renewal was already under way. The proof was the Awakening itself. The split between new and old lights was the real last battle; soon all would be new. Whitefield's tours of the colonies, for example, were reversing the long-standing American trend in which sects forever subdivided themselves, each trying to be purer than the sect that spawned it. Whitefield had no interest in sects, or in superior purity: he preached to Presbyterians, Congregationalists, Episcopalians, Catholics, Quakers, Moravians. While many preachers were less ecumenical than Whitefield—especially regarding Quakers and Catholics—people from warring sects and mutually hostile colonies were growing united in a new, shared faith. There had long been a folk belief that in the last days, the sun would rise in the west. Now this prediction seemed to refer to the ascendancy of faith in North

America. No longer the Puritans' city on a hill, American society was the stage for a cosmic struggle, climaxing in this generation.

From the 1740s on, millennium in America was a call to action. Work would be consecrated, greed would die, union flourish, and the idea that God's love is a particular love for you—though helpful as a step in accepting forgiveness—transcended: Salvation of the whole society was the goal. Passivity was error. Inclusion among the saved required taking on the work of redemption and actively pushing history toward the coming kingdom. Twenty years before the revolution, Jonathan Edwards predicted a union of American colonies under a charismatic leader. In the 1770s, the next generation of Evangelicals, increasingly committed to liberating the working class, would do more to realize that union than liberal theologians and university rationalists—natural allies of creditor-class revolutionaries—would ever admit. Evangelicals opposed greed and luxury, supported paper finance, and worked for general salvation. They viewed the American union as instituting freedom and equality for all people and George Washington as the avatar of a cosmic, not merely a political, change. In 1775, Continental troops mustered in Newburyport, New Hampshire, before marching to the Canadian Maritimes to solicit support for American independence. George Whitefield had died in Newburyport five years earlier. Before starting their mission, the troops went to Whitefield's grave, dug up the coffin, and pried it open. On the bones, the clerical collar and cuffs were intact. The soldiers took the preacher's clothing to carry as a standard in the struggle for liberty.

In the 1740s, young Husband became convinced that schisms between old and new lights presaged the biblical millennium. The book of Daniel seemed to be saying that all dead churches would be redeemed by the spread of one small, enlightened church, which the adolescent Husband imagined resembling the primitive Christians after the Crucifixion. It was his duty to join that group.

The only problem was finding it. He split with his father's Anglicanism to join the Presbyterians, split with old-side Presbyterians to join the new side, and then discovered the Quakers, to the horror not only of polite Chesapeake society but also of his new-side brethren. The theologian Jonathan Edwards warned against new lights' unhealthy obsession with spiritual independence. For years Herman Husband, searching for what he described as the drop of leaven in the parable, which over time fermented a whole sea, embodied that obsession. The truth Husband yearned for was so uncompromising that it couldn't be found.

Throughout his twenties and thirties, however, he did remain an active Quaker, a member of the East Nottingham monthly meeting near the Maryland-Pennsylvania border. Quaker theology was radical enough for Husband to embrace. Quakers described the Holy Spirit as indwelling love; that idea matched the blissful intimations Husband sometimes received of the holiness of creation. Too, Quakers resembled early Christians for having been horribly persecuted in England and New England. They had a conception of universal brotherhood that recognized people living, as Husband put it, even in China as children of God, and thus they strongly opposed slavery. Their worship indulged no ritual forms or shows, and while they defied conformity imposed from outside, they were pacifists, radically loyal to the precept to love one's enemy. He served on management committees of the Society of Friends, the Quakers' tightly structured organization, setting standards of conduct for the main meeting and its local weekly subsidiaries. He married, had children, bought his own plantation in Maryland, and became rich, as many American Quakers did. He was a land speculator and part-owner of two copper mines and a smelting business, an investor in a Caribbean shipping firm. Those who later knew Herman Husband as the barefoot ancient of the Alleghenies would have been startled to get a look at him in his thirties, a diversified Maryland planter and businessman like his father, yet religious like his grandfather, owning no slaves, eschewing frivolity, and taking no public office. He managed all his operations with diligence and aplomb and made enormous profits. Meanwhile, with many others rich and poor, he prepared for the millennium.

Yet he would end his forties in tumult, a fugitive traveling under aliases, a radical leader of the people's movement. The change began with a move to the backcountry. The western forests of North Carolina, at first barely settled but soon filling with home-steaders and squatters, became in the 1750s a site of intense land speculation. Husband first visited the area as a bargain hunter, buying up thousand-acre parcels for himself and other members of a Maryland consortium. Over the next few years, he visited Carolina again and bought more land. He would become one of the area's largest landowners, with more than ten thousand acres along the Sandy Creek and the Deep River. Even before he moved there to live, the new, wild land seemed to Husband not merely a fine busi-ness opportunity but also a natural place to encourage human lib-erty, especially of the religious kind. He wrote to Lord Granville, who owned the upper half of the colony, importuning him to block the Anglican church from establishing itself as the legal religion of the backcountry and stifling, as it had in Maryland, religious free-dom. He also hoped Granville would stop western landbuyers from bringing slaves into the backcountry. The abominable institu-tion had practical detriments that Husband could explain from experience. He pointed out to Granville a grim irony: planters mur-dered American natives, forced African natives to work stolen land, and left poor whites unemployed. In the backcountry, Husband hoped for a new and better home. In 1762, following his wife's death, he moved his children to western North Carolina—permanently, he thought. He joined the Cane Creek monthly meeting, and married a local Quaker.

Yet even as he established himself as a leading backcountry planter, his spiritual absolutism began reasserting itself. Husband's first fight in North Carolina wasn't with government but with the Society of Friends. He'd long been disturbed by the way every church, in the end, denies its members the right to voice revelations of the Holy Spirit when those revelations conflict with procedures of the church. Perpetuating itself as an institution, a church fails its original purpose and dies spiritually. Quakers' roots were in the religious enthusiasms of seventeenth-century England, when the most extreme Puritanism had fractured. Back then, Fifth Monarchy Men proclaimed millennium, Levellers demanded wide access to the franchise, Diggers invited all to share goods and plant on common lands, and Grindletonians, a tiny sect from the village of Grindleton in Yorkshire, predicted heaven on earth. Ranters ranted, Baptists baptized, and Quakers, naked and daubed with shit, quaked as they invaded high Anglican services to call out the pharisees. Persecution inevitably followed, and the Society of Friends had spent a century developing a strict discipline to rein in violent enthusiasms. Quakers now enjoyed some toleration by respectable society. Pumped-up new lights of the Great Awakening, adding to Quaker numbers, glorified the old fervency and threatened to revive a ranting spirit that the society had worked hard to dispel.

At the Cane Creek meeting, Husband rose one day to condemn Quaker discipline. He confronted the assembled members with what he termed the impossibility of following the discipline while also following the dictates of conscience. He was expelled from the Society of Friends.

For twenty years, in accordance with his own intimations and the mysterious visions interpreted by Daniel, he'd hoped to live amid the one group that could bring on the millennium, the drop of leaven to ferment a sea. Midlife, he was unchurched. His excommunication placed him in a state of dejection. Even hopes of the millennium now seemed in doubt. He was forty.

While Husband suffered the pain of excommunication, Great Britain imposed the Stamp Act on the colonies. Backcountry people, hundreds of miles from the seaboard where colonial furor coalesced, had little to do with protest, petitioning, and assembly battles over the Stamp Act, but Husband, in his spiritual loneliness, read newspaper articles and pamphlets against the act and saw something that began to clarify all he'd been confused about. To his surprise, when anti–Stamp Act writers wrote of liberty, they evinced intense spirituality. They might not be talking about Christ, he thought, but they seemed inspired by what religious people call

Christ. He'd always viewed civil government and religion—wrongly, he saw now—as separate entities: religion the force that gave true meaning to creation, civil government the small, dry offshoot, necessary, perhaps, but dismayingly corrupt, rightfully the province of kings, nobles, scholars, and lawyers, not of people possessed of revelation. He returned with excitement to the book of Daniel. Now he began to understand it. The book was about government. Daniel's interpretations of mysterious dreams, the miry clay from which all vegetation grows, the beasts of the field and of the sea, the horns and the mountain—these gave a key to the history of government and described in symbolic form something Husband began thinking of as good government. Good government would, in itself, bring about the millennial climax of humankind. And the biblical authors knew this.

Wielding this new idea, Husband emerged as a powerful figure in a field he'd long avoided: public action. By the end of the sixties he was a folk hero, elected by his neighbors to the provincial assembly while carrying out a comprehensive politics of resistance. He led protests, wrote demands, and was repeatedly jailed. Despite the refreshing effect on him of the Stamp Act writers, Husband wasn't protesting a remote British government's interference in the colonies. His targets were local gentry who served as officials of a government no more distant than the East Coast, often those same anti-British Whigs whose words had inspired him. Oppression in the backcountry took the form of taxes levied by provinces, exponentially more unjust, from any objective perspective, than the imperial taxes on trade complained of so bitterly by rich merchants in port cities. In the backcountry, taxes drew maximum cash and physical effort (there were labor taxes for things like road building) from the mass of ordinary people for the flagrant benefit of a rich few. The rich were often exempted from taxes, which they had the job of collecting and at times liberally embezzling; they had the job of repossessing tax delinquents' property, which they stole. All public positions were occupied, through a patronage system, by gentry compensated not by salary but by a multitude of high commissions and fees, supposedly defined by law yet often defined by the officials themselves, who had a captive market and benefited from eastern governments' lack of interest in fairness for the back-country. Every transaction required the services of clerks, registrars, notaries, and other officers who did little and charged what they wanted. Sheriffs repossessed property at many times the value of delinquent taxes. Town commissioners gave friends and family contracts for public improvements, which were always intended to improve life and trade for the few.

In response, Regulators, as Husband's constituents began calling themselves, went beyond traditional blackface attacks and court riots. The Regulators' rioting was indeed memorable, especially at one court session in Hillsborough, North Carolina, where they occupied the town for days, beat and dragged officials through the streets, conducted a mock trial, and destroyed all the property of the most reviled official, whose elegant house they dismantled brick by brick. Husband, having plunged headlong into public life, helped lead that riot. Yet he was still a pacifist. He struggled with his allies' penchant for violence; he preferred confrontational petitions, speeches, and lawsuits, and in that context the Regulators articulated, in a series of petitions, a call for a complete economic restructuring of the province. They wanted a public land bank for easy credit; they wanted currency emissions to let them pay taxes in paper; they wanted direct public scrutiny of sheriffs' tax lists, collection records, and fee schedules. Land titles must be granted to improvers of land, not absentee landlords. Government must punish overreaching local officials. Court costs must be eased. Qualifications for voting and officeholding must be lowered. Most radically of all, they wanted taxes proportional to wealth. These demands were made not against the king but against a colonial government that, though operating under the king, the Regulators believed was violating the spirit of the English Constitution. Regulators wanted more government, not less, and they wanted it dedicated to protecting the liberties and opportunities of ordinary people.

Husband could irritate the Regulators. He still urged nonviolence; sometimes he made deals with the government, censoring himself to avoid jail time. But he also shuttled long distances to pursue the Regulators' agenda, both as an elected assemblyman in the tidewater capital of New Bern, North Carolina, where he was becoming a striking and controversial figure, and as a leader of resistance action in the west. Quakerish ways made him immune to finery, even to grooming. His graying hair was famously a mess. In his forties he already had the authority of old age.

In one assembly session, Husband introduced a radical Regulator petition, but backcountry issues were forever being swept aside by eastern merchants' struggles with the mother country. It was the governor, Lord Tryon, not merchants opposing British interference, who showed some sympathy for the plight of western settlers. Tryon visited their region and brought prosecutions against corrupt officials. In return, he wanted the Regulators to agree to disband. Husband and others were sure they were getting these weak concessions only by applying extreme and constant pressure. If anything, now was the time to escalate.

Husband was jailed and released three times in a tense series of riots, trials, and standoffs. The governor, meanwhile, kept trying to negotiate with the Regulators, who kept rebuffing him. During one of Husband's arrests in the backcountry, seven hundred Regulators marched on the prison to free the prisoner; terrified officials let him go. In New Bern, he rose in the assembly chamber to castigate the body and announced that if he was arrested again, men would come to release him. This was too much. Husband was stripped of legislative powers, expelled from the assembly, and arrested. Regulators did muster to march on the capital itself. Husband was acquitted, and the Regulator attack on New Bern was averted, but now the governor readied the provincial militia for serious action.

Husband had no illusions about how things would go if Regulators challenged the governor to a military contest. He argued for moderation, but the Regulation had become self-destructively defiant. In March of 1771, Tryon called out the militia and marched it west. Regulators armed themselves and mustered.

Tryon offered to withdraw troops if Regulators would only sign loyalty oaths and disband. Husband involved himself in the negotiations, hoping for compromise, but he was high on the list for hanging, no matter what ensued, and the Regulators, though outnumbered and outskilled, only mocked the governor's offers. The Battle of Alamance commenced. Two hours later the few Regulators who hadn't fled or been killed were captured. One was summarily hanged on the spot to mollify the troops; six others were hanged after a trial. Less than two months later, six thousand Regulators signed loyalty oaths and were granted an amnesty for past crimes. The North Carolina Regulation was over.

Husband, having failed to prevent the battle, fled on horseback just as it began, a fugitive from justice at forty-six, his new community shattered, his comrades hanged, his plantation seized by troops. He was alone again, a marked man. Yet he didn't sink into dejection. He drew resilience from hopes he'd recovered in the Regulation's struggle for justice in the backcountry. He'd been widowed again in North Carolina; not surprisingly, given his ardent nature, he'd married a third time. He had a large family, children whose ages spanned almost a generation. For Husband, unconsummated sexual tension was the most creatively fecund state—an image of Christ's relation to His church—and the crown of creation was the first stage of sexual passion between a man and a woman. He knew well the penalties for consummation: marriage, with the repetition and exclusivity that can silence the Song of Songs, followed by too many children. He loved his children and took good care of them, considering what was becoming a very high-risk lifestyle. Yet he was sure that if people were allowed to consult both nature and their consciences, they'd find a way of regulating their own reproduction. His third wife was another Cane Creek Quaker. Her name was Emmy; she was expelled from the Cane Creek meeting for marrying the excommunicant. Together they'd added children to those from his earlier marriages. Only twenty-seven when Husband fled the Battle of Alamance, Emmy was a Regulator too, a resourceful administrative talent and a partner in Husband's vision.

Pregnant and under surveillance by provincial authorities, Emmy managed to follow the fugitive north with her children and stepchildren and keep in touch with him without causing his capture. Husband had fled home to tidewater Maryland, where he stayed briefly with family and friends. When he learned that a childhood friend had established a hunting camp in the wildest part of western Pennsylvania, he resolved to seek refuge there from North Carolina law enforcement. After Husband left Maryland for the west, Emmy brought her family to Maryland, settling briefly in the farmland near Hagerstown in the western part of the state, southeast of the mountains, where she gave birth to another son, sent messages to Husband, and waited to hear from him.

The fugitive had meanwhile traveled west to Fort Cumberland and then northwest, ascending the Pennsylvania Alleghenies. Over the crest of those mountains, and partway down the west side, he arrived in an unsettled area known as the Glades, whose only tiny village was Bedford, where a low, small fort stood on the banks of the wild Juniata River. Though east of the Forks of the Ohio, the Glades' loneliness made them frightening to some, and strikingly beautiful to Husband. The country was rolling and thickly timbered, with bottomlands that grew bluegrass as tall as a man. Above and to the east, hills and then ridges shot upward, full of boulders, ancient trees, cliffs. A paradise for hunters and trappers, the Glades had long been a temporary home for hunting parties both native and white, who camped and took bear, deer, and beaver for the skin trade. Packs of skinny wolves, drawn by hopes of leftovers, nosed around the camps and bayed all night.

Husband began by using the Glades as a hideout and ended by civilizing it. Taking the alias Tuscape Death, he joined his childhood friend and another hunter in their rough wilderness camp. Both hunters agreed to bury his identity further by referring to him only as "the Quaker," a designation fitting his style of dress and refusal to carry arms. Husband wouldn't hunt, but he made himself useful at camp by dressing skins and adding crops to the hunters' scratch potato farming. When he began taking up his old development interests, the hunters laughed at him. He was buying and claiming Glades property, long considered too wild to farm, and registering it under the name Tuscape Death. To the hunters' further amusement, he expected to improve his land, raise crops and livestock there, even build a commercial gristmill. Most absurd seemed his plan to bring a young wife and a lot of children into this transient, all-male hunting and camping culture.

Husband had only the use of his horse and some basic cutting and digging tools. Yet he cleared acres and built a cabin and shed. He sent Emmy word to name their new son Isaac Tuscape Husband. He planted. When the farm was ready, he traveled to Hagerstown and rejoined his family at last. He described bluntly the ruggedness of the situation at the Glades. Emmy repeated what she'd told him by letter: she planned to settle with him there. Husband's grown sons didn't share his optimism about Indians and wild animals. Husband wouldn't raise a gun against other human beings, but as the family walked through the mountains with packhorses, his eldest son, John, only a few years younger than Emmy, carried one gun, John's brother Herman another.

Before long the family needed two log stables to house their livestock and a barn with a threshing floor for the grain they were growing in abundance. Herman Husband was becoming one of the biggest landowners in the Glades. Change came quickly and irreversibly. By the mid-1770s, more farmers than hunters lived in the newly erected county of Bedford. One settler's farmhouse boasted a four-hundred-pound metal stove. Trees had been felled and the turf plowed and planted; grazing livestock pushed out game, and hunters with it. When wolves, starved of leavings, began attacking hogs, humans organized posses to control wolves. Absentee land speculators, inevitably, also became interested; a local political ring, centered around the courthouse in the village of Bedford, represented creditor and landlord interests, with strong bonds to eastern officialdom. When politicians started receiving lucrative public offices in Bedford County, it was clear that minions of the Antichrist were starting to control local politics, even in the Glades.

Yet Husband kept a low profile. He was still in hiding. He explored the most forbidding parts of the Alleghenies, seeking easier passes east that would help develop the region. He began drawing elegant maps, perfectly scaled on grids, displaying visual and verbal information with precisely plotted longitudinal and latitudinal degrees, beautifully integrating neatly handwritten annotations. He studied the mountains' complex geology and vegetation. Husband and his horse, wearing protective suits of thick hide, fought their way through tangles of laurel and thorns. Tiny figures beside fallen, overgrown timber and huge rocks, they hauled surveying rods and chains down ridges, clambered up dry creek bottoms, walked outcroppings that opened on range after range of tree-covered mountain. Birds wheeled. In the humid, gusty days of early fall, the trees swayed high overhead, and chestnuts socked the turf while Husband, measuring his home, cut new trails.

In 1776 his aliases became unnecessary. The provincial government that had made him a fugitive was replaced, abruptly, by an independent entity known as the state of North Carolina. Even more miraculously, with its own independence, Pennsylvania restructured itself along the lines of what Husband considered good government. In creating a constitution with no upper house, easy access to the franchise, frequent elections, and close regulation of officials, Pennsylvania was beginning to make real what had once been Husband's demands. Many former Regulators, despising rich eastern revolutionaries, went Loyalist. But Husband had allies among the delegates to the convention that created the radical Pennsylvania constitution; the convention appointed him collector, in the Glades, of a new kind of tax, whose funds were earmarked for poor families of rural revolutionaries. Then his neighbors elected him to represent them in the Pennsylvania assembly.

In office in 1778, Husband was no longer an insurgent but among a majority that hoped—though embattled by the creditor faction—to use the new state government to change the world. To Pennsylvania radicals, this war, for all its grimness, revealed the wild dreams of Diggers, Levellers, and other seeming utopians as constitutional and republican, hard-nosed yet suffused with holy spirit. Husband had experience with legislative process, and many others in this revolutionary assembly were new to elected office, so at times he took a leading role. Trying to stabilize the crashing wartime economy, the assembly carried to new extremes populist measures that gave Bob Morris hives. They instituted the price-control regulations that Morris fumed over in the confederation Congress; they passed resolutions against profiteering merchants and the lust of avarice. They broke up a lead-mining monopoly. They considered a radical scheme, set forth by Husband, not only to tax property—and tax it in proportion to the quantity of property owned—but actually to tax income.

If those ideas seemed extreme, Husband had others. The scarcity of gold and silver, along with the paper-currency inflation that was sinking Pennsylvanians deeper in debt and foreclosure, inspired him to develop a full-scale monetary plan. Its most novel feature was a proposal to disconnect paper currency completely from gold and silver. Paper would always fluctuate unpredictably, Husband believed, if backed by metal, which was persistently overvalued. He envisioned a currency system tied to no external standard. Depreciation would of course occur, but the creditors' horror of any and all depreciation, and their concomitant obsession with gold, were actually making depreciation worse, Husband suggested. If money were taken off the gold standard, inflation, accepted as natural, could be limited and steadied, regulated by a thoughtful, centralized policy.

The creditors never had to withstand the horrors this plan would have caused them, because Husband's allies, though approving of many of his tax ideas, disliked the excessive regulation his monetary plan would require—and the idea of a paper currency without an ultimate gold standard was simply baffling. Despite his grave and authoritative mien, Husband's thinking lent him an aura that struck even fellow radicals as strange.

He left the body at the end of the session and returned to the

Glades. His neighborhood was suffering terribly from the deepening poverty of the wartime economy. The terror of British-inspired Indian attacks kept western people in their cabins or fleeing to forts. The outcome of the war was far from secure. The winter of 1779 brought a blizzard that lasted forty days, burying the Alleghenies deep in snow. Still, Husband's hopes for the revolution remained high.

Then they soared. That June, he was exploring an Allegheny pass when his life underwent yet another change. Like George Washington, Husband had been determined to connect the west to the east, but he thought roads built to serve private interests were impractical. That day he was looking for a natural highway, something passable because of its geological formation, which would allow those he called the princes of the east to come easily westward. All at once his road-building survey was swept into something engulfingly big. The vision he'd been awaiting all his life was given to him.

Herman Husband saw, very suddenly, where he really was. These Alleghenies, which he'd been exploring with such intense interest, formed the eastern wall of the New Jerusalem, the redeemed city of God described in the books of Daniel, Ezekiel, and Revelation. He was in the twelve-gated city. Like John, he was walking in Jerusalem. The Bible described the city symbolically, but he saw that it existed literally, on a massive scale, here on the North American continent. Now he knew why he'd been drawing, mapping, and surveying with such passion and precision. Up on this eastern wall, the four famous gates were really specific mountain passes; and if he followed this wall southward—as he immediately planned to—he would come to its intersection with a range that stretched toward the Pacific Ocean. Ultimately, all four walls might be surveyed, as well as the interior of the city, whose meaning for life in an independent America would be revealed.

Back at the farmhouse, he began reading with new eyes. Up in the forests he took long bushwhacking trips. One winter, when Indian raids sent everybody at the Glades to safety at Fort Cumberland, he traveled back to North Carolina to see his grown sons John and William, who had returned there to live, and to explore the Virginia mountains on the way. In 1784 he traveled to Canada. Ultimately he covered hundreds of miles, mapping and taking notes. It emerged that the four walls of the city stretched southward from the Hudson Bay to the southern end of the Appalachians, from Georgia westward to the foot of a north-south range running parallel to the Pacific, from the northern end of that range eastward to the Hudson Bay. He backed up these observations with intense and patient study. For historical context he used an oddball book attributed to Voltaire, deliberately employing the work of a rationalist because he didn't want bias in favor of religious vision. Ezekiel gave the best blueprint of the city: Husband was amazed to find that Ezekiel's dimensions for fields, walls, and gates, as given in cubits and furlongs, precisely matched Husband's own punctilious surveying, once units were modernized and scaled up to the size of the mountains. Daniel remained essential: The prophet's climactic symbol of the glorious mountain evoked the whole upthrust Allegheny area, with its astonishing ridges, hundreds of miles in length, and flat tops like the walls so carefully measured in Ezekiel. John's Revelation describes the eastern wall as made up of twelve kinds of precious stone. Husband saw that John meant valuable deposits of stone and mineral, six of which—sandstone, limestone, marble, salt, coal, and iron ore—the naturalist in Husband had already identified on travels through the woods.

There was nothing new in the literary world about a close reading of biblical prophecy as applied to contemporary settings and events. Isaac Newton had published a famous one, as had dozens of other philosophers, theologians, and scientists before and after Newton. What made the vision of New Jerusalem especially satisfying to Husband was the way it linked the ongoing war against England with social justice, millennial redemption for America, and a new understanding of the western country he'd come to live in. Husband tracked Daniel's history of government through the development of the modern states and interpreted Daniel as predicting the current revolution. Ezekiel had foreseen the exact locations and characters of the thirteen states. In the Prophets and in Saint John, the western country was specially blessed, the revolution divinely inspired.

Now Husband began writing. Publishing as "the Philosopher of the Allegheny," he predicted the war's draining British public finance. As "Hutrim Hutrim," he published a series of one-liners making patriotic prognostications. Husband described the philosopher of the Allegheny as an elderly wilderness prophet, tall and skinny, with piercing eyes and long white hair and beard. The philosopher lived in a cave, studied the stars, and interpreted dreams. In real life, visitors to the mountain farm found the rich, sixtyish Husband, a major Glades landowner with many horses and head of cattle, barefoot and unkempt, in old clothes. In spite of his unassuming dress and increasingly prophetic image, or perhaps because of them, he retained the respect of his farming and laboring neighbors. With the war over, his constituents elected him county commissioner. In his sermons he began to speak to them directly of biblical prophecy. Fulfillment of the visions he'd been chasing since his teens seemed at hand. Independence meant redemption.

For Husband was a nationalist. He wanted unity and a strong national government. In the 1780s, as he entered his own old age and the infancy of American independence, he called for regulation of local officialdom and fair and equal access to political power, but unlike many at the radical end of the revolutionary spectrum, he believed that the Antichristian powers of creditors and conservatives needed greater vigilance, planning, and control than anything state power would resist on its own. Husband envisioned the New Jerusalem as a powerful federal system. In contrast to the federal government endorsed by Alexander Hamilton, Husband's was designed to obstruct the concentration of wealth. Mixing biblical prophecy with the work of the English political writer Richard Price and other sources, Husband came up with a three-tiered federal structure. The thirteen states, at the lowest tier, continue to oversee their own counties and townships, but laws regarding property ownership are set by constitutional fiat. Titles must be granted to those dwelling on and cultivating land, not speculators. The state is responsible for granting each man a maximum of three hundred acres, with a wife owning an additional two hundred and each child receiving an additional one hundred at birth. While larger land-office titles may be granted, they are limited to two thousand acres and revert to the public if purchasers fail to use them. Inheritance laws prohibit large entailments to any single heir.

To ensure proper oversight of these and other laws, the next tier of government sorts the states into four large regions. Each of the four regions is operated by a senate, to which the unicameral assembly of each member state appoints a number of representatives apportioned by population. These four senates monitor laws of their member states, vetoing any that violate fairness and freedom. Finally, at the highest and most refined level of government, sits an executive body of twenty-four men—the four-and-twenty elders of Revelation—six appointed by each of the four regional senates. Elders hear appeals on vetoes of state laws, appoint judicial systems for the four regions, and buy, instead of steal, Indian lands. Western expansion is not a free-for-all dominated by those with cash and muscle: new lands are granted in the normal fashion to those who work them, and the elders form new states and regions by orderly process. When enough new states are formed, elders create a new region and place the states under a new senate, subject to the federal system.

Elders receive no salaries. They make decisions by majority rule. They hold their property communally. Appointees are between the ages of fifty and sixty and have risen through purifying lower levels of government. They serve ten-year terms, with one elder retired by lot every other year, to ensure rotation, and replaced by the appropriate senate.

Husband saw this federally structured kingdom of heaven, with its broad foundation and increasingly pure upper levels, both as a government and as the image of the restored temple of Jerusalem. It featured things like a progressive tax on wealth; an income tax; rules against nepotism; public promotion of arts and sciences; profit-sharing for workers; and paper currency, pegged to no gold standard, with a slow, centrally managed rate of inflation. It allowed no slavery. It made peace with the Indians. Thinking like this made some call Herman Husband "the madman of the mountains." Millennial interpretation might have been common, but linking it to a vision of a nation state, committed through dozens of administrative mechanisms to the welfare and advancement of all citizens, with the most successful and privileged bearing the larger portion of responsibility for all—to some this made old Herman Husband manifestly insane. But he didn't seem insane to those of his neighbors who listened with growing fervor to his sermons. In 1789, they sent him again to the assembly.

By then, however, all his visions and hopes were shredded. In the eleven years since he'd served in the radical assembly, the struggle had gone on between the creditors and the radicals. The creditors had won. The U.S. Constitution had been ratified. When it was first published, Husband had begun reading it with great excitement, in part because George Washington, whom he'd long considered a model of disinterested judgment, an elder, had worked on its framing. He finished reading in horror and disgust. The thing was an obscene fraud.

Washington had betrayed the people by endorsing, in pursuit of national pomp, the return of tyranny. The Constitution, inverting Husband's own idea for a federal structure—a broad foundation, with levels successively purified—had a top-down authority, with an elite, unelected upper house, the whole thing clearly intended to extinguish ordinary citizens' only hope for direct representation: their state legislatures. Husband too had wanted to see the states managed from above. But the U.S. Constitution created unlimited freedom within the states for precisely the wrong people, making the creditor class solvent and giving it the private use of a whole nation's strength.

Then the Pennsylvania assembly called for a convention to revise the revolutionary state constitution, reestablishing traditional relations. Quickly following that debacle came Alexander Hamilton's plan of national finance. The Beast, not merely resurgent, was ravenous as never before. The west, now holiest of holies in Husband's spiritual geography, was being opened to exploitation by the seacoast landjobbers, speculators, and other merchants, whose expensive educations had been purchased solely for the purpose of freeing them from doing any useful work. They were already beginning the demolition of the west, where Jacob had told Joseph the children of Israel would bless all nations. The federal government organized the infidels in an almost irresistibly powerful system. The courthouse ring in Bedford, the elites of Pittsburgh: these were the advance guards of degeneracy, harlotry, the rule of Antichrist. The idolatry natural to mankind—even Samuel's sons, Husband preached, were made judges and took bribes—had surfaced in the official corruption that Daniel called the abomination of desolation, now flooding the federal government. Profit-sharing and equal land distribution weren't on the minds of the industrialists who had invaded the west. Landless workers were nearly slaves. Hamilton's finance plan was a declaration of war on the holy city, whose people were already becoming captive.

Back when Husband's hopes for American transformation had been so thrillingly high, he'd embraced even the urban seaboard in his vision of good government: Unified with the transformed federation, the east might look up to the west as an image of the temple; judgment would be gentle. But by the early 1790s, with the passage of the finance plan, the east had exposed itself as incorrigibly wicked and degenerate. The resurgence of luxury and vice was all the more bitter because it followed a moment of hope for fundamental change.

Husband's long commitment to nonviolence faltered. The Alleghenies had come to seem a fortification against the earthly kingdom of the east.

In his sermons, he began telling the western people that a body of free laborers, militiamen, and voters, being numerous, has the physical power to overcome a sinful few. In the last days, he reminded them, a laboring, industrious people would prevail over the armies of kings and tyrants, who rob the people and live in idleness on their labor. Husband identified the industrious people with local militias—freemen democratically electing their officers, armed for regional defense. Salaried hirelings were everywhere in the westerners' midst, yet the militias, like the Jews when in the infant and virtuous state of their own government, could throw off the yoke of tyranny anytime they chose. Hirelings could be identified. Every person must watch for them.

Your old men shall dream dreams, prophets had said. As Herman Husband approached his seventieth year, far from depressed, he was preaching a long-promised millennium that waited only for the last battle with the Beast. People were listening. The militias were drilling.

CHAPTER FIVE

The Neville Connection

The man appointed to collect the whiskey tax in western Pennsylvania was General John Neville, an entrepreneur and commercial farmer, whose plantation, which he called Bower Hill, sprawled on a mountaintop a few miles south of the Monongahela above the valley of Chartier Creek. Despite his wealth, the high style in which he enjoyed it, and the control he exercised over the local economy, General Neville had been fairly popular with the people of the Forks of the Ohio, where he'd lived for almost ten years. That popularity began dissipating quickly when, in the spring of 1791, the general received an appointment as inspector of the revenue for the fourth survey of what was now termed, for purposes of federal excise collection, the district of Pennsylvania.

For General Neville was also a large-scale distiller. The leading local beneficiary of the tax had been given the job of enforcing and collecting it.

With passage of the excise law in March of 1791, the executive branch had divided the nation into federal districts, each corresponding to a state. The larger states were further divided into surveys, whose inspectors' responsibilities included hiring deputies, registering stills, monitoring production, coordinating collection, and reporting violators. General Neville's wasn't just any survey. Comprehending Pennsylvania's four westernmost counties— Washington, Allegheny, Fayette, and Westmoreland—as well as Bedford, in the highlands just to the east, it placed under Neville's purview the heart of distilling in America.

Sixty when he received the appointment, testy and fearless, Neville was Virginian by birth and ancestry and had long been known to the president as not only ambitious and rich but also tough. He differed in significant ways from most of his neighbors. Before moving here, he'd served his native state in the border war. Of English, not Scots-Irish or German, stock, he took pride in his Elizabethan ancestors and their forebears of the Wars of the Roses. An Episcopalian, he eschewed both low-church grimness and religious enthusiasm. Hunting, riding, and dynasty were his pursuits, and in his background was an element of romance: his father had been kidnapped from England to the colonies; his mother was a cousin of Lord Fairfax, who had owned a large part of Virginia. Neville had been attracted to the west from a young age and first reached the Forks as a Virginia militia officer under the command of his tidewater neighbor George Washington, in General Braddock's failed expedition against the French and Shawnee. Later, when the militia got into the border skirmishes with Pennsylvania, John Neville received for his service to Virginia five hundred acres near the Chartiers Creek.

In the spring of 1775, news of the battles of Lexington and Concord came to the Shenandoah Valley, where Neville was living, quickly followed by orders from the Continental Congress: Captain Neville, known to have experience and property in the western region, was to march one hundred Virginia militiamen to the headwaters of the Ohio and occupy Fort Pitt, abandoned by British troops yet vulnerable to their return from Canada. Neville and his men arrived that fall at the confluence of rivers and took command of the wet, dilapidated fort, with the job of defending the west from natives.

Pennsylvania partisans weren't pleased to see the Virginia militia at Fort Pitt, but while Captain Neville negotiated treaties with Indians, he also declined a commission as justice of the purported Virginia county of Yohogania. He would remain a Virginian by sentiment. Yet in that period of flux, he guessed that allying himself too tightly with any state might turn out to be foolish.

When Congress sent regular troops to relieve him at Fort Pitt, Neville joined the Continental Army as a lieutenant colonel. He commanded the twelfth, eighth, and fourth Virginia regiments and saw action at Trenton, Germantown, Princeton, and Monmouth. He wintered at Valley Forge. He led troops in the southern campaign. He was imprisoned in Charleston. Exchanged in time to serve in the decisive victory at Yorktown, he left the army with the brevet rank of brigadier general. Now he wanted to live in the area where he'd speculated and held brief command. With the border war resolved by the Congress, General Neville believed there was commercial potential across the mountains, as well as a chance for a lavish and domineering lifestyle, harder to come by in settings already civilized.

He'd married Winifred Oldham, also from a prominent Virginia family and notably game. General and Mrs. Neville, having come to a place where some tidewater planters were loath even to visit, lived large. Like Jefferson at Monticello, they built on a hilltop.

By the time he received his appointment as revenue inspector, Neville had a ten-thousand-acre plantation, a place not just to inhabit but to develop and profit by. Bower Hill was a diversified commercial farm, nothing like the subsistence smallholdings owned and rented by so many of his neighbors. It had large barns and other farm buildings, fields near and far from the mansion, livestock, transport, complicated deals and contracts—and slaves. Slavery was hardly unknown in Pennsylvania, even in the far west; still, slaveowners stood out. The assembly had instituted a policy of gradual abolition. Quakers and certain Presbyterians vocally opposed the institution. Many people at the Forks were simply not rich enough to own slaves.

General Neville's slaves lived in outbuildings set away from his home. The fanciest home in that part of the west, Bower Hill was a showplace where the Nevilles entertained in a style that might have seemed adequate to the Bob Morrises of Philadelphia and would have stunned any visitor expecting rustic simplicity. Two stories high, sheathed in clapboard, the mountaintop home was adjoined by a square log kitchen roofed with shingles and a broad veranda for enjoying the rugged charm of hills, ravines, and sky. When log houses were standard even for comfortable farmers at the Forks, the Neville family walked down halls with plaster walls and ceilings, on wood floors carpeted with rugs. Wallpapered rooms held elegant furniture and framed pictures. There were five feather beds, lots of china plate, silver, and glass; there were a spyglass, books, maps of the world, and advanced novelties like mirrors, a Franklin stove, and an eight-day clock in a mahogany case. As a sportsman, the general stabled many horses—he also kept pistols, swords, and fowling pieces—and Mrs. Neville liked to ride about the country at her husband's side.

The general's son Presley, in his thirties when his father became excise inspector, had attended the University of Pennsylvania in Philadelphia and served in the revolution; around Pittsburgh he was something of a blade. Presley had studied law with Mr. Brackenridge, but he'd given it up as a profession not befitting a gentleman. Mr. Brackenridge regretted losing his student; he considered Presley the one Neville with any potential for usefulness. Presley now owned a large brick townhouse near Mr. Brackenridge's and a country residence on the banks of the Chartiers, precipitously below his father's; a swath through steep woods between mansions let father and son use visual signals to communicate up- and downhill.

From Bower Hill, the general presided over the Neville Connection, a family and business clan that pursued diverse industrial, mercantile, and social interests centered on Pittsburgh. An important member of the Connection was Isaac Craig, a veteran and entrepreneur married to General Neville's daughter Amelia. Like the general, Craig had first come to the west as an army officer; he'd invested in a glassworks and other large projects, which he was skilled in managing for maximum personal benefit while offering bland assurances of integrity, timeliness, and quality. Major Abraham Kirkpatrick, sometimes hotheaded, was a Pittsburgh investor, creditor, and businessman married to Mrs. Neville's sister. John

Woods, the professional competitor and enemy of Mr. Bracken-ridge, who attended the Green Tree meeting as a Neville Connection spy, served as Neville family counselor. The Brisons, the Days, the Ormsbys, and other industrialists, speculators, commercial farmers, and merchants ran ironworks and boatyards, grew grain on big spreads, brokered deals, and worked on their seaboard cronies to sew up west-flowing patronage and trade for the Connection.

The Nevilles were an army family. The Connection, though eager to work any angle, was largely an army-supply operation. The Ohio headwaters remained strategic. In the winter of late 1791 and early '92, Pittsburgh was becoming the staging area for a military expedition, from which Forks residents hoped to benefit. Forts were slung from Pittsburgh down the Ohio Valley; the army would soon launch itself from the old treaty line on the river and penetrate Indian country. The old fort at the headwaters, soggy and decrepit and never thoughtfully situated, was scrapped. A new fort, Fayette, was under construction in town, east of the point and near the Allegheny side. Soldiers and other personnel were converging on Pittsburgh, some to be garrisoned for fort construction, others to boat downriver to the wilderness forts and the coming Indian war.

This first martial seriousness on the part of the United States gave the struggling economy at the Forks a reliable local customer for food, drink, horses, tar, iron, blankets, lumber, brick, fodder, boats, and labor. The Neville Connection was eager not only to feed and support the army but also to dominate and control the process of doing so. Eastern patronage was the key. Just before General Neville received his appointment as excise inspector, his son-in-law Isaac Craig became deputy quartermaster for the troops garrisoned at Pittsburgh. Soon the general's brother-in-law Major Kirkpatrick would run the commissary at the fort; Craig would soon be project-managing construction of a blockhouse that, as far as Secretary of War Henry Knox was concerned, ran infuriatingly over budget and behind schedule. The Neville Connection was gaining control over buying at the garrison to which it sold.

One of the most important products of army supply was whiskey.

General Neville could expect to start outselling his small competitors on a grand scale—if the tax was enforced and illegal whiskey made unconveyable to the army. Meanwhile, as tax enforcer, he would draw not only a Treasury Department salary of $450 per year but also a 1 percent commission on what he and his deputies, also paid by commission, collected from their neighbors. Neville had railed, at first, against federal excise. Then he'd taken the collection job and changed his mind. Naturally some at the Forks imagined he'd been corrupted by salary and commission.

Yet the general's wealth made his salary less important than the way his appointment embodied—even reveled in—what ordinary people saw as yet another wrap in a tightly cinched system. The overarching purpose of federal law seemed to be to funnel money from a growing military establishment into corrupt mercantile cartels. The government enriched eastern bondholders and local entrepreneurs, reducing the struggling people of the Forks to a kind of peonage. If the Washington administration had set out to incite violent resistance, not just to the whiskey tax but to all eastern government and policy, it couldn't have made a better choice than John Neville for inspector of the fourth survey.

Secretary Hamilton sent all excise inspectors a standard-operating-procedure manual, into which he poured his love of tight process, precise recordkeeping, and diligent follow-through. In the manual, consistency and documentation are everything.

A survey inspector hires deputies and assigns each deputy a county in the survey. A deputy locates stills in his assigned area and inspects still capacities; he places a mark in a conspicuous place at the still to show that it's been registered. From distillers paying the flat, still-capacity tax, the deputy collects the single annual payment; from distillers taxed per gallon of whiskey actually produced, the deputy must, before removal of any product from the still, collect the duty, either in cash or by bond. Before a distiller moves product from a still, the deputy gauges the proof in every cask, using a standard-issue treasury hydrometer, and then marks every cask with a unique number, assigned to casks in succession. Also marked on each cask: the name and location of the distiller; the type of beverage (rum, grain whiskey, brandy, etc., per approved abbreviations listed in the manual); the gauged proof; and the actual number of gallons in the cask. Information for each cask is also entered in a ledger kept by the deputy. Having collected the duty or secured the bond, the deputy then issues a certificate stamped with a Treasury Department seal.

The certificate is the prize. It travels with the whiskey, proving to buyers that duty has been paid. Certification makes the product legal.

West of the Appalachians, none of that happened. Even finding deputies willing to start locating and registering stills caused mayhem. General Neville's first hire was Robert Johnson—waylaid, tortured, and humiliated. Prominent local enemies of the Neville Connection meanwhile gathered at the Green Tree Tavern for the purpose, General Neville believed, of obstructing operation of the law.

As leaves changed and flew and chilly winds disturbed the Ohio, enforcement efforts deteriorated. Johnson had recognized among his attackers Daniel Hamilton and others. The information was communicated to Philadelphia. In October a deputy federal marshal named Joseph Fox arrived in Allegheny County to serve the suspects with warrants on federal charges. Far from home, Fox was keenly aware that the crime for which he was supposed to be serving processes involved attacking a federal officer like himself. What would have happened if Fox had actually served his warrants became academic when Fox explained his trepidation to General Neville.

Fox's very life was in danger, the general agreed. Then he made a surprising suggestion: send the warrants by proxy. Even more surprising, the proxy Neville recommended was an ancient cattle drover named John Connor, widely considered stupid if not senile. Deputy Fox agreed to the plan with great relief. John Connor was given the warrants and instructed to serve them to Daniel Hamilton and a number of others.

Many who deplored what came next considered it inevitable. If

General Neville, so sharp and decisive, had wanted to enforce the law and have arrests made, people wondered, why did he send old John Connor out with a fistful of warrants? For when word spread that Connor was trying to serve papers in the Johnson case, Washington County's recommendations regarding the treatment of tax collectors kicked in. The old man encountered a gang that took him into the woods and began by using a horsewhip on him. His naked body, stripes new and raw, received the blistering tar. He was stuck with feathers, tied up, and left in the woods in agony, his horse, money, and warrants seized.

Fox got news of his process server's fate and fled the area. No warrants were served that fall.

General Neville added the atrocity to a list and began sending the Treasury Department urgent complaints about tax resistance, calling for serious assistance. Only an armed force, the general said, would be capable of ensuring federal tax collection at the Forks.

Later that month, a young man named Robert Wilson appeared in the area. Seemingly refined and well-educated, Wilson claimed to be looking for work as a schoolmaster, but it soon emerged that he was some kind of spy, a shadow inspector for the Treasury Department. He snooped around farms and community stills and worked casual conversation around to who had or hadn't registered. Late one night, Daniel Hamilton and a gang came to where Wilson was staying, rousted him out of bed, and took him five miles through the dark woods to a blacksmith shop, where coals were glowing. Someone placed an iron in the fire and worked the bellows. The gang was blackfaced. They stripped Wilson naked, tossed his clothes in the fire to burn, and held the hot iron to Wilson's flesh, demanding that he swear to stop spying. Hot tar was being prepared for the next step—but for all his refinement, Wilson was no coward. His dedication to the government, and to the job he'd undertaken on its behalf, was so complete that no matter how horrific the pain he refused to swear anything at all, wouldn't renounce the tax law or grovel for mercy. Amazed, the men began to tar him, and though submission was the only thing, the ritual thing, to show when being tarred and feathered, Robert Wilson fought so hard that in the melee, tar stuck to attackers, feathers stuck to tar, and backlit by the flickering fire, the tussle might have been taking place among shadowy, winged creatures in a nightmare.

Still Wilson wouldn't swear. The feathered gang had to either kill him or stop, so they stopped. Wilson, too, they abandoned, naked and injured. He'd been staunch, but unlike Robert Johnson, Wilson had no superior to take his troubles to. General Neville didn't know who this man was. The Treasury Department in Philadelphia hadn't heard of him either. Robert Wilson, it emerged, wasn't a tax inspector or a federal spy. He only desperately wanted to believe he was, and he'd been willing to die for his belief.

Appearances to the contrary, reason could prevail at the Forks of the Ohio. Or so Mr. Brackenridge believed. Winter put a temporary end to resistance and collection efforts, and early in the new year of 1792, Mr. Brackenridge left Pittsburgh for Philadelphia on a mission to prevent further excise-related violence. He wanted to act alone, before things got worse.

In the end, he hadn't put his name to the Green Tree Tavern petition. He'd made his opening speech and proposed his resolutions, but John Woods, the Neville family counselor, called some of Mr. Brackenridge's language—"until our remonstrance shall roll like a tempest to the head of government"—treasonable. Mr. Brackenridge thought Woods lacked the taste to distinguish between literal threat and figurative language. Between Woods's criticisms and the committee's revisions, the document got so carved up that Mr. Brackenridge had to disclaim connection with it.

The petition was sent to Congress and the Pennsylvania assembly. It deployed the old English tropes, in which any excise necessarily infringes liberty, which Hamilton had demonstrated to Congress this one did not. It did also make a specifically western protest: Despite supposed uniform operation throughout the nation, the excise discouraged small operators and hit westerners hardest; it was thus a selective tax, the petition said, levied more on some than on others; the tax was also bad for domestic manufacture, something the petitioners implied the federal government had a responsibility to foster. Still, the petition contained little that was likely to persuade federalists in Philadelphia to repeal or reform the tax.

Riding the ridges and icy valleys eastward through the short days, Mr. Brackenridge hoped to succeed where the petition failed. Unhindered by local committees, and by enemies like Woods, he would persuade Congress and the secretary of the treasury to repeal or at least substantially adjust the tax, forestalling a crisis that he believed need not occur. He had two worst-case scenarios. In one, the federal government, obstructed by blackface violence, tacitly gives up enforcing law at the Forks, effectively abandoning the west and ending the dream of a great American future there. In the other, the federal government doesn't abandon but further suppresses the Forks, leading to full-scale civil war, another kind of ruination. Mr. Brackenridge was forever getting stuck between terrible extremes like these. It was a position he found anything but neutral. Rejecting, for all the obvious reasons, extremism, he was both a federalist and a republican, a populist and an elitist. He therefore found himself perpetually at odds with federalists and republicans, populists and elitists.

Things had seemed to be developing nicely back in 1786, when he'd been elected to the Pennsylvania legislature and, as an assemblyman from the Forks, returned to Philadelphia to sit in a chamber hallowed by Congress's having used it a decade earlier to declare independence. This was one of the great rooms in Continental politics, and Robert Whitehill and William Findley were squaring off with Robert Morris and James Wilson over paper finance. Mr. Brackenridge, elected as a western populist, worked hard in committees to promote greater equality for the west, including Mississippi access and the establishment of Allegheny County, with Pittsburgh as its seat. Yet he declined to pander, putting it mildly. He worked on the law that made new-state agitation a capital crime. In the floor fight over the radicals' plan to let rural people pay land-bank mortgages with Pennsylvania's bonds,

Mr. Brackenridge heard Robert Morris out and concluded that Morris had a longer-range perspective than that of western voters. He'd promised to vote for the populist plan, but he changed his mind and followed Morris in supporting a cash-only payment policy. He also voted to restore the charter of Morris's bank, persuaded that, despite many abuses by bank directors, national banking could be a good thing for everybody.

Defending his reversal, Mr. Brackenridge presaged James Madison's idea, in *The Federalist*, that an elected official rightly acts on behalf not of his constituents' interests but of their judgment, which voters assign, temporarily, and under limited circumstances, to somebody better equipped to exercise it. Representatives don't act as instructed delegates. Sincere debate, conducted far from the pressures of voter influence, shapes the represented judgment of the people. Mr. Brackenridge had never claimed to be consistent. He was trying to learn and think.

Western voters didn't see it that way, not that their assemblyman bothered persuading them to. At home, letters attacking him appeared in the *Gazette,* and in Philadelphia, representatives from the Forks met at a private house where his fellow politicians confronted Mr. Brackenridge. They cited the will of the people as a reason to vote against Morris. Stung, Mr. Brackenridge phrased his philosophy in the negative: the people, he snapped, are fools. William Findley, the weaver from Westmoreland County, had been seeking a chance to bump Mr. Brackenridge aside as the leading Forks politician; he wrote to the *Gazette* to report the lawyer's remark.

Mr. Brackenridge's reelection was therefore far from likely when, in the next session, things got worse. The assembly had again moved upstairs, now giving space to the Constitutional Convention. Debate on establishing a state ratifying convention, which would adopt or reject the controversial Constitution, became chaotic. Anti-federalists, hoping to prevent ratification, or at least delay it, denied the body a quorum by staying away, but a creditor posse broke into the boardinghouse bedrooms of two members and hauled them onto the floor for a vote. Mr. Brackenridge, famous now for being the only frontier federalist, led debate in favor of hurrying the ratifying convention, and with the session over, he returned to Pittsburgh and wrote a series of articles for the *Gazette*, in which he urged the people of the Forks to imagine the benefits for the west of a national government. He didn't realize that his political career was over.

When he offered himself as a delegate to the state ratifying convention, he suffered the humiliation of seeing his anti-federalist enemy William Findley chosen instead. Despite Findley's efforts, Pennsylvania did ratify the Constitution, as Mr. Brackenridge had known it should, and when the Constitution became law, he celebrated by giving a poetic oration to an outdoor audience in Pittsburgh. He got an enthusiastic response, but orating couldn't restore his career as a politician. Forks settlers believed that, dazzled by the vices of the capital, he'd been bought off by Robert Morris. William Findley encouraged that idea. Mr. Brackenridge tried courting local federalist support instead, but federalists had never liked his republican opinions; he'd never liked the local federalists led by General Neville. Between what he saw as populist demagogues and greedy mercantilists, Mr. Brackenridge could find no political home.

Having been kicked by both parties out of the political process, he returned the favor and withdrew from it. He began to distinguish himself as a dismayingly deadpan humorist. His remarriage raised some eyebrows. In the fall of 1787, the wife he'd brought west had died, leaving him with a son not yet two. Riding between courts in a company of lawyers one hot day, he saw a wild-looking girl, darkly beautiful, tending cattle. When one of the cows broke away, the girl gave chase. The lawyers stopped to watch. Coming to a fence, she didn't stop, or even vault it, but leaped the fence without touching it and kept running. Women wore only loose garments under their dresses. Mr. Brackenridge considered. If she does that again, he thought, I'll marry her. She did. A few days later, he was taking shelter from a storm in a farmhouse and there she was, the farmer's daughter. Her name was Sabina Wolfe. Her father pointed out that he needed her for a job in his fields that otherwise would cost ten dollars. Mr. Brackenridge paid up. After a stint in Philadelphia, where the lawyer sent her to be educated in the ways of polite society, Sabina returned to Pittsburgh and took up duties as the second Mrs. Brackenridge.

Meanwhile he began working up satires of the ignorance and foolishness of ungrateful backcountry settlers and their conniving, backbiting leaders. He was returning to an early ambition, writing a book, which he entitled *Modern Chivalry*, the first American novel. Picaresque and episodic, it was published in a series of volumes; the third, printed not in Philadelphia but in Pittsburgh, was the first book published west of the Appalachians. In *Modern Chivalry*, Captain Farrago, an amazingly reasonable and amiable man, travels Quixote-like through frontier America accompanied by his self-aggrandizing, comedy-Irish servant Teague O'Regan, encountering clowns and charlatans who engage in low political chicanery and pursue bad ideas that doom their pitiful efforts at betterment. Broad regional dialects fill the book, for which Mr. Brackenridge apologized to his readers: he'd hoped, he said, to create an American character who was neither African nor fresh off the boat from Ireland—but sadly such Americans just don't exist in real life. He worked especially carefully on a verbal portrait of William Findley, in real life a perspicacious, hardheaded Irish immigrant, lacking Mr. Brackenridge's delight in the awful ironies of human comedy, and possessing, possibly as a result, political skills the lawyer could only mock. Findley appears in the book as Traddle the Weaver, a rude mechanical with a knack for thudding banality. Cracking himself up writing *Modern Chivalry* gave Mr. Brackenridge many happy hours.

Yet for all his disdain for pandering populism, Mr. Brackenridge remained scornful of high-federalist decadence, embodied now in Pittsburgh by the Neville Connection and liberated as never before by the triumph of the Constitution, which Mr. Brackenridge had helped bring about. In local courts, he defended rioters, squatters, and Mamachtaga. When creditors in the Pennsylvania assembly called the convention to revise the radical Constitution, Mr. Brackenridge opposed revision. When Alexander Hamilton's finance plan was revealed, Mr. Brackenridge published *Gazette* essays criticizing it as socially and regionally unfair and politically shortsighted. By the time the federal whiskey tax was passed, he'd come to believe that, whereas populist extremists failed to appreciate the gift to human liberty that the Constitution had built into the federal government of the United States, federalist extremists were abusing that great document by subverting it to low ends. Stuck in the middle, understood by neither side, he'd been growing bitter.

Now, riding toward Philadelphia, he felt a renewed desire to take part in political life, not just satirize it. Alexander Hamilton's excise tax, he thought, tended to remove political equality from the large class of people whom—though he mocked them—Mr. Brackenridge still saw as the best hope for the future, independent western smallholders. Attacks on collectors were grotesque, but what would the people, knee-jerk anti-federalists anyway, not resort to if the Washington administration kept confirming their suspicions that drafting the Constitution, and even gaining independence from Great Britain, had been nothing but tricks for liberating rich merchants and landlords to prey on settlers who improved land and built economies?

The tax was irrational. Irrational responses to it were inevitable. The middle position, to which inveterate realism had long cursed him, might allow Mr. Brackenridge to explain the two sides to each other. He'd begun thinking about running for Congress in the next election. His period of withdrawal was coming to an end.

The whiskey tax had opened Congress to a barrage of petitions and complaints. Now Mr. Brackenridge, wintering in Philadelphia, published in the *National Gazette*—the nation's opposition-party organ—a number of reasons and arguments for adjusting the whiskey tax, addressing his thoughts directly to the secretary of the treasury as well as to the Congress. The essay began in humility, pointing out that obstruction of the river forced western farmers to convert an untaxed product, grain, into a taxable one, whiskey. But it ended with a vision of the fulfillment in the American west of the ideals of a democratic republic. Leaving the excise far behind, Mr. Brackenridge swept himself into a paean to a new way of looking at American culture.

He didn't sweep Hamilton along with him. In March of 1792, the secretary reviewed petitions and complaints against the whiskey tax. From large-scale distillers and his own inspectors he accepted some suggestions for revising the law. But he rolled western arguments slowly around in his mouth and then, with pursed-lip disgust, spat each soggy bit out. Digesting this stuff wasn't on his mind.

Hamilton wasn't in a good mood. Funding, assumption, excise, and the central bank—his triumphs of the year before—had led not to greater successes but to the permanent resentment of opposition politicians and voters. Many of his plans were faltering. He'd hoped to follow up the national finance system by inspiring large-scale national manufacturing, but the House had ignored his impassioned call for government participation in industrializing America. Even as Hamilton was considering the antiexcise petitions, financial ruin was hitting the New York markets. Fantastically overvalued bank stocks and government bonds had started sliding. Both the rise and the fall were the work of a crowd surrounding an ethically vacuous insider named William Duer, who would go to debtors prison while ruined investors demanded his head. Unfortunately for Hamilton, Duer had for a time been his top assistant in the treasury, part of the national web of federalist speculators, officials, and hangers-on. Worse, Hamilton had put Duer in charge of an especially cherished part of the national-manufacturing concept—a showcase factory town of the future, privately owned by a consortium, drawing energy from the Passaic Falls in New Jersey. Duer had embezzled that project dry. Hamilton would expend great effort in trying to salvage it, but moneyed men on its board were losing confidence.

He was also subject to attacks, unfair and unremitting, on his private and public lives. The *National Gazette*, where Mr. Brackenridge had published his essay on the tax, had been founded to print such attacks. There was a move on in Congress to launch an investigation to remove Hamilton from office for misconduct or, more likely, and just as good to his enemies, destroy him in the process of failing to prove anything at all.

The creative phase of Hamilton's career was coming to an end. A defense-and-enforcement phase was beginning. Optimism and charm crashed periodically into a cold rage that did not rob him of energy and orderliness. He had, in Philadelphia, a department taking up a city block, complete with both the largest on-site bureaucracy in the government and many collectors and inspectors in the field. The executive branch had power to enforce its revenue-collection measures. Even as General Neville made the case for using military action to collect the tax, a militia act, supported by Hamilton, was being developed in Congress. In a situation in which federal law was so obstructed, within a given state, that ordinary judicial process broke down, the president would be empowered by the militia law to bring irresistible force against a local insurgency. If the relevant state's militia refused to serve, the president could—on his own discretion, if Congress wasn't in session—call out militias of other states.

So if there was an opposite to what Hamilton evinced, in his report on the petitions, it was sympathy for western tax resisters. Only after demonstrating, exhaustively, once again the invalidity of traditional antiexcise arguments when it came to this excise, and referring to advantages given by the law to domestic over foreign produce, and agreeing to importers' and big distillers' requests for leakage allowances, shipwreck drawbacks, and protection of trade secrets, did he turn, as if in postscript, to address what he called some complaints of a local complexion.

He began by demolishing the idea, put forth by the Green Tree petition, that western dominance in whiskey production made the tax unequal. Any tax on a domestic product would of course be experienced that way by somebody, he said—yet nothing was consumed more equally throughout the country than whiskey. This point held the key to Hamilton's rejection of western complaints. Defining the excise as taxing consumption, not production, he avoided any discussion of the small producers whom the tax stifled. If the people of the west were greater consumers of whiskey than people elsewhere, as he deftly misread the complaint to suggest they were, all they had to do was cut down on their drinking; equality would be restored.

He also dismissed Mr. Brackenridge's explanation that westerners were unique in being forced by economic circumstances and government policies to convert a nontaxed article, grain, into a taxable one, whiskey, merely in order to sell it. So what? Hamilton asked. Consumers pay the tax, not producers. Westerners pay only on their own drinking.

When it came to scarcity of money in the west, he doubted it. But it wouldn't make a difference: because scarcity of cash could be invoked in support of objections to any tax, the real purpose of invoking it could only be to promote the dissolution of government. The supposed scarcity of money was obviated anyway by the Indian-war ramp-up, Hamilton said: in the past year, the army's spending, in Pennsylvania's four western counties and Kentucky alone, added up to more than five years of whiskey-tax collection there. He didn't mention new modes of army buying and selling he was working on, meant to keep that army cash outlay in a very few hands. It was true that major customers for western liquor had always been armies; officers had carted batches of whiskey from open marketplaces or sellers' stills. But now, in concert with the excise tax, Hamilton was launching from the treasury a reform of the army-supply system, dispensing with small, independent sellers. He created commissary offices willing to buy only in bulk, with responsibility for delivery shifted to the sellers.

That reform offered large-scale producers yet another means of underselling anyone smaller. Merchants with access to big transport—not distillers at all, in some cases—could buy up small batches of whiskey cheaply, from farmers suddenly bereft of markets, and sell them in wagonloads to the commissary. The system offered simplicity and efficiency. At Fort Fayette, for example, the commissary was run by General Neville's brother-in-law Major Kirkpatrick; Neville's son-in-law Isaac Craig served as deputy quartermaster; the general himself, along with many in his cohort, was both a large-scale distiller with ample means of transport and an enforcer of the whiskey tax.

A complaint that Hamilton did address inspired him to make an important revision in the tax law that not only benefited big producers but also pursued his highest goals for American industry. The revised excise law of 1792 removed the distinction between city and country producers. Whether located in towns or in the country, any distiller could now choose to pay either on still capacity or per actual gallon produced. Big distillers everywhere took advantage of the new option, choosing to pay on capacity; constant innovation would ultimately reduce their real tax to a sixth of a cent per gallon. But the option couldn't help small producers, mainly in the country and already taxed on still capacity: given their brief and occasional processes, the capacity rate was already raising their tax.

Whichever way they turned now, small producers were further overtaxed by the government and undersold by big competitors, and with the new army-buying procedures in place, they lost their best local customer just as it started bringing government money to the west. Hamilton did propose one reform to the law that he presented as a concession to small distillers. You could get a cheaper, monthly license to distill. It would cost you 10 cents per gallon on the still's capacity; you'd be prohibited from operating at any other time. With big distillers steadily reducing their real tax toward fractions of a penny, this revision did nothing to encourage competition.

What Hamilton wanted from the new law was enforcement. A central excise office was to be opened in each county; distillers must go there to register stills; failure to register would mean forfeiting the still, and the fine was raised to $250. Nonpayment too was now a lien on the still. The earlier law had exempted the smallest stills, with under forty-gallon capacity, not from the tax but from registration. That exemption was removed.

Congress debated and passed the new excise law on May 8, 1792. During the debate, William Findley, now in the U.S. Congress, argued for lowering the tax and succeeded in getting a 1-cent reduction, too little too late, he believed, for his constituents. Perhaps more significantly, he also objected to Hamilton's rationales being read aloud as arguments on the floor of the House. With the doggedness that Mr. Brackenridge mocked in Traddle the Weaver, Findley rose again and again to declare the procedure out of order. Only members of the House with local knowledge should provide information, Findley said: Reports from what he called the secretary's closet were drawn from collectors—unelected bureaucrats of the permanent government—as well as from interested parties like the Nevilles. The reading of Hamilton's arguments was stopped. Findley had distinguished himself as an enemy in the eyes of Hamilton and the administration.

Mr. Brackenridge had failed to mediate. His arguments, made in a national paper in the capital, had done nothing but irritate the secretary of the treasury. Hamilton's report had decisively rejected every grievance of small western operators; the revised law had arranged to further disable the rural whiskey economy. It was summer, season for enforcement and resistance. New outbreaks of violence could be expected not only at the Forks of the Ohio but elsewhere up and down the frontier.

Hamilton began musing aloud about enforcing the law not through normal judicial process but through a military expedition directed by the executive branch. As he contemplated using troops against the citizenry, Hamilton would often resort to an unaccustomed delicacy, which inspired euphemism and recalled his subtlest letters to Washington during the Newburgh crisis. The thing must, he declared in July of 1792, be brought to an issue. Just as Mr. Brackenridge feared, certain people at the Forks of the Ohio, less inclined to euphemism, were coming to the same conclusion.

CHAPTER SIX

Tom the Tinker

The armed body of free militiamen could, Herman Husband preached, throw off the yoke of eastern tyranny and bring on the millennium in the west. Even as Alexander Hamilton began considering ways of bringing a federal military presence to the Forks of the Ohio, five hundred men calling themselves the Mingo Creek Association emerged as a power at the Forks. They had a shrewd and ambitious idea, which involved the armed bodies Husband was talking about. In meetings at the Mingo Creek church—a small log structure on comparatively flat ground near the creek, where the four western counties converged—the Mingo Creek Association began setting official militias at odds with the government.

The association had a long ancestry. Men who became members and allies of the association had, in the years leading to ratification of the U.S. Constitution, closed roads to towns where debt cases were heard and foreclosed property was auctioned; they'd enforced boycotts on liquor brought in from the east. They'd corresponded with Virginians and Kentuckians on the need for western unity. At the recent Washington County meeting, they'd condemned federal tax collectors and sent delegates to the Green Tree convention; they'd participated in attacks on Robert Johnson, John Connor, and Robert Wilson. They were inheritors of attacks on British soldiers, carried out in the 1760s by the Indian-clad "blacks," and of squatter associations that had escorted Pennsylvania's sheriffs out of the area in the early seventies.

Now the association set goals far broader than attacks on collectors. It planned to unite the four western counties, add Bedford County, and bring General Neville's survey and the whole trans-Appalachian west into armed opposition to eastern oppression. Conveniently for the association's plans, the sanctioned state militia, which organized and armed all able-bodied adult white males, was subject to extreme degrees of popular democracy.

Militia musters were the scenes of drills, drinking, debating, caucusing, and electioneering. Armed service, a sometimes onerous requirement of citizenship, offered the only officially sanctioned arena for community action outside state and federal elections. From colonels down, officers were elected by the militiamen themselves, including by landless men and dependents in others' households. Anyone possessed of charisma and effectiveness, even if lacking gorgeous uniforms, proud mounts, gleaming arms, or money, could rise in the militia system.

Using the democratic process, the Mingo Creek Association perpetrated a takeover, from within, of the authorized militias of the Forks. The association didn't merely use militia musters to recruit men to the antitax cause. It turned the militia itself inside out. The nucleus was the battalion commanded by Colonel John Hamilton. Almost every member of the Mingo Creek Association also served in Hamilton's militia battalion—but the two entities did more than overlap. The association gave itself eight subdivisions, corresponding to the battalion's eight companies, and gave those companies the task, to be carried out at official musters, of electing representatives to the association's leadership, which held regular meetings at the Mingo Creek church to plan obstructions of federal tax law. Company captains received copies of the committee's resolutions, speeches, and endorsements for public office. Those records were to be kept secret among the militia companies. Colonel John Hamilton presided, so far without objection, over the merging of his battalion with the association: he'd been present at the attack on Robert Johnson and was in sympathy with the goals of the attackers. But the beauty of the operation lay in the fact that, had an officer objected, he would have been stripped of command by vote of the men under him. Attaching itself to and replicating the militia, the association turned official resources—arms, armaments, and hierarchies—and official purpose, armed defense of the region, against officialdom.

The association took an even more radical step. The revised, conservative state constitution had ended popular elections for local judges. The governor appointed judges. Creditors had been finding debt cases easier to bring and win. So the Mingo Creek Association constituted itself as a court of law. No citizen in John Hamilton's militia district, the association announced, was to bring suit in county court against any other citizen in the district without first applying to the association for what it presented as mediation. Mediators would be chosen by popular elections, held outside sanctioned political process.

Not surprisingly, given the association's identity with the local militia, and the assaults for which it was becoming known, lawsuits for debt collection in the county court dropped off sharply. Going to law to collect debts or bring foreclosures suddenly took courage, even foolhardiness. And the association's ideas spread quickly. A similar association in Allegheny County was soon imposing an extralegal court too.

The Mingo Creek Association began making its desires felt when General Neville took out an ad in the *Pittsburgh Gazette* in July of 1792, seeking to rent space for the registration offices now required by the revised excise law. Almost nobody was willing to rent to him, but he did get one bite. Captain William Faulkner, an officer in the army at Fort Fayette, owned a house in the town of Washington, where he and his wife lived and operated a tavern. Faulkner offered to rent Neville a room in the house.

A number of people came to visit Faulkner to suggest politely that this was a bad idea. Faulkner insisted on his right to use his private property in any way he chose; Neville made the deal and ran another ad in the *Gazette*, informing the distillers of Washington County that twice a week, Neville himself—he was finding it almost impossible to hire deputies—would be in attendance at Faulkner's to register their stills. The first excise office at the Forks seemed to be open for business.

One day William Faulkner was riding near Pigeon Creek, hoping to find some of his soldiers. (Preparations for the Indian war hadn't been going smoothly; desertions were common.) Faulkner's search was interrupted by Robert Morrison, who farmed near the Mingo. Confronting Faulkner on the road, Morrison showed him a copy of the *Gazette*. There was General Neville's ad, announcing an excise office at Faulkner's house. Irate, Morrison demanded that Faulkner accompany him to discuss the matter further with a man named Benjamin Parkinson.

Intimidated, Faulkner went with Morrison to Parkinson's house. Parkinson, a tall, red-haired former justice of the peace, passionate and influential, was already known to Faulkner, who had enjoyed more or less cordial relations with him. Inside, Morrison handed the paper to Parkinson, who looked at it a long time before speaking. Then Parkinson asked if it was possible that Faulkner was such a damned rascal that he'd given consent for an excise office in his house. "Never in my company again," Parkinson told Faulkner. Repeating the deliberately insulting expression "damned rascal"— both were fighting words—he noted that the ostracism he'd just imposed meant that nobody else would speak to Faulkner either.

Faulkner stalked out into the daylight. Parkinson and Morrison followed him. In the front yard, Parkinson took a more reassuring tone. He'd just been giving Faulkner advice, he said, Faulkner had nothing to fear; simply being in Parkinson's house gave Faulkner protection. They went back inside. Faulkner went out. They kept going in and out: Faulkner, trying to leave, feared outright bolting, and Morrison, acting as enforcer for Parkinson's interrogation, repeatedly managed to escort Faulkner back inside without resorting to outright violence.

Finally Parkinson came to the point. Throw Neville out of your house, he ordered. The demand would not be made again, he said; it was coming not from Parkinson alone but from five hundred men for whom Parkinson spoke, and they would be only too happy to turn Faulkner into an example. Faulkner must not only evict General Neville as a tenant but also announce in the *Gazette* that he'd done so. Nothing less, Parkinson said, would satisfy the association.

Faulkner didn't know what this association might be. The group hadn't yet written its constitution, for which the Washington County resolves for violent treatment of taxmen served as founding principles. To demonstrate the association's scope and power, Morrison and Parkinson escorted Faulkner to the home of another of the Mingo Creek Hamiltons, David, brother of the wild Daniel, where they read the Washington County resolutions to Faulkner. They put it to him in a friendly and logical way. What would happen to him for having rented space to General Neville? He would, they answered themselves, be tarred and feathered and have his house destroyed.

Soon Colonel John Hamilton arrived, along with Daniel Hamilton himself. Informed of the existence of an excise office in Faulkner's house, Daniel gave a sudden whoop and grabbed the hair on top of Faulkner's head. Tugging on Faulkner's scalp, Daniel asked if the tavernkeeper understood the meaning of that. Faulkner did. The men repeated the demand: Faulkner must announce the discontinuance of the excise office in his house or see his house destroyed and suffer himself. Daniel took Faulkner outside and reviewed the situation again, with vehemence. Then he sent Faulkner on his way.

This treatment was emblematic of the association's approach. Faulkner, though considered a lowlife as a tavernkeeper and army officer, wasn't a federal official or tax collector. He was a local abettor. The association intended to bring all such people, throughout the region, to an understanding. Anybody suspected of serving as a hireling for the Nevilles and their federalist masters must now publicly avow loyalty to the people of the Forks.

Yet Faulkner chose to ignore his day of intimidation. A few days later, Mrs. Faulkner, tending bar at the tavern, had to put up with some loud antiexcise talk; later the same day, a gang galloped up to the tavern door. Wheeling and shouting, the gang tore down the sign advertising the excise office. Mrs. Faulkner watched them gallop away.

Still Faulkner wouldn't take the hint, and to Forks moderates like Mr. Brackenridge, the context in which the association finally did attack Faulkner's house was even more frightening than the attack itself. An anonymous ad in the *Gazette* called another convention to meet in Pittsburgh to discuss problems with the excise law. This time the call didn't come from prominent men. Means of representing townships and counties was even less clear than before. The convention that gathered in late August of 1792 was crowded with nearly forty delegates, and moderates were outnumbered by a new and vocal group. In fact, the most prominent of the moderates deliberately stayed away. Both Mr. Brackenridge and his nemesis William Findley declined to serve.

One new and prominent moderate did attend: Albert Gallatin. He'd been at the first, casual meeting in Brownsville, where the plan for delegating the Green Tree meeting had been adopted, but he hadn't attended the Green Tree meeting, and this more extreme convention was his debut as a local delegate. Gallatin was a Swiss immigrant and American patriot whose intellectual background surpassed even Mr. Brackenridge's. He'd been dandled on the knee of Voltaire himself. A committed republican and anti-federalist, he'd moved to western Pennsylvania and settled on an estate he called Friendship Hill. He'd fought the creditor interest in 1790, as a delegate to the convention to revise the Pennsylvania constitution; he'd been representing Fayette County in the assembly for two years. A student of finance, Gallatin vociferously opposed federal debt service and thus the whiskey tax. But he was equally sure that violence and lawlessness could only further isolate and impoverish the west.

His voice was weak. It was the Mingo Creek Association that dominated the second Pittsburgh convention. Joining the returning delegate Colonel John Hamilton were newcomers Benjamin Parkinson and John's relative David, at whose homes William Faulkner had been intimidated. These Mingo Creek men were joined by another Washington County resident, David Bradford, a wealthy lawyer with the fanciest house in Washington, who had attended the Green Tree convention. Bradford wasn't a member of the Mingo Creek Association, but despite his wealth, he'd long involved himself in road closings and other antigovernment activities; he'd been a participant in the radical Washington meeting, whose resolutions founded the association. David Bradford badly wanted to keep common cause with laborers and farmers.

The convention made a list of radical demands, including the replacement of the whiskey excise with a progressive tax on wealth. They wanted hirelings of the federal government disabled. They demanded the resignation of General Neville, who couldn't, the petitioners believed, be replaced; nobody would take the job now. They created committees of correspondence to reform government and unite the entire Forks in militia-structured resistance. Most significant, first for William Faulkner, and soon for other civilians who abetted or even complied with the law: they backed up demands with a resolution to support any action taken against any resident of the Forks who aided federal officials.

That's what gave moderates true cause for fear. A document purporting to represent the people of all four western counties enshrined the radical and violent ideas of Mingo Creek. Albert Gallatin would regret signing the convention's resolutions.

Two days later, thirty armed men rode up to William Faulkner's house. Their faces were painted a variety of colors. Aiming their guns at the tavern sign, with its representation of George Washington's head, they opened fire. The president's features splintered and flew. Then they battered the door of the house until it split.

Faulkner was out. They threw the beds all over the floor and went everywhere in the house, including the tavern, where they threatened to smash up the bar. Some said they'd shave Faulkner's head and tar and feather him. Some said they'd take a limb; some said they'd kill him. One man called for burning the house, as it was at a distance from others and wouldn't start a town fire. Another said that for community safety the house should be torn down, not burned. After breaking everything in the house, they rode away. David Bradford threw a jubilant celebration for the attackers. The next day, when Faulkner finally did publish in the *Gazette* his decision not to allow an excise office to operate in his home, jubilation overflowed. Unity was growing at the Forks.

"If the plot should thicken," Alexander Hamilton was musing, "and the application of force should appear to be unavoidable, will it be expedient for the president to repair in person to the scene of commotion?" This anticipation, in which, as during the Newburgh crisis, he imagined moving the great man like a chess piece, came to Hamilton in the first week of September 1792, while he was writing to John Jay, chief justice of the Supreme Court. Jay wrote back to advise caution: warlike preparations, he reminded Hamilton, might only inflame matters on the frontier. That didn't faze Hamilton, who was busy conjuring for the president the benefits of an armed military suppression, somewhere, of whiskey-tax resistance and the promising features of the Forks of the Ohio as the scene for such action.

Hamilton had given western North Carolina serious consideration too. But the attorney general of the United States, Edmund Randolph, had reviewed the situation in North Carolina and found no evidence for federal prosecution there, let alone for a military expedition. Most surveys beyond the mountains were making it impossible to collect the whiskey tax—revenue inspectors in North and South Carolina were resigning, no tax had been collected in Kentucky—and decisive action at the Forks, Hamilton told Washington, would serve as a good example for all. The Forks were a special embarrassment, he added, as the region was in the same state as the seat of government; it was convenient for suppression because of the army presence there. Indecision, Hamilton reminded Washington, would make the executive branch look weak.

Washington found petitioning at least as disturbing as attacks. He authorized Hamilton to push Attorney General Randolph to get indictments against attendees of the second Pittsburgh convention, whose daring extralegality, Washington assured Hamilton, would be checked by the full force of executive power. Randolph, however, noted that while the attack on Faulkner's house did provide a cause of legal action, the Pittsburgh convention did not. Assembling to remonstrate, Randolph reminded Hamilton, is among the rights of citizens.

A tense disagreement was developing between Randolph and Hamilton in competition for Washington's judgment. Unbidden, Hamilton whipped up a presidential proclamation—the natural prelude, he said, to a new course of conduct—in which the president not only condemned the Faulkner and other attacks but also warned the people of the Forks not to hold meetings like the Pittsburgh conventions. In Hamilton's draft, the president flatly threatened the use of federal troops if order were not restored. Randolph, reviewing the draft, crossed that part out as inflammatory, and Washington signed the proclamation with Randolph's modifications. Hamilton pushed: issuing a proclamation means resolving to act on it, he reminded Washington, with all the powers and means enjoyed by the executive—another of his and Washington's euphemisms for using military force on citizens.

In a private letter, Washington counseled Hamilton in terms that were not, for these two, unfamiliar. The subject was the highly problematic nature, no matter how lofty the end, of using the army as a political means. Washington expressed no doubt that the proclamation was likely to fail, and military action—here he called it "ulterior arrangements"—would have to be taken. But the law and the Constitution must rule, he insisted, and in the event, citizen militias and not regular troops should be used if possible. He and the federalists had been pushing for a regular peacetime army, and Washington could do a pretty accurate impression of the knee-jerk opposition. "'The cat is let out,'" he imagined it squalling, "'we now see for what purpose an army was raised.'" Using troops against citizens must, Washington reminded Hamilton, always be a last resort.

Hamilton understood that. He'd told John Jay, when imagining a military suppression, not that force would be unavoidable but that it would appear unavoidable. Now he began bringing the thing, as he put it, to an issue.

The first step was to send George Clymer, federal revenue inspector for all of Pennsylvania, out to Pittsburgh. Had Hamilton meant to give the people of the Forks a view of the executive branch as disinterested and fair, governing all the people, acting with restraint yet fully capable of enforcing federal laws throughout the nation, the choice of Clymer would have been a strange one. Any inspector from the east would have been viewed with suspicion over the mountains. George Clymer offered the people of the Forks a crude caricature of their worst fears about the real nature of the Treasury Department, the federal government, and the east.

By traveling in manifest terror, Clymer managed to make an impression even before arrival. He'd been at the Forks in 1778, when he'd started land speculating; the area, he'd noted then, was a good place to do penance in. A fifty-three-year-old Philadelphian of the Robert Morris type, wealthy even before independence, he'd profiteered successfully throughout the revolution and become one of the richest men in Pennsylvania. He'd opposed the state's radical constitution, supported the conservative revision of 1790, participated in the federalist victory at the ratifying convention for the U.S. Constitution, and was now deeply involved in western Pennsylvania land speculation. He was therefore under the mistaken impression that he was famous throughout the state.

To remain incognito, on his way west he introduced himself as Henry Knox, secretary of war. While Clymer was not, in fact, well known, Henry Knox was known at least to be fat, and the traveler was skinny. People whom Clymer encountered had no idea who he was, but knew he wasn't Henry Knox, and word spread of a mysterious man on a badly concealed errand.

As Clymer rose into crisp mountain air, it distressed him to learn that news of his approach had preceded him. He came up with a new alias—the time-honored "Smith"—and traded roles with his servant, giving his good mount to the man and taking the poorer horse himself. Role reversal meant he had to handle the stabling at a tavern, where the tavern's groom announced that Smith had no idea how to take care of a horse. Word spread again. By the time Clymer, now almost unbearably frightened, rode down from the highlands, ferried the river, and appeared on Pittsburgh's mud streets, he'd donned yet another disguise. He'd beaten up his hat; he slouched in the saddle. He took lodgings at the Indian Queen, a tavern depressingly unlike the gentleman's lodging house of the same name back in Philadelphia. Then he went straight to Fort Fayette, still in its slow and chaotic state of blockhouse construction, the staging area for efforts to defeat Indians in the northwest. Within the gates, safely among soldiers, Clymer doffed his disguise. As a federal officer, he asked the commander to provide security for an official stay in the area.

Riding from the fort with soldiers assigned to his protection, Clymer could at last relax. He checked out of the room at the Indian Queen and moved up to the fancier Bear Inn.

He thought that he could not, for his life, leave the marginally civilized confines of the village and fort. Though he'd seen nothing personally to support the impression, he'd already decided that the counties he was supposed to inspect were in a state of outright insurrection. He therefore sent a message to the district judge, Alexander Addison, asking Addison to take depositions to provide names of attendees of the Pittsburgh convention. Judge Addison was no judicial nullifier—he'd been appointed by the state governor, under the new constitution, not elected by the people, and he could be a tough enforcer—but as a Pennsylvania-rights man he was a stickler for what he saw as constitutional process. He pointed out to Clymer, with asperity, that a state judge had neither jurisdiction nor responsibility to become the agent of a federal investigation. Had Clymer come to him as an officer of the court, Addison said, that would be one thing; but Clymer was trying to delegate federal judicial process to a state court, turning a state into a federal department. Addison couldn't allow it.

Clymer concluded that the insurrection was even worse than he'd thought. Local judges were in on it too.

That conclusion was important. From it would follow a further conclusion, critical to invoking the president's powers of suppression under the militia law: If state judges were described as insurgents, then Pennsylvania law enforcement had no chance—no inclination—of enforcing law at the Forks. Judicial process could be said to have broken down beyond repair.

Clymer did get justices of the peace in Washington County to take depositions from Faulkner and witnesses to the ransacking, and Faulkner named some attendees of the latest Pittsburgh convention. Meanwhile, General Neville confirmed for Clymer in person everything the general had been writing in letters. People throughout the entire area weren't only insurrectionary and anarchic, Neville and Clymer agreed. The people were drunk, depraved.

Clymer galloped out of Pittsburgh like a man pursued by nightmares, the hooves of his cavalry escort beating retreat. He'd been in town only a few days. His impact was lasting. As an emissary from the luxurious east, at first traveling in disguise like the secret agent of a hostile nation, then moving officiously about with an armed guard, he gave the people of the Forks a clear picture of their government as remote and ostentatious, timorous, slippery, and, though entirely incompetent, in command of thuggish dragoons.

As the Mingo Creek Association expanded its mandate, General Neville redoubled his attempts to get military help from Philadelphia. Both Neville's and the association's efforts devolved on a man named Benjamin Wells, the deputy collector for Fayette and Westmoreland counties. If Benjamin Wells couldn't stay in business as a collector, nobody could: So eager was Wells to make money—not only by rake-offs on commissions but also by rewards for turning in unregistered stills and giving testimony against resisters—that in hopes of founding a kind of junior Neville Connection, he had one of his sons in the quartermaster's office at Fort

Cumberland in Maryland and wanted to see his son John in the potentially lucrative collections business.

Wells was poking around a mill belonging to a man named James Wigle when he was confronted and punched out by Wigle's son Philip, a landless veteran, like so many in his generation at the Forks. Wells dusted himself off and went on with his job, complaining to both General Neville and Clymer that his neighbors' scorn made him live like a dog, yet eager enough for the bounty on reporting unregistered stills that throughout 1793, he kept snooping. He took voluminous notes. He was repeatedly attacked. He saw the house in Uniontown where he was trying to operate an excise office stoned and its windows smashed; he had to run from the place, while moderate citizens held off the attackers. In April, when he was away from his house, men visited his wife, threatening violence against her and her husband.

Wells was undeterred. In November his house was again attacked by a disguised gang. He was home this time, and under threat of the usual punishments, he did turn over to the gang his excise commission and record books and publish his resignation in the *Gazette*. The association and its allies were interested in this kind of formal resignation of office and published recanting. Such gestures signified the gathering unity of the Forks under a new, self-appointed officialdom based on militia elections. In accepting Wells's papers, they assumed administration of his office, which they nullified.

Wells, by the same token, believed there was a loophole to his public disavowal of tax collection. He got General Neville to give Wells *fils* the coveted excise commission to carry on the family trade.

Neville used the Wells situation in his ongoing push, and Alexander Hamilton's concomitant pull, for military intervention. In 1793 alone, Benjamin Wells traveled three times to Philadelphia to give the Justice and Treasury departments names of delinquent distillers and testimony against his attackers. Meanwhile General Neville made a record, in a steady flow of letters to the Treasury Department, of the imminent likelihood of his deputies' quitting under threat of violence and their prospect of no earnings. He cajoled deputies into staying on and urged them to keep offices open. He tried to find homeowners and tavernkeepers who would rent him space, and he urged his deputies to do the same. He tried to add to the corps of deputies. He orchestrated Wells's trips east to give testimony.

Yet unhappily for Neville and Hamilton's shared plan to bring military enforcement of the law to the Forks—it had seemed on the verge of fulfillment in Hamilton's communications with the president in 1792—the cabinet found itself beset by bigger problems, and a military solution had to wait. The king of France was decapitated. Algerian pirates harassed American shipping. A new war with Britain seemed more and more likely. The French minister to the United States tried to recruit Americans to the French cause, sparking a craze for French extremism that made George Washington, who had proclaimed U.S. neutrality in the French-British conflict, fair game in the press for the first time. People mobbed the Philadelphia streets; then yellow fever broke out, forcing the evacuation of anyone who could afford to leave, panicking survivors, shutting down government operations and mob restlessness alike. Hamilton contracted the disease and barely survived it.

Meanwhile, the resistance movement at the Forks found a new leader. Tom the Tinker, joyously violent, seemingly everywhere yet visibly nowhere, had begun writing personal notes to individuals who seemed less than fully committed to the cause. You might find a note posted on a tree outside your house, requiring you to publish in the *Gazette* your hatred of the whiskey tax and your commitment to the cause; otherwise, the note promised, your still would be mended. Tom had a macabre sense of humor and a literary bent: "mended" meant shot full of holes or burned. Tom published on his own too, rousing his followers to action, telling the *Gazette*'s editor in cover notes to run the messages or suffer the consequences. He was always sorry to have been forced, by someone's waywardness, to pay a visit. But nobody was exempt from his service, he reminded his readers. He asked his victims to imagine his fires making the hills give light to the vales.

Little indeed could make a more decisive point, on a black and frigid night, than a blazing barn. In January of 1794, men who saw their barns burn weren't tax collectors, nor had they rented space to tax collectors. Their crime was merely having registered their stills. For large-scale distillers to exploit the advantages Hamilton was giving them, they had to sell whiskey legally. Hamilton and the army had deliberately started buying whiskey from Kentucky and Virginia, hoping to compel Forks distillers to register or suffer, splitting the resistance. But the message of barn burnings was clear. Compliers with the law were now as traitorous as collectors. Stored crops and precious tools and machines, even the animals themselves, could be destroyed in such fires, which spread and caused terrible damage. Soon all compliers met with such treatment: stillhouses were burned, pot stills shot full of holes, barns and gristmills ripped down.

The gangs called themselves Tom the Tinker's Men. They huzzaed Tom at gatherings and made victims do the same. While nobody believed Tom existed, everybody knew that he did. His author, some said, was the veteran resister John Holcroft, who had served in the Shays Rebellion—but Tom wasn't an alias for a person. He was the stark fact that loyal opposition to the resistance was disallowed. Tom was Mingo Creek personified.

Now the Neville family came under direct attack. A General John Neville made of straw was hoisted and lit on fire that spring at a muster and militia election held just south of Pittsburgh where the Youghiogheny flows into the Monongahela. Presley Neville watched his father's effigy burn for the delight of an armed and rowdy crowd. One evening not long afterward, the general, Mrs. Neville, and their small granddaughter were riding home from Pittsburgh when they were accosted. The family had pulled up and halted; the general had dismounted to tighten his wife's saddle girth. Two men came riding by and passed into the woods; then a man and woman rode up and stopped. The man asked the general if he was John Neville. Neville said that he was. The man leaped from his horse and ran at the general, who responded with alacrity, pouncing on the man, wrestling him to the ground, and beating him. Mindful of the riders who had just passed, the general silenced the attacker by throttling him until subdued. The woman, and then the man himself, begged to be allowed to go. Neville let the man up, and as the couple rode quickly away, Neville, dusting himself off, filed away the man's name: Jacob Long, a German immigrant and subsistence farmer. Back at his mountaintop mansion, the general began planning for a direct attack on his home.

By May of 1794, liberty poles were rising. Up to a hundred feet tall, these were symbols of the trees under which, most famously in Boston, but in other villages and towns as well, the revolutionary committees of correspondence had organized to resist Great Britain. Where there were no appropriate trees, rebels of the seventies had erected poles. Often the poles had displayed symbols of resistance, the snake saying, "Don't Tread on Me," striped flags showing the unity of townships. British occupiers in Boston and New York had cut them down. Patriots had erected them again.

The appearance of liberty poles in the western country thus had a meaning that was clear to everyone. Rebellion against tyranny was under way. Attacks by blackface gangs had been one thing, but the formal establishment of the Mingo Creek Association, the forced recantings in letters to the *Gazette,* the extralegal court system, the takeover of the militia, Tom the Tinker's acts of destruction—these were something else.

The Revolution of '76 was breaking out again. Many signs announced that this time it would be completed. At Bower Hill, General Neville armed and drilled his slaves, and as summer approached, he burned candles through the shortening nights.

CHAPTER SEVEN

The Hills Give Light
to the Vales

The president was perturbed and indignant. Congress had investigated the treasury secretary; the opposition, always reading Hamilton wrong, had failed to prove he'd used public money for personal gain. But the inquiry had been rushed, and rumors wouldn't stop, so Hamilton asked for a new investigation, the more comprehensive, he said, the better. A congressional committee responded to that challenge. It asked the secretary under what authority, four years earlier, he'd diverted funds, earmarked by Congress for paying foreign debt, into stabilizing a domestic project, the central bank. Only a direct order from the president could have legitimized such a change.

The president, Hamilton told the committee, had indeed given authorization, but verbally; no written evidence could be presented. Hamilton offered to give the committee some letters showing the general spirit in which he and Washington normally handled such matters. Then he tried to stall the committee by arguing that the question itself was out of bounds. He needed to speak to the president.

Washington had meanwhile exploded. He'd received backchannel word that Hamilton was claiming, in a congressional investigation, to possess letters from the president authorizing, as Washington took it, something improper. Washington insisted passionately that no such letters could possibly exist. It was a difficult meeting when Hamilton showed Washington the letters, which turned out to be not very damning, or even germane. They related to authorizations other than the one at issue. Hamilton therefore tried to jog the president's memory—known in the cabinet as sometimes sluggish—and get him to agree on the nature of specific discussions of four years earlier. Hamilton needed a public letter from Washington saying that the redirection of funds had been authorized verbally.

Uncomfortable with trying to remember, and resenting Hamilton's importuning tone, Washington retreated to magnificent reserve, giving Hamilton a potentially serious problem. Congress was requiring a written report on the matter. Hamilton wrote it and sent Washington a copy, with a cover letter meant to persuade Washington that the report contained only what they'd discussed in their memory-jogging conversation of a few days earlier. The president, keenly alert now, sent the report to Edmund Randolph for legal reading. Randolph, formerly attorney general, had taken over as secretary of state when Jefferson resigned. He was Jefferson's relative; the high federalists led by Hamilton saw him as a knee-jerk, if weak-willed, apparatchik of the Jeffersonian opposition. The opposition, for its part, saw Randolph as a spineless idolater of Washington, neither bright nor trustworthy.

Edmund Randolph was not a forceful man, but he was learned and articulate. He considered issues on their merits and made personal and professional loyalty to the president his first concern. Only Washington, Randolph believed, could wield a balance between Jeffersonian and Hamiltonian extremes. He informed Washington that Hamilton's report, far from merely suggesting that the president had acquiesced in the secretary's judgment, seemed to embrace Washington in blame by suggesting that he'd actively rendered an opinion that applying funds to the bank was legal. Washington must refrain from signing on to any of the report's implications, Randolph urged, yet dispute nothing specific.

The presidential letter Hamilton had asked for—written, actually, by Randolph—therefore offered no vindication at all. It said only that whatever the secretary had alleged was probably accurate, but that the president couldn't specifically recall authorizing any particular redirection of funds.

Hamilton was horrified. He begged Washington to revise the statement. He complained that the president was leaving him vulnerable to ruin and implied that Randolph was turning the president against him. Washington declined to make any changes in the letter. Opposition congressmen at last saw a chance of bringing Hamilton down. James Madison gleefully reported the flap to Jefferson: this only showed, Madison said, how far Hamilton's wangling had outstripped the president's ability to direct or even understand what went on in the treasury.

But the committee soon realized it was stymied. The issue now turned on the quality of the president's memory, and publicly exploring the quality of the president's memory was out of the question. With nothing else on Hamilton, Congress took the safe course of fully vindicating him, yet again, and only two weeks later, Hamilton, undaunted, was asking Washington for a new authorization. Now he wanted to apply some of an appropriated three million florins to paying down Dutch debt.

Washington pounced. People were worrying about his memory and suggesting his command had slipped. He went to his files and discovered that he'd already ordered, at Hamilton's request, all three million of the appropriation applied to domestic debt, not to Holland. The president shot Hamilton a note demanding clarification. Hamilton replied that he'd simply forgotten all about Washington's order—he'd had yellow fever—and pointed out that, since the order had never been entered in the treasury's books, Washington could simply reverse it now and let the money go to Holland. Otherwise, Hamilton added, the United States would experience financial embarrassments.

No, said Edmund Randolph. Changing this appropriation without out Congress's knowledge would be highly improper; at the very least, the treasury secretary must specify what the supposed financial embarrassments might be. Hamilton, compelled for the first time to justify a finance recommendation, responded instantly, drowning Washington in elaborate rationales full of numbers and concepts that both men knew were beyond Washington's scope. Washington countered, again on Randolph's advice, by saying that if paying Holland was really so important, Hamilton had permission to take the whole matter back to Congress.

Checkmate. Hamilton sent back a list of good reasons for not getting Congress involved and finally, out of options, had no choice but to let the matter drop.

So Washington did have the focus and consistency, when furious and worried, to regain a kind of control over a project of his bustling treasury secretary. Yet the enormous effort he'd expended had really only exposed the queasy news that Hamilton, in the one case where Washington had looked closely, was relying on presidential forgetfulness and, when that hadn't worked, had tried to sneak a seedy idea past Washington's treasured sense of propriety. There was nothing for Washington to do with this awareness. Gone were the days when an irritable general and chafing staffer could snap at each other, split up, and get back together later. In 1794, every consequence was dire.

Edmund Randolph, meanwhile, was becoming a Hamilton irritant. With Jefferson gone, Hamilton enjoyed unopposable dominance in the cabinet. Henry Knox, secretary of war, was not an energetic politician. William Bradford, who had taken over as attorney general, was becoming a shrewd ally of Hamilton, with a subtler understanding than the treasury secretary's of the uses of public perception. Randolph posed no concerted threat, but as the only Virginian left in the cabinet, he was increasingly Washington's adviser, even—to the extent that Washington confided anything—a confidant.

Hamilton had announced an intention to retire from the treasury as soon as his name had been cleared by Congress, but now he sent Washington two important letters. In the first he withdrew his name from consideration for the job of envoy to England. Washington had already told people that Hamilton was too unpopular for such a sensitive diplomatic assignment; knowing he was out of the running, Hamilton allowed this letter to reflect petulance. (Soon he'd be working on the mission anyway, sending instructions to the envoy that neither the president nor the secretary of state would see.) Staying home had advantages. Hamilton had projects. He wrote another letter, this time telling Washington that he would remain in the cabinet after all.

That was in the spring of 1794. In April the president received a remonstrance from a group calling itself the Democratic Society of the County of Washington in Pennsylvania, which drew the cabinet's attention abruptly back to matters at the Forks. Washington had already been giving much worried consideration to the political clubs that had formed up and down the seaboard in excitement about the French Revolution's culmination in terror and beheadings. Self-styled "democratic societies" denounced monarchical tendencies in the federal government; in smoky taverns they wrote letters to editors and addresses celebrating *égalité, fraternité, liberté*. Washington called the clubs self-created, in that they tampered extralegally with the only legitimate popular expression, elections; he saw them as gatherings of anti-federalist politicians trying to inflame ordinary people to mob violence and sedition with loose talk about guillotining aristos.

The Washington County democratic society's officers included the wealthy lawyer David Bradford and his business partner James Marshall. The remonstrance they sent the president, which actually originated in Kentucky, complained mainly of unfairness to westerners. When it appeared in Philadelphia, the remonstrance was reviewed and abominated by everyone in the cabinet: Not only was this the latest example, the cabinet inferred, of a disturbing craze for all things French; it was also the worst imaginable example of that trend. General Neville had been reporting attacks on tax collectors and tax compliers. Those attacks now seemed to be explained by an inflammatory society in Washington County.

Had the president envisioned the real situation at the Forks, he would have discredited it as a garish nightmare. He was correct in believing that the bug for glorifying French violence had infected the west as everywhere else. The Washington County society was indeed a gentlemen's club, like the societies in eastern cities, for political discussion, petitioning, and electioneering, and David Bradford and James Marshall, having flirted with radicalism for years, were exactly the sort of ambitious opposition politicians the president had in mind for censure. In the *Pittsburgh Gazette* too, writers proffered the guillotine as a political solution. Even Mr. Brackenridge, member of no society, had in a fit of republican flamboyance published a piece titled "Louis Capet Has Lost His Caput," exploiting for comedy and shock value the decapitation of the king of France. The national fad for French terror mixed easily in the west with regional grievances and old-fashioned reverence for natural English liberties.

But the Washington County democratic society wasn't directing the attacks General Neville had been reporting. It met only twice. The Mingo Creek Association inspired and led those attacks, and the association was something President Washington couldn't imagine. Its roots were in actions and attitudes that predated not only French fever but the French Revolution itself. The association met regularly, it wasn't a club, and it wasn't self-created, exactly, but something far more destabilizing, having taken over a state-created body, the militia. The association was forcing prominent men, especially supposed radicals like David Bradford, to confront the growth of a radicalism not literary but militant, not French but American, not controlled from above by opposition politicians but originating among small farmers and landless laborers.

Ordinary people, operating an extralegal court, regulating an entire region, challenging the prominent on the nature of their commitments: this picture didn't coincide with Washington's experience of ordinary people, especially those of the Forks. Washington felt he knew the Forks well. He'd been getting immensely frustrated with the major project of his life, western land speculation. In five decades, that speculation had given him a total of sixty thousand acres across the Appalachians. His efficiency and commitment had been unremitting. As Virginia's young militia commander, he'd stalled petitioning the governor to make good on land claims to militiamen, buying the claims from soldiers whom he led to believe the governor's promise would never be kept. He'd deployed land scouts with instructions to break and get around laws limiting tract size. He'd threatened and bullied people who were eyeballing plots to which, by virtue of having eyeballed them first, he claimed title. When the royal proclamation of 1763 prohibited land purchases west of the mountains, he told his agent to buy there anyway. The War of Independence legitimized his titles by overturning royal injunctions. After the revolution, he showed no patience for illegal possession: he spent much energy bringing actions against squatters, disdaining their idea that title—or at least affordable rents—should be offered to those willing to live on and improve the land.

He needed full rent. He had a constant need for cash. Making Mount Vernon pay for itself was always a problem, and his late mother had been a carping, ungrateful drain on his slim cash resources. He'd hoped to gain solvency through collection of western rents and then—when canals and roads were supported by the government and built by his own company, when Indians were suppressed by the United States Army, when regional government became what he called well toned—make a fortune by selling those lands, which would, in the meantime, have become extraordinarily valuable.

But his hopes for the west were growing dreary, his patience thin. The land was still squatted on; rents went uncollected. The absence of cash in the west—for all of Hamilton's skepticism about it—was well known to Washington: he had to accept grain and other barter as rent, which always sold, through his agents in the west, for less than he knew it was worth. The sluggishness of his agent at the Forks in sending cash, and even in responding to Washington's voluminous questions—the agent didn't answer letters for up to a year, sometimes claiming lamely not to have received them—

suggested that it might not be realistic to expect consistent rent collection at the Forks. Government there was anything but well toned, and the irresponsibility, disregard for law, and disaffection with the east that Washington saw as inherent in the character of western people were turning his land into an actual drain.

He planned on replacing his agent—he had in mind General Neville's son Presley—but really he was considering giving up his dream. The land wouldn't fetch, now, a fraction of what it someday might when canals, roads, and governmental authority linked west to east. Still, he needed income, not outgo. Recently he'd been writing his friend James Ross, in Washington County, about finding buyers for his land.

For Washington, dire personal matters were inseparable from dire national ones. The western land bubble would soon burst for everybody if lands appeared not to be under effective control of the United States. Especially painful was the military vulnerability of the frontier. Diplomatic efforts, as well as the deployment of a small, problematic army, had failed to subdue a confederation of native tribes centered around the lakes. The English, no longer simply failing to vacate western forts, were engaging in military buildup at Detroit and had established a new fort south of the western end of Lake Erie. Spain had been negotiating with Creeks and Cherokees, and Britain and Spain seemed to be developing a joint understanding in which all American settlement west of the mountains might be deemed theirs. Yet what really made both Indians and Europeans so dangerous sprang from a tendency on the part of western Americans to take independent action. Separatist attitudes made both cogent diplomacy and reliable defense impossible. At the headwaters of the Ohio such attitudes were especially destructive. The United States held vast lands beyond the Forks; those lands would be cut off by any permanent disaffection around Pittsburgh. The region was supposed to be serving U.S. military efforts, not obstructing the federal government.

The whole problem was becoming encapsulated for Washington in the western people's resistance to the tax law, which hadn't been enforced anywhere over the mountains, from Kentucky to the Northwest Territory. Failure to collect a national tax imposed an embarrassing limit on the national reach. Tax resistance also had the practical effect of weakening big creditors' confidence in the financial stability of the United States, which had promised to pay bondholders interest derived from excise revenues. To make up the shortfall, Hamilton had been forced to propose new federal taxes: excises on snuff, sugar, and carriages, as well as stamp taxes and new import duties. Because such taxes shifted burdens back to eastern merchants and creditors, now even high federalists were worried about excessive taxation.

The awful national weakness, in all its military, legal, financial, and public-relations aspects, had a source, the president was beginning to believe, in the calculations of western opposition radicals, like those of the Washington County democratic society. A display of overwhelming force at the Forks of the Ohio might serve multiple purposes.

Hamilton did not need to believe that prominent men were leading a deluded rabble to violence. Though he endorsed and defended the president's certainty that democratic societies were to blame, he was eminently capable of seeing the situation the other way round—a resistance movement driven from the bottom up. The Mingo Creek Association too was becoming known to the government: the U.S. attorney for Pennsylvania, William Rawle, was building a file on the group, based on reports from a spy at the Forks. Hamilton called the Mingo Creek Association a democratic society. Yet as he and Robert Morris had complained in the 1780s, politically ambitious elites often weren't inciting but actually pandering to the organized resistance of ordinary people.

There was time at last to revive the plans of '92. This time Hamilton wouldn't fail to send troops to the Forks. With the help of Attorney General Bradford and U.S. Attorney Rawle, he devised a procedure with more than one original twist. The tax man Benjamin Wells was called, yet again, to Philadelphia to give information on still owners who hadn't registered; Wells was promised half of the $250 fine to be collected from each defendant. A list of recalcitrant distillers was compiled from Wells's voluminous papers and from information sent by General Neville and other Pennsylvania inspectors over the past year. On the list were seventy-five violations for Pennsylvania. Only fifteen were for distillers east of the mountains.

The idea, which appeared straightforward, was to send the federal marshal for Pennsylvania to serve summonses to the people on the list. Hamilton officially described the operation as a means of testing the law's effectiveness in prosecuting offenders. Its real purpose, however, wasn't to develop prosecutions. The writs required defendants to appear in court in August; courts were closed then. Attorney General Bradford noted privately that anyone who received a warrant and agreed to register a still on the spot wouldn't actually be charged. What was being tested was the reaction of people at the Forks to being served warrants. As Hamilton, Bradford, and Rawle knew, people at the Forks, less and less likely to respond peacefully, better and better organized for panregional action, were likely to respond with the kind of violence that would justify a federal military suppression. And with Congress in recess, the president would be empowered by the new militia law to call out the largest possible force on his own discretion.

Yet even as Hamilton, Bradford, and Rawle were developing this plan, Congress was busy setting more lenient rules for trials of excise defendants. William Findley had argued for this reform. To people accused of nonregistration of stills or nonpayment of tax, travel over the mountains to federal court in Philadelphia meant many weeks away from work and family, new and overwhelming expense, even the failure of farms. It all seemed punishment in advance of judgment. Court costs were prohibitive enough; the huge fines were designed to be ruinous; nothing had caused deeper bitterness among the people of the Forks, Findley said, than being forced to stand trial in Philadelphia. It was a truism of common law that nobody must be hauled from a vicinage for trial among the strange people of another region. The west's sense of itself as a distinct region, whose problems were persistently ignored and misunderstood by easterners, amplified passion for this principle.

So a new tax law, though involving tougher enforcement provisions, would allow the federal judiciary to establish court sessions in the countryside, using local courts to hear federal tax cases, just as William Findley had hoped. This leniency might give people being served warrants a feeling that their government was heeding their most deeply felt grievance. They might be less apt to explode with the kind of violence that would justify a military suppression.

U.S. Attorney Rawle rushed the warrants into the May 31 docket. He just beat passage of the more flexible law, signed on June 5. The warrants could be served under the old law. They would impose the travel requirement. This masterstroke contrived to deliver the sting that the people considered the nastiest.

Meanwhile, in the June 7 *Pittsburgh Gazette*, General Neville took out an ad giving names and addresses of excise officers for each county and calling on all distillers to register stills before the end of June. What happened was predictable. The rebels moved instantly to shut down all tax offices and punish not only officials but also civilian collaborators. Contrary to General Neville's wishful advertising, Benjamin Wells's tax office had already been shut down, but in June, Wells's son and deputy John opened an office for Westmoreland County in the home of Philip Reagan, who was officially subdeputized a tax inspector as well; that house was fired on and stoned almost continuously throughout the month of June. John Wells's own barn and crops were burned. Reagan and John Wells defended Reagan's house, shooting back and refusing to close, but they couldn't operate.

Meanwhile John Lynn, who ran an inn in a house he rented in Canonsburg, foolishly sublet a room to General Neville for Robert Johnson's Washington County tax office. A gang of ten or fifteen men in blackface came at night and called to Lynn to come out. He fled to an upper room and barred the door. The gang shouted that unless he came out, they'd burn his house; if he complied, he wouldn't be hurt. Yet when Lynn came out, the men beat him, tied him up, and took him to the woods, where the usual mixture of whiskey-fueled wildness and ritual deliberation ensued. They chopped off his hair, shaved his head, stripped him naked, and poured the fuming tar on his head and body. Stuck with feathers, Lynn passed the night in the woods, tied to a tree. He was released in the morning.

John Lynn wasn't a tax collector. Yet after his tar and feathering, he was shunned with astonishing unanimity. His tavern was empty of customers. After part of the house was torn down, the landlord ordered Lynn off the property; Lynn had to seek refuge at the home of Robert Johnson, who, facing new threats himself, and not making any money, kept telling General Neville that quitting the tax-collection business might be the only option. By the end of the month, when Neville was supposed to send money and information east, he hadn't been able even to get reports from some of his embattled deputies. The life of anyone cooperating with Neville could be made unlivable.

In this volatile environment, Hamilton and Attorney General Bradford introduced the spark. David Lenox, the U.S. marshal for Pennsylvania, left Philadelphia in mid-June to begin issuing summonses to delinquent distillers. After serving his few writs for the eastern counties, Marshal Lenox crossed the mountains in the bright days of early July. On the fourteenth he rode into Pittsburgh in time for a chat with Mr. Brackenridge.

The lawyer insisted on having hope. If everybody listened to reason, processes might be served at the Forks without undue incident. The marshal must behave properly; the people must respect him.

When Lenox confided relief at having encountered no trouble, so far, in serving processes, even in the west, Mr. Brackenridge expressed surprise that the marshal was so relieved: people here might attack a tax man, but surely they would accept the authority of a sheriff or marshal. He chose not to mention the mobilizing of militias by the Mingo Creek Association, the closings of all tax offices, the liberty-pole raisings that recalled and presaged revolution. Getting reason to prevail meant emphasizing the prevalence of reason.

The marshal had only a few more writs to serve, but they were for southern Allegheny County, not far from the Mingo Creek headquarters. Mr. Brackenridge advised the marshal that people's anger had been focused on General Neville and suggested that leaving the general at home might avoid confrontation. Lenox didn't take the advice, and the next morning, with dawn breaking, the marshal and the general left Bower Hill, rode down through the woods, and started south along the Washington pike. It was harvesttime. Men, women, and animals were in the fields; scythes were swinging. People shared whiskey, and the presence of Neville and a federal marshal on the high road excited comment.

The two officers visited four farms as the day warmed. Lenox read out his summonses while General Neville looked on from the saddle. By noon it had already been a long day. Lenox was no hysterical Clymer but a brave, upwardly mobile hero of the revolution. Yet he was shocked: each of the people to whom he read a writ expressed loud contempt for the government he represented. One man had to be found out in a field, working with other sweaty reapers, who stood listening with menacing hostility to words that meant not only fines and legal fees, which could never be afforded, but also the crushing expense and insult to liberty of being carried away to stand trial among strangers. News of the marshal's presence traveled through the forests and farms. A hastily gathered posse of thirty or forty militiamen began tracking the two federal officers, at a distance.

Around noon Lenox and Neville rode up the lane of William Miller's farm and stopped in the dooryard of the log house. Miller was supervising about twenty men who were working his harvest; interrupted, he stood and listened as the marshal, who had dismounted, stood before him and read out the summons. As insects hummed in the noonday sun, Miller found himself desperate. He wasn't a rebel. He'd supported the Neville Connection; he was a war veteran who had fought Indians near the Forks throughout the revolution; he was a cousin of the general's brother-in-law, Abraham Kirkpatrick, with whom he'd done business. But he wasn't rich, and he couldn't believe what was happening to him. All his hopes had lain in selling his farm, right after this harvest, and moving to Kentucky. Now he was required not only to pay an impossible $250 but also to spend more money and time traveling to court in Philadelphia in order to pay it. The fine and the trip killed his move to Kentucky. His pulse pounding, Miller considered the fact that General Neville, still atop his fine mount, had deliberately piloted the marshal to Miller's door. Every time Neville had run for office, Miller had voted for him.

"William Miller, you are to put aside any manner of work and excuses . . ." But Miller was lost in a heart-pounding heat of rage and desperation and refused to accept the writ. He began cursing the marshal. Lenox, stung by an outright display of emotion—the day had been harder than any other on his overlong journey— responded by giving Miller an angry lecture. The two men were arguing when General Neville called out to Lenox to hurry: the shadowing posse, leaving the screen of woods, was advancing across a field toward the main road, where it would cut off Lenox and Neville and trap them in Miller's lane. Mounting up, Lenox left Miller in his doorway and caught up with Neville. Reaching the road ahead of the posse, the two men began riding away toward Bower Hill. The snap of rifle shots made them pull up, wheel, and face the posse, at whom they shouted angrily. The posse stopped too. Black smoke drifted. It wasn't clear to Lenox whether the shots had been meant to hit or only to frighten. Neville, who knew that these men could have hit the left eye of a squirrel at long distance if they'd wanted to, warned Lenox that confrontation was not advisable. Lenox did loudly warn the gang against interfering with federal officers. The gang shouted back in accents that Lenox found incomprehensible. Neville and Lenox, turning to ride again, agreed that Neville should head for Bower Hill, not far away, and already fortified; Lenox would ride to relative safety in Pittsburgh.

Meanwhile, at the Mingo Creek church, another group of militiamen had been meeting to respond to the call for soldiers for the army's expedition against Indians; the brigade inspector had been hearing appeals for exemptions from this service. Evening was falling, and the meeting was breaking up, when a man rushed into the church with news of the marshal's errand in the region and the confrontation at the Miller farm. Business was instantly suspended. Tactics were debated. The men arrived at a plan to arrest the federal marshal. They would bring him back to Mingo Creek, question and try him—the Mingo Creek Association being also a court—and what they did after that would depend on the marshal's testimony.

The men elected John Holcroft, of Tom the Tinker fame, to command. Holcroft selected a cadre, many armed with rifles and muskets, others only with clubs. This unit would go to Bower Hill, where the militia was betting the marshal would be. A separate party was dispatched toward Pittsburgh, to station itself on the high southern ridge overlooking the river and the village and, should the marshal be there, pen him in. "Fire if fired upon" was the order. Destroy all impediments. At all costs take the marshal.

It was midnight when Holcroft's men left Mingo Creek and moved through the dark woods toward the promontory of Bower Hill, about ten miles from the church. They climbed through the rocky woods high above Chartiers Creek and reached the mountaintop in the gray predawn of midsummer, emerging on Neville's wet lawn and surrounding the quiet house. Only now did they see that the house had been barricaded. There were thick planks nailed over the expensive glass windows.

General Neville had just awakened. In the house were Mrs. Neville, the Nevilles' small granddaughter, and a young female friend of Mrs. Neville. Though the general had drilled his slaves for defense of Bower Hill, summer work began in the dark, and slaves were already away on distant fields.

Neville called out to the men, demanding that they identify themselves. Holcroft, assuming Neville was the marshal, shouted an offer: the marshal should avail himself of the protection of this guard from Washington County. "Stand off" was Neville's reply. Then he fired. His ball hit William Miller's young nephew Oliver. The boy went down. The wound would be fatal.

Fired upon, Holcroft's company followed orders. Rebel balls ripped the planks on the windows and lodged in the wood frame. Neville had left the front door open, but Holcroft, noting the quality of fortification, decided against a massed charge: the door might be commanded from inside by a cannon. For twenty-five minutes, therefore, the men pounded the house with gunfire. Inside, the general was relying with confidence on his position, his fortification, and his own ranks. The Nevilles' granddaughter lay on the parlor floor. Mrs. Neville and her friend rapidly loaded guns. The general fired from posts at various windows, passed a gun back for reloading, took a newly loaded one, fired again. He didn't need to send out a barrage. He selected targets. He thought he wounded four more of the men who were firing in ranks on his lawn.

In the brightening morning, Holcroft realized that his men were making no headway. Neville's castle apparently held plenty of powder and shot. The rebels had perforated the frame building, but Neville had the position, the skill, and the apparent willingness to pick them off one by one. They'd already taken a terrible loss in young Oliver Miller; now they had four other casualties.

Holcroft called retreat. The men went down the mountain, falling back to Couch's Fort, an abandoned redoubt of the French and Indian War, nestled partway down a long, gentle slope about four miles from Bower Hill. Only twenty-four hours had passed since Marshal Lenox and General Neville had left Bower Hill to serve writs. Everything had changed.

In his office, Mr. Brackenridge found himself trying hard to get General Neville's son Presley to exercise some judgment. Presley was demanding the support of the Pittsburgh militia: he had a note from his father saying that a more concerted attack on Bower Hill must be imminent. The rebels, Presley was afraid, expected the general to deliver up his commission as tax inspector.

"Deliver it, then!" was Mr. Brackenridge's advice. The bitterness Mr. Brackenridge felt for the rest of the Neville Connection didn't extend to his former law student. Now that the worst had actually happened, he tried to reason with Presley. If the weak Pittsburgh militia would come out at all—and it might not—rebels would trounce it and sack and burn Pittsburgh, or put the town under siege and starve it, or take Fort Fayette. When a federal army marched in response, as it must, the situation would be civil war, which would lay the region to waste and wound, perhaps fatally, the entire Union. With things like that at stake, the lawyer tried to explain, handing over some papers meant nothing. Once an outbreak had been avoided, and the situation was back in hand, let sheriffs and courts deal with wrongdoers.

To Presley, the outbreak had already occurred. He stormed out of the lawyer's office, and soon two associate judges, who were also the town's militia commanders, appeared in Mr. Brackenridge's office to ask whether, at Presley Neville's request, they could legally call out the Pittsburgh militia. (Such judges only assisted a district judge and weren't always trained in the law.) No, said Mr. Brackenridge: only the governor could do that. The judges went away and came back. Could they, as judges, raise a posse from the county? No, Mr. Brackenridge insisted. But he admitted the county sheriff could. The sheriff pointed out—by now they were all in a tavern—that raising a posse seemed a bad idea, since the mob now *was* the posse, at least out in the countryside.

Mr. Brackenridge agreed. Persuasion was the thing, not threat. And seeing himself, when there was any persuading to do, as the man for the job, he volunteered to ride out to Couch's Fort, where the rebels were said to be planning a full-scale assault on Bower Hill, and address them. Instead of threatening dire consequences, he would appeal to reason. Fired by a hope that he still might prevent the worst for the Forks and the nation, Mr. Brackenridge mounted up and rode down to the Monongahela waterfront, the judges and the sheriff riding with him. As they waited impatiently to cross by ferry, the peacemakers encountered Presley Neville again. Now he had a crew of two other rich men's sons, flagrantly armed, eager to cross; they were accompanied by Marshal Lenox. Peacemaking clearly wasn't on their minds.

Mr. Brackenridge didn't know what Presley knew: A detachment of soldiers, led by General Neville's brother-in-law, Major Kirkpatrick, had left Fort Fayette and was hurrying to Bower Hill. Presley, the marshal, and the crew of bloods were on their way to join the defense.

Hoping to stop what he saw as an escalation, the lawyer picked out the youngest of the men, John Ormsby, whose parents he knew. "What, armed?" he said. "You will not ride with us armed." "Ride as you please," the young man retorted, "I am armed." "We are not all born orators," Presley told the lawyer. He sat on a gray horse, pistols in his belt, and the chivalric stance didn't speak well of his judgment, the lawyer thought. The groups took separate ferries, and when in the low water of a dry summer his boat hit a sandbar and stuck, Mr. Brackenridge jumped his horse over the rail and swam it across the channel. Soon joined by the sheriff, he rode up the high barrier ridge, and when the two judges caught up, the men hurriedly conferred.

Mr. Brackenridge feared the rebels would be patrolling the roads. If they spotted judges and a sheriff, they'd think this was a posse. The sheriff said he knew a back way to Couch's Fort. The peacemakers hurried down the south side of the steep mountain and rode into the countryside.

After John Holcroft's cadre had retreated from Bower Hill to Couch's Fort, militia regiments overlapping with the Mingo Creek Association had called out themselves and other militias in the region. Throughout July 17, about six hundred men gathered at Couch's Fort. Decision making was democratic. The group voted in favor of bringing more assertive action against Bower Hill. When some brought news that soldiers of the Army of the United States, led by Major Kirkpatrick, were on their way to defend Bower Hill, the rebels voted to face down those troops and make two demands.

The marshal must hand over his remaining writs. General Neville must resign as excise inspector. If the demands were met, violence would not ensue.

No blackface now, no wild disguise. This wouldn't be a raid by a gang but an expedition by a large, disciplined fighting force, mobilized without orders from any legal authority, offering to do battle with a division of the U.S. Army. A ripple of misgiving at what was turning out to be a very late date passed among the ranks. Two members of the gentlemanly Washington County democratic society—David Bradford, who had treated the Faulkner ransackers to a party, and his partner, James Marshall, who had signed the society's remonstrance to the president—declined to join in the attack. Perhaps more notably, John Hamilton, though commander of the battalion from which the Mingo Creek Association derived its structure, and a tormentor of Robert Johnson and intimidator of William Faulkner, refused to take this next, potentially fatal step. He would not go to Bower Hill.

A committee of three, led by the association's Benjamin Parkinson, asked James McFarlane, a militia major and local hero of the revolution, to command the operation. McFarlane's acceptance of command was a decisive event. Nobody evinced more dramatically than he the direness of the situation that had developed at the Forks in only forty-eight hours. James and his brother Andrew, brave, enterprising, and no strangers to armed conflict, had come to western Pennsylvania as youths from Scotland in the late 1760s; they'd traded with Indians and made money. During the Virginia-Pennsylvania border war, Andrew McFarlane had been held prisoner in Virginia for two years; later he'd served in the Eighth Pennsylvania Regiment, which marched home across the mountains from Valley Forge in an awful winter to protect Forks families from gruesome Indian attacks. When Andrew was captured by Indians in 1777, the Indians delivered him to the British, who imprisoned him. James had meanwhile been with General Washington, in the First Pennsylvania Regiment, which saw action in the most grueling theaters of the revolution. His talents were such that he rose to the rank of lieutenant. In 1780 he traveled to Quebec, where he'd learned his brother was being held, and brought about a prisoner exchange. The McFarlane brothers left Canada, traveling first to Andrew's wife's home in Virginia, where she'd fled, and then back to the Forks and their expanding lands and businesses. Unlike many others, they'd continued prospering, enjoying the respect of all classes of neighbors. By the 1790s, Andrew was living on the banks of the Monongahela, James near the Hamilton clan, high above Mingo Creek.

Lately, though, like so many other disappointed war veterans at the Forks, James McFarlane had become involved with the Mingo Creek Association. His home seemed again under attack from a distant, oppressive force, which seemed to have made the most cynical use of the commitment of men like the McFarlane brothers to the war for American independence. Shots had been fired. People had been killed and maimed. In the late afternoon, James McFarlane, embodiment at the Forks of the deepest sacrifices and greatest glories of the War of Independence, led ranks out of Couch's Fort to confront U.S. troops at Bower Hill.

Mr. Brackenridge and his peacemaking party, going as fast as they could, were noticing with dismay that harvesters working in the late-afternoon light were all women. When the party stopped at a farm along the way, hoping for news, the place seemed eerily quiet. A woman was in the house. "Are you of Neville's party?" she asked, suspicious. Mr. Brackenridge, full of misgiving, hurried his party toward Couch's Fort.

Major Kirkpatrick's troops, meanwhile, arrived at Bower Hill ahead of the rebels. They took up positions in the house. General Neville positioned himself just below the house, in a ravine in the woods, where he could observe the battle.

The force of six hundred rebels arrived on Neville's broad hilltop at five in the afternoon. Unarmed men were ordered to hold the horses at the rear. Men in arms began a formal muster in front of the house. Drums beat a tattoo. Orders were shouted. What the general could see from his hiding place was at once impressive and distressing. Ranked men paraded and drilled with discipline on his lawn. With troops deployed and ready, James McFarlane and a committee of three retired to a high point for command.

McFarlane began by sending a messenger to the house with a truce flag. At the house, Major Kirkpatrick met the messenger, who demanded that General Neville come out and give up his commission. Kirkpatrick replied that General Neville wasn't home. The messenger came back to McFarlane, then returned to the house with a demand that six militiamen be allowed to search for Neville's official papers. According to the messenger, Kirkpatrick refused. According to Kirkpatrick, he agreed to the demand but was then told that his soldiers must come out and ground their arms; this he could not allow. Either way, it was an impasse. But the messenger and Kirkpatrick did agree that women should now leave the house. The women emerged and ran downhill to Presley Neville's house at the foot of the mountain.

Some rebels, restive, began setting outbuildings on fire. They also fired desultory shots at the house; then both sides opened fire in earnest. As the gun battle went on, and black smoke again obscured the view, militiamen were still coming up the hill and reporting for duty. Some had received word that failure to appear for this event might have unpleasant consequences.

Now too came Presley Neville, his friends, and Marshal Lenox. But since they were approaching the rebels from the rear, they had no way of aiding the defense of the house.

Presley was still in chevalier mode. "If any of you is a gentleman," he shouted to rebels in the woods at the rear, "come out and speak to me!" Marshal Lenox winced at this pointless challenge. Militiamen confronted Presley and his friends and placed the whole group, including the marshal, under guard. Presley could only watch as balls tore into his father's house and smoke hung over the grounds and farms.

Firing from the house abruptly ceased. Through the smoke, rebels saw a white flag waving from a window. At his high command post, James McFarlane stepped from behind a tree to tell the men to hold their fire.

A shot was fired. Someone in the house had picked McFarlane off. Hit in his groin, he fell. He'd survived the War of Independence. He died on the ground at Bower Hill, a few miles from where he lived. In shock, the rebels, robbed of command by what seemed the grossest treachery, resumed firing. Neville's slaves started shooting at the rebels from their quarters. The rebels lit more outbuildings ablaze.

Inside the battered mansion, Major Kirkpatrick could see fire spreading quickly toward him. Flames, not shooting, would soon make defending the mansion impossible. The heat was becoming unbearable. The house and everyone in it would burn. Kirkpatrick had no choice. When he came out and surrendered, the militia, so abruptly victorious, dismissed Kirkpatrick's soldiers, who left, and arrested Kirkpatrick.

It was evening. Militiamen entered the house and surveyed the shambles. Fine furniture lay splintered. Mirrors and windows were shattered, ornate plaster smashed on carpets. The rebels broke out the general's whiskey, and as darkness gathered they made a massive bonfire of General Neville's entire Bower Hill plantation. They ran through the house smashing what hadn't been smashed. Barns, fences, grain, and crops went up in high flames. Soon the mansion was ablaze too; an orange brightness lit clouds of smoke drifting over the deep Chartiers Valley. Men ran through flaming barns and stables. They shot stamping, rearing horses, a cow, a pig. Slaves were pleading with the rebels to spare the slave quarters, as well as the smokehouse where the slaves' food was kept, and when it was all over, slave quarters and smokehouse were the only things left standing at Bower Hill.

Only a few miles away, Mr. Brackenridge and his party, cresting a hill, saw the glow in the sky. They'd already turned back, having learned at a house along the way that they were too late. They could hear whoops and shouts as rebels dispersed up and down the steep forest. Some were carrying James McFarlane's body to his brother Andrew's house. Some were escorting prisoners to Couch's Fort. Some were going home.

Mr. Brackenridge had failed, again, to mediate. Disaster had come at last. He and his companions nudged their horses on toward Pittsburgh.

Meanwhile, Marshal Lenox was being hustled on horseback into the rebel fallback at Couch's Fort. A shot was fired, just missing Lenox: drunk militiamen were there, and Benjamin Parkinson and his committee were trying to impose order while deciding what to do with Lenox. Two men with knives approached Lenox and slashed his coat. The committee removed Lenox to a nearby house for safekeeping, where Lenox found Presley Neville, also captive. Lenox was deeply regretting Presley's loud challenge to the rebels at Bower Hill.

Yet the killing of James McFarlane and the burning of Bower Hill hadn't removed the original demands from the committee's mind. Negotiations began. Marshal Lenox swore to serve no more writs west of the mountains and to surrender himself to the committee on demand. Presley agreed to sponsor the arrangement: should Lenox default, Presley would suffer in his place. With business concluded, the committee assigned a guard for the prisoners' safe passage to Pittsburgh and released them.

Out on the road in the darkness, Lenox and Presley were making their way through the dispersing crowd when some drunk militiamen aimed guns at them. Their appointed guard, following orders, stayed between them and the drunks, but the drunks were having none of that and began forcing the whole group back toward Couch's Fort. The situation could not end well, Lenox saw. He spurred his horse and bolted into the woods. Arriving at about three in the morning at the Monongahela, he rowed himself and his horse to town. Presley soon escaped too; he arrived in Pittsburgh shaken but unhurt.

Major Kirkpatrick had been taken by another group of rebels, who were saying that he'd personally shot James McFarlane. David

Hamilton, calmer brother of the wild Daniel, joined the group, and Kirkpatrick, knowing David, felt safe enough to start berating his captors. But when David told him quietly, "I'm putting my life at risk trying to save you," Kirkpatrick fell silent, and David found a way to let Kirkpatrick too escape. The major arrived in Pittsburgh, where the whole Neville Connection, distraught, was gathering around General and Mrs. Neville, who now owned literally nothing but the clothes they wore. The Nevilles were staying at the home of their daughter and son-in-law, the Craigs, while the Connection tried to absorb the losses of the night and the peril of the immediate future.

General Neville had been warning the Washington administration for years that law at the Forks of the Ohio needed the immediate, armed help of government. Isaac Craig wrote hurriedly to his boss, Henry Knox, in the cabinet in Philadelphia.

James McFarlane's marker would stand out on the steep hillside across the road from the Mingo Creek church, where only children had been interred before him. The burial, a day after the destruction of Bower Hill, became a crowded scene of grief and rage, at once a funeral and a meeting of militias and the association, led by Benjamin Parkinson's committee. Mourners were talking about more fire. This time they wanted to burn the town of Pittsburgh, where the Nevilles and their friends were gathered with the marshal. The committee chose to send the calmer David Hamilton and another rebel, John Black, to collect the warrants that the marshal had already served and demand the resignation of General Neville. If these conditions were met, Pittsburgh might be spared.

Meanwhile, at the village on the point, some were saying that surrendering the Nevilles and the marshal to the rebels might be the only way to escape destruction. When David Hamilton and John Black crossed the river that evening, fearing arrest, they told people that the rebel committee was waiting in a nearby tavern. Townspeople walked restlessly in the dirt streets and stared across the river at the ridge. Rumor had it that a thousand men were up there, ready to rush down, ford the river, and sack the town.

David Hamilton met with General and Presley Neville and asked for the general's resignation as tax inspector. Even Presley now advised his father to comply with the demand: the Nevilles' home, their animals, their fields and harvest were nothing but charred hulks. The general wrote out and handed David Hamilton a resignation full of conditions and haughty language. Hamilton refused to accept it. It seemed calculated, he said, to insult—as if Neville actually wanted to incite the rebels to march on Pittsburgh.

Mr. Brackenridge, in his office, found himself mediating a disagreement that he could hardly believe was taking place. The rebels and the marshal were arguing over what had been agreed to the night before. The rebels Black and Hamilton said that the marshal had agreed not only to serve no more writs but also to hand over the writs he'd already served. The marshal insisted that he was under oath to return all served writs to Philadelphia. The lawyer watched in amazement as a dispute of almost monstrous irrelevance unfolded before him. Pandemonium threatened the nation while the marshal argued, rightly, that a writ is only a summons, not a judgment in itself, and John Black wondered whether people's lands would be seized and sold in Philadelphia if the marshal returned the writs. Black wanted to hear from Brackenridge whether the marshal was really bound to return them.

Mr. Brackenridge could have laughed, but he was beginning to see the trouble he was in. These rebels, fretting over trivialities like the return of writs, fearing their lands could be seized, were probably guilty of the capital crime of treason. The Nevilles and the marshal, for their part, clung to papers, offices, and pride in the face of the threatened burning of Pittsburgh and the outbreak of civil war in the United States. If the lawyer told Hamilton and Black that having their lands seized was the least of their problems—that they'd probably all hang—rebel desperation would spill over. Nor could he advise the marshal to do the simple thing, give up the writs, defuse the conflict, save the town. Asking a federal officer to relinquish his sworn duty might, in Lenox's eyes, place Mr. Brackenridge among the group to be hanged.

Gamely, the lawyer offered to render an opinion on the question. He stayed up all night studying the excise law and the language of the writs, and in the morning he wrote out a formal, if useless, statement: The writs were summonses to show cause why process should not issue, not judgments in themselves; yes, the marshal was on oath to return them, but no lien could ensue from their mere return. He gave a copy of the opinion to the marshal, another to Black and David Hamilton. But the committee, Hamilton said, wouldn't accept this. If the rebels had known that the marshal meant to return the writs, they would have killed him when he was their prisoner, and Presley Neville was surety for the marshal's not leaving town.

Mr. Brackenridge made a final suggestion. If the rebels allowed the marshal to leave with the writs, in any ensuing prosecution for tax evasion—as if that were really the thing to fear now—Mr. Brackenridge would appear for the defendants and get them off. If he failed, he'd pay any fines for unregistered stills out of his own pocket.

Hamilton and Black agreed to nothing. They did ask Mr. Brackenridge to come present his idea to the rebel committee, which they claimed was waiting only four miles away; they wanted an escort out of town anyway. The lawyer, though sleepless and exhausted, was committed to seeking reason. He agreed to go. Crossing on the ferry, David Hamilton expressed doubts about prospects for peace. He seemed more gloomy and worried than fervent: there were moderates on the rebel side too, apparently. He told the lawyer that the people at McFarlane's funeral had been ready to burn the town, an event that his and Black's trip to town had been meant to forestall—but the people would come to Pittsburgh sooner or later, he warned. They would arrest General Neville and the marshal. There was no escape. All roads out of town were now being patrolled by rebel militias.

Another man had come along on this trip. The excise officer Robert Johnson, tarred and feathered three years earlier, was fed up at last with trying to enforce the law and had agreed to hand over his commission to the rebel committee. The group stopped at Johnson's house while Johnson wrote out his resignation. Now Hamilton and Black admitted that the rebel committee wasn't really nearby. It was still at Bower Hill, they said. Arriving on those heights in the afternoon, the party saw the smoking skeletons of what had once been the most elegant home and prosperous plantation at the Forks. The slaves were there, but the rebel committee wasn't. It was really down in the headquarters at the Mingo Creek church, Black and Hamilton confessed; they'd come to Bower Hill only to look for a dead rebel body.

At this, Johnson refused to go further. He handed his resignation to Hamilton and Black and agreed to publish it in the *Gazette*. Mr. Brackenridge was fed up with the rebels' deceptions too. If Johnson left, no witness could vouch for the lawyer's reasons for traveling with outright insurgents. Downhearted, he said good-bye to Black and Hamilton.

As Mr. Brackenridge and Robert Johnson rode down from the remains of Bower Hill, thunder rumbled. Wind whipped leaves inside out. At the Monongahela riverbank, Johnson took the lower ferry, and as Mr. Brackenridge turned north for the upper one he was hit by a blast of rainy wind, blowing up quickly into the most drenching storm he'd ever seen. He took shelter in the ferry house. Flashes lit the sky. Out on the Ohio, a boat carrying two soaked federal officers and an escort of soldiers went bobbing past the point. General Neville and Marshal Lenox were taking their best chance of escaping Pittsburgh.

CHAPTER EIGHT

A New Sodom

No calm followed that storm. Four days after the general and the marshal flushed themselves down the west's biggest drain, Mr. Brackenridge was standing before a grim crowd in the Mingo Creek church. The meeting, called by the committee that had overseen the attack on Bower Hill, was turning into a tribunal, at which the people put a direct question to the rich and educated.

Benjamin Parkinson, tall and red-haired, stood before the crowd. "You know what has been done," he cried. Mr. Brackenridge heard a kind of anguish in his voice. "We wish to know," Parkinson said, "whether what has been done is right or wrong."

Not to attend this meeting: that had been the lawyer's fondest hope. After the escape of Lenox and Neville, rebels had been saying that prominent men who failed to support the rebellion would be treated in the same way as the general. The eyes of the rebellion were on Mr. Brackenridge. Tom the Tinker, suspicious of the lawyer's commitment to the rebel cause, wanted him in the front ranks. Isaac Craig and others in the besieged Neville Connection, for their part, wanted the town to take a stand against insurgency; at times it seemed as if they didn't care if the town burned. Craig had insisted on keeping the Pittsburgh excise office open as a signal of defiance. Mr. Brackenridge started a rumor that five hundred militiamen were coming to close down the office, and Craig took down the sign with a degree of haste that the lawyer, for all his apprehensiveness, found satisfying. The Neville Connection were eyeing Mr. Brackenridge with suspicion too.

Yet it was at the urgent, personal request of Presley Neville that Mr. Brackenridge had come to the Mingo church meeting. A written invitation had been delivered to Mr. Brackenridge's office from David Hamilton, the gloomy moderate of the rebel side, who seemed to think the lawyer might help the rebels succeed without excessive violence. Frightened now of anything connecting him with the insurgency, Mr. Brackenridge tore the invitation in pieces and tossed them into the chaos of an armoire. But Presley came into the office and asked the lawyer to go to the meeting, pressing it as a personal favor. Presley, Mr. Brackenridge remembered, had been the guarantee against the marshal's leaving town. Mr. Brackenridge insisted on taking witnesses who could vouch for his reasons for attending the meeting, and Presley gratefully agreed to vouch for him too.

When the Pittsburghers arrived at the church, they were distressed to find not the small committee they'd expected but a mass gathering. A narrow road dropped steeply from forested heights and passed the church on the Mingo. Dozens of men were already outside, dozens more were arriving; and across the road was the tilted graveyard, with James McFarlane's grave freshly dug. Among the waiting attendees was James's brother, Andrew, silent and drawn, with a black band on his arm.

Country people observed the arriving Pittsburgh contingent with subdued rage. Nobody spoke as they waited for the meeting to begin. Men paced around or lay on the grass.

One of the Pittsburgh group had brought a letter from Presley Neville. When the crowd had entered the church and the meeting began, the letter was read from the chair, and Mr. Brackenridge, seated in the crowd, cringed. If the young man had meant to inflame, he'd succeeded. His letter praised the valor of the hated Major Kirkpatrick, suspected assassin of McFarlane. The crowd grew furious. After making an argument (surprisingly cogent, the lawyer thought) for the marshal's being no longer bound by any agreements, and Presley's being thus released from his own obligations as forfeit for the marshal's escape, the letter went on to brag.

Presley had so much property, the letter said, that he didn't care if the rebels did burn him out. Men glared at the Pittsburghers, who had nowhere to look.

Then, in answer to Parkinson's question—was it right or wrong?—the rich Washington lawyer David Bradford addressed the crowd. Though he'd always been a populist, the actions he'd engaged in had merely obstructed creditors, made law enforcement difficult, intimidated collectors, pushed government away; they hadn't been acts of war. Bradford had declined to participate in the attack on Bower Hill, and in the days since, rebels had been accusing him of encouraging them. When he denied it, they threatened him. On the way to the meeting at the church, he'd conferred with his business partner, James Marshall. Other rich men were wringing their hands too; there was no prominent supporter of the kind the rebels were asking for. Addressing the crowd, David Bradford made a fateful decision.

He vehemently supported the attack on General Neville. He reviled the government of the United States. He called for organized regional self-defense. He praised the French terrorist Robespierre. And worst of all, for Mr. Brackenridge and the Pittsburgh moderates, he called for an immediate vote, here in the church, to see who truly supported burning Bower Hill and arresting the marshal and who was a hypocrite. On calls for yea or nay, people must literally stand up and be counted.

The crowd responded avidly. Many who had wavered before Bower Hill were now fully enlisted in the cause. All eyes were on Mr. Brackenridge as he walked to the middle of the aisle in a tense silence. Faces were angry and suspicious; he feared immediate attack. Feeling a need to warm up the room, he did an impression of Isaac Craig hurriedly taking down the excise sign. Mockery of the Neville Connection was something he could share with his audience. He got laughs. Quickly now, he slipped in the idea that he and his colleagues couldn't possibly participate in any vote, as the Pittsburgh contingent was not here as a delegation from the town, but he did volunteer, simply as a personal friend of the country, to answer Parkinson's stark question: right or wrong? Burning Bower Hill, he said, might (he emphasized "might") have been right—morally. But it was wrong legally. He went further. It was treason. He pushed this painful idea against the crowd's apparent disbelief. Under the Militia Act, he told them, the president of the United States was now empowered to call out an army against them.

The church was silent. The people seemed amazed. Many in the militias apparently possessed only the weakest conception of how far their actions had taken them. They expected to be left alone to force officials to resign and flee, to winnow out overactive creditors and engrossers of business and property, and to impede distant government with acts of regional self-defense. They didn't seem to understand that state and federal governments had recently been restructured to cope with just such outbreaks—that those governments had, to a great degree, come into existence specifically to do so.

Having scared them, the lawyer offered a way out. If they couldn't make a revolution, he warned them, they would only make a rebellion, and a rebellion would be crushed; this meeting didn't have the official support of all of western Pennsylvania, or western Virginia, or the Kentucky territory. But the Washington administration, he advised them, had always been pathetically eager to prevent war at all costs. The president was likely to agree to an amnesty for crimes committed, if the rioters made a statement of full submission to the laws. He gave them his best impression of fat Henry Knox, in broken-English parley with the Seneca chief Cornplanter. People were too disconcerted to laugh much. The lawyer explained his point: if mere Indian tribes could exact leniency from the president, the westerners might expect no less.

This idea, a statement of regional submission and a plea for amnesty, would become the best plan of the prominent moderates at the Forks, who would go on hoping, with growing desperation, that destruction and civil war might be prevented. At the church, however, Mr. Brackenridge saw anger pass across Benjamin Parkinson's face in response to the lawyer's proposing that those not involved in the Bower Hill attack be appointed to ask the president for amnesty on behalf of the attackers. This was hardly the univocal support that Parkinson and his committee were demanding. Other militiamen were shaking their heads. The meeting took a break. People wandered around outside, talking angrily. Daniel Hamilton approached Mr. Brackenridge, to whom the mercurial Daniel seemed to have taken a sudden liking, and confided that Parkinson and Andrew McFarlane were excoriating the lawyer. Mr. Brackenridge began moving his colleagues onto their horses, and to avoid being put on the spot in a vote, the Pittsburghers rode off.

Then, fearing that such a quick exit might reveal outright dissent, the lawyer changed his mind, rode back quickly, hid his horse near a stream, walked up to the church, slipped inside, and began mingling and chatting as though he'd never left. But there was nothing more he could do here. With Bradford now in the lead, the meeting had responded, in a way the lawyer hadn't intended, to the idea that broad regional support was lacking. The rebels now called for a grand western congress two weeks hence, a gathering of all four western Pennsylvania counties, plus Bedford, and as many Virginia counties as would join in the defense of the region. The lawyer had prevented a vote that might have brought immediate destruction on Pittsburgh. But he'd failed to push back rebel rage, which kept seeking broader avenues. He slipped out of the church and rode for town.

Alexander Fulton was a wealthy distiller in his thirties, a veteran officer of the revolution. Before Bower Hill, he'd loudly derided the rebels, whom he scorned as a faction. Men who blackened their faces and disguised themselves had to be ashamed, a mob, nothing for the likes of Alexander Fulton to fear. He'd openly claimed a connection with General Neville; he'd offered Neville the use of his house and the support of his person, should Neville's home ever be attacked. Fulton was, in other words, just the sort of propertied, educated man of whom the rebels were now demanding demonstrations of wholehearted loyalty to the western cause. Fulton prided himself on knowledge of military tactics, and the rebellion needed just such expertise.

So what Fulton had once considered his unassailable pride had been replaced by bowel-loosening panic. He could barely master his shame. He'd been in a tavern, drinking wine—not whiskey—when local moderates had come in with the news of the rebel defeat in the morning attack on Bower Hill. Fulton had expressed pleasure in the news, and learning that the rebels were gathering at Couch's Fort, believing too that radicals were now out of power—in any event, he was sure they'd never have the effrontery to attack Neville in force—he thought he'd go to Couch's Fort. He could play on the crowd. He could disperse the rebels. On the way, however, he went to his uncle's house and fell asleep.

At eleven in the morning his uncle awakened him, alarmed. Word was out. Fulton must go to Couch's Fort, and not as any kind of peacemaker: if he stayed away, his property would be destroyed. Flustered by his abrupt change of status, suddenly afraid for his farm, distillery, and home, Fulton arrived at Couch's Fort to find the militias gone, already marching to Bower Hill. The march must be bravado, he thought. The mob couldn't really mean to strike, undisguised, at the vitals of government. He went after them anyway. When he caught up, self-assurance washed away. This wasn't a mob but a force, six hundred strong, hardy war veterans led with discipline by those he once would have called respectable people: Benjamin Parkinson, James McFarlane. Civil war had broken out. Incredibly, Alexander Fulton was on the wrong side. His property and even his life appeared to be in danger. As the line marched by, two militia officers offered Fulton a command.

He declined. He'd come, in fact, unarmed, a violation of a call to arms: if you owned weapons, you were required to bring them. The officers returned with a request from James McFarlane himself that Fulton accept the rank of brigade major. Fulton again declined. A murmur broke out along the line: Fulton had offered aid to General Neville and must be here as Neville's spy. McFarlane, riding up in person, asked Fulton to take a command. Miserably, Fulton averred that, having never held militia command, wouldn't it be considered assuming if he took one now?

McFarlane rode off, and an officer told Fulton that if he refused command he'd be a prisoner. Amplifying Fulton's discomfort, Daniel Hamilton, commanding a company of his own, made his always intimidating presence felt. Not only was Fulton a prisoner, Daniel informed Fulton, but if he tried to escape he'd receive far worse treatment. Daniel had a way about him. Fulton agreed to lead the march.

At Bower Hill, after hanging back with the unarmed horse guard, Fulton fled to a high field to watch the battle. He saw the surrender of Major Kirkpatrick, then the burning and mayhem. Now he understood. This would happen to anyone boasting a connection with General Neville. In the days after Bower Hill, Fulton went around boasting instead of faithful service to the rebel cause.

After the Mingo church meeting, therefore, when James Marshall asked Fulton to come to a meeting at David Bradford's, Fulton had no choice. He was one of them. Arriving at Bradford's elegant brick home in the town of Washington, Fulton was further amazed. Bradford had followed up his speech at the church by expanding the rebellion's base. Writing to leaders in the Virginia counties that bordered Pennsylvania, he asked them to send delegates to the upcoming grand congress. He'd also decided to examine and police local commitment to the rebel cause. Two days earlier, on the post road twenty miles east of Pittsburgh, men sent by Bradford had waylaid the carrier of the U.S. mail and stolen bags of letters. The purpose was to take action against anyone writing for federal help.

Now Bradford, Marshall, Benjamin Parkinson, and the discomfited Alexander Fulton opened the mail. Members of the Neville Connection, they discovered, had indeed been writing to the government in Philadelphia to describe not only the burning of Bower Hill but also—treacherously to this committee—Bradford's rousing antigovernment speech at the Mingo Creek church. Bradford, Marshall, and Parkinson decided to go to Canonsburg to review these letters with others and consider what measures to take against Presley Neville and the treasonous cohort.

Alexander Fulton made excuses. He fled home. The committee followed him. They insisted he come with them. Awash in fear and shame, Fulton could do nothing but comply.

In a room at Canonsburg, the letters were pulled from saddle-bags and read by a larger group. All other letters were put carefully back in bags to go to Pittsburgh and be mailed again. The traitors' letters were heatedly discussed. Fulton, availing himself of copious drafts from the whiskey cask, was in a weird state of terror and drunkenness. With Bradford, Marshall, Benjamin Parkinson, and others, he shakily put his signature on a circular letter to all militia commanders in the region.

What this once-proud aristo had signed was a revolutionary document. It called out all the militias of the region. Only the governor could do that, but Bradford's committee was now openly usurping military authority, just as committees of safety and correspondence had done in the seventies. A regionwide force, dwarfing the one that had destroyed Bower Hill, was to muster near Pittsburgh. It would arrest the letter writers and their sympathizers, place them in the Pittsburgh jail, and attack the garrison at Fort Fayette. Like the Massachusetts militias in '75, like the Green Mountain Boys at Fort Ticonderoga, the people would seize the oppressor's arms and use them for the defense of what Bradford was now explicitly calling the western country. Braddock's Field, where the British general had been defeated in the 1750s, and where the militias were now ordered to muster, would take its place in glory.

Yet even David Bradford wavered on the verge. The orders he was giving could only mean armed, outright secession. Moderates receiving the circular argued vehemently with him, and three days before the muster, he sent a new circular, weakly countermanding the order. Munitions the rebels had planned on seizing were meant for use in the Indian war, Bradford said; best to leave them there, no need to turn out after all.

His supposed followers weren't buying this. Armed militias converged on the town of Washington, filling the streets and jamming the courthouse for an impromptu meeting. Moderates too tried to seize on the unplanned moment, which might be the last chance to argue for calm. U.S. Senator James Ross of Washington, a friend of the president himself, spoke at the courthouse for two hours, trying to dissuade the people from mustering at Braddock's Field; other moderates joined him. Even James Marshall, too far in with Bradford to turn back, suggested not mustering; and John Hamilton, commander of the Mingo Creek militia that was the movement's core, tried to order his men not to march. But the crowd, furious now, threatened immediate violence, and when David Bradford himself arose to speak, he was very much back on task.

He expressed outrage at being accused of countermanding orders. He'd done no such thing, he said. He was their leader; orders to rendezvous at Braddock's Field would be obeyed by all. The crowd acclaimed the plan. Later that night, James Marshall found the door of his house covered with tar and feathers. The message was clear. Everyone was going to Braddock's Field.

Bradford's committee had ordered troops to bring four days' provisions to the muster. Country people started coming into Pittsburgh to buy those provisions; they muttered about high prices, predicted the town's gouging would soon come to an end, and tried to trade produce for large stocks of flint and powder. Strangers were seen hanging around the streets. The militias were said to be considering alliances with Britain that would bring in substantial armaments from Canada. Country women were said to be looking forward to living in the rich people's houses, country men to getting new hats and clothes free of charge. Pittsburgh was now called Sodom, and it was said that this time Sodom would be leveled by fire not from heaven but from earth.

Mr. Brackenridge was ruing the day he'd been so witty about King Louis's lost head. Word had it that David Bradford had taken to calling himself the Robespierre of the west. Troops at the Fort Fayette garrison—overwhelmingly outnumbered, should all militias turn out—were fortifying and laying in stores. Isaac Craig brought his family into the fort. Presley Neville fortified his own house. Townspeople were nearly hysterical with anxiety.

The region's moderates now consisted of a small, embattled group of well-known citizens who kept trying to reason with David Bradford as hours counted down to the muster. With Mr. Brackenridge in Pittsburgh were his friends John Wilkins and Wilkins's father, John Wilkins, Sr., an associate judge. Moderates outside Pittsburgh included Albert Gallatin, the Swiss republican from Fayette County, now in the U.S. Congress and regretting signing the resolutions of the second Pittsburgh convention. George Washington's friend Senator James Ross lived in Washington County, the heart of rebel territory: Ross had Neville ties, and his wife was sister to John Woods, the Neville family counselor and Mr. Brackenridge's enemy. Yet unlike many in the Neville Connection, Senator Ross knew there was no choice, at this point, but to negotiate with the rebels. The state judge for the district, Alexander Addison, though no friend of federal overreaching in state law, was keenly aware of the foolhardiness of thinking the region could defeat the United States in any armed conflict—or that, if it could, the region would be better off. William Findley, Mr. Brackenridge's old enemy and a U.S. congressman, had argued vociferously in Congress against everything Alexander Hamilton proposed, and he'd attended the first, nondelegated antiexcise meeting, but he'd managed to stay aloof from the Pittsburgh conventions while retaining credibility with his constituents. Mr. Brackenridge might lampoon Findley as *Modern Chivalry*'s plodding Traddle the Weaver. Yet as disaster developed, Findley was managing to thread the eye of a tiny needle.

For all their differences, each of these men wanted peace and reason. Many considered the excise tax misguided; some were in favor of it. Some had attended the Pittsburgh antiexcise conventions; all believed such meetings were legal, that laws should be changed through peaceful petition and the electoral process. Their hope was that a regional statement of submission to the law and a plea for amnesty from the federal government for past outbreaks of violence would end the crisis without carnage or a rift in the Union.

But now they found themselves negotiating desperately just to keep Pittsburgh from burning. In Washington, Senator James Ross finally prevailed upon David Bradford, who did make an offer. Pittsburgh must officially banish the following people: Presley Neville and Major Kirkpatrick; treasonous Neville Connection letter writers John Gibson, James Brison, and Edward Day; and Major Butler, commandant of Fort Fayette. With these demands, Bradford attempted to cut Pittsburgh's strongest ties to the east and break up the military-industrial cartel. In the new west, a Neville Connection wouldn't be tolerated. In return for the banishments, Bradford would try to keep the people from burning Pittsburgh.

Another condition: men of Pittsburgh must march enthusiastically out, in militia order, to join with the people in the Braddock's Field muster. The new west must be of one mind.

Pittsburgh's moderates could see no course other than compliance. In the long night before the scheduled muster at Braddock's Field, a large, anxious town meeting appointed a committee that included Mr. Brackenridge and his friend Wilkins, Jr., to negotiate with messengers from David Bradford. The demand to evict Major Butler was withdrawn—nobody thought the town had the power to evict the fort's commandant. To take over civic operations during the emergency, the meeting created a committee of twenty-one, which sent word to the other banishees that they must leave. Giddy with a mixture of terror and hope, the committee of twenty-one also drew up a resolution to find and expel anyone else who opposed what they now called—amid some sickly laughter in the room—the common cause. They resolved to appear in force the next day at Braddock's Field, and even to bring along handbills expressing support for the rebels. The *Gazette* editor volunteered to stay up all night printing the bills in his log shop.

The meeting broke up late. Candles burned through the summer night. People anticipating mayhem worked in fear and grief to hide valuables, bury cash, and burn official records. First light brought only confusion. Many had been up all night. Women were still hiding money and household possessions as men suited up to march. Some just stared into space. Jumpy already, people were startled by the arrival of a man who came shouting through the streets on horseback, waving a tomahawk. "It is not the excise law only," he screeched at frightened citizens, "that must go down. Your district and associate judges must go down, your high offices and salaries. A great deal more is to be done. I am but beginning yet!"

The ambassador from Herman Husband's New Jerusalem rode off, and at nine o' clock, the evictees Brison and Kirkpatrick complied with the town's instructions: smarting, yet agreeing to leave for the good of the town, they rode to the river and were seen ceremonially across by Wilkins, Sr., who could hardly believe he was participating, as an officer of the town, in the banishment of citizens. Presley, Day, and Gibson were refusing to leave; worse, just as Wilkins was mounting up for the muster, an express rider brought an urgent letter from Governor Mifflin. The governor ordered Wilkins, as associate judge, to spare no effort in arresting the Bower Hill rioters.

Wilkins hid the letter. Sickened, he prepared to join those very rioters in an operation that might end with an attack on Fort Fayette. There was nothing else to do. At ten the men of Pittsburgh marched in glum formation away from the convergence of rivers to join the rebels on Braddock's Field.

Throughout the Forks, men were riding and marching in militia units up and down hills, fording the river, arraying themselves about the vast plain on the bank. By midafternoon nearly seven thousand were on Braddock's Field, a broad plain on the Pittsburgh bank of the Monongahela, about eight miles east of town, two long bends up the river.

Some of the assembled men were full of fear and misgiving and had appeared only on pain of punishment. But many were parading with enthusiasm, even with hope. Only about a third of these men owned stills. Most owned no property at all. The strange rider of the morning had announced it: Distilling and tax payments were not the main thing on most people's minds. The expulsion of the Neville Connection from Sodom portended a reversal of society. High-salaried officials and monopolizing army contractors were being driven back to the vicepots of the east where they belonged. Pittsburgh, many hoped, would soon be the people's own, a Sodom redeemed. Women had come with the militias to aid in any household looting.

The Pittsburgh militia, terribly jittery, approached from the west and halted to close ranks a few miles from the field. The committeemen planned their entrance. Mr. Brackenridge, more and more eager to demonstrate the utterness of Pittsburgh's submission to rebellion, thought they should advance waving a white flag. Others thought this would show mistrust, not the enthusiasm the rebels demanded. They sent a man ahead to distribute their rousing handbills. When it was reported that the bills had been received well, Pittsburgh advanced to the field. The twenty-one committeemen rode at the front, unarmed, to show the town's official submission to the rebels. They were followed by officers and men in arms, showing readiness to fight for the rebel cause. As the Pittsburghers crossed the field, they found it hard to see anything or hear any orders. Black smoke hovered above the ground and floated over the river. Thousands of men from the countryside were firing their weapons.

The Pittsburgh group was ordered to halt, stand, and arrange itself. All around the plain, whiskey was passed as muskets and rifles fired again and again. The rebels used balls to hit marks and powder alone to shoot into the air. They were mostly dressed in buckskin hunting gear and wore handkerchiefs around their necks—the outfits they wore to battle Indians. Various parades started up. Men made harangues condemning traitors not to tar and feathers but to the guillotine. The Pittsburghers, rudely challenged again and again, by men they did not know, on their loyalty to the new west, loudly deprecated the citizens they'd banished, agreed to further banishments, cheered on the most extreme plans of violence, and wondered if they'd survive the day. They had the impossible task of showing total conversion to the cause while persuading rebels that there was really no need to burn Pittsburgh, since it was being cleansed of all offenders.

Mr. Brackenridge applied all his talents as a writer and an actor to conjuring a mood of camaraderie and submission. He passed among the men, sharing whiskey and cracking nervous jokes that denigrated the Nevilles and Pittsburgh. But he kept seeing the bereaved Andrew McFarlane glowering at him; other rebels seemed unsure of the lawyer too. Groups debated, in his presence, whether to make him governor of their new state or burn his house in Pittsburgh. There was constant talk of taking Fort Fayette. The lawyer was asked repeatedly, "Are we to take the garrison?" He always enthusiastically answered that they were. "Can we do it?" men asked, and hoping to deflate interest, the lawyer kept saying they could do it with ease: only one thousand killed, maybe only five hundred wounded.

As he smiled and entertained he snuck glances of horrified amazement at David Bradford—Major General Bradford now—astride a big horse, in a gaudy uniform, with a flashing sword and a hat with plumes. Bradford rode about the field with staff and supporters, cheering on his rowdy men, who had taken to worshiping him with extravagant compliments, praising him as a Washington of the west, bringing him cool water to drink and begging for commissions and offices in this freakish form of western army. Bradford seemed to bask not only in command but also in the delusion that he could control, with precision, just how far the rebels would go. Mr. Brackenridge thought that if Bradford had tried to restrain them at all, his supposed adorers would hang him to the nearest tree without a thought.

The militias bivouacked that night on Braddock's Field. The Pittsburghers, relieved that a tense and eerie day was over, started to return to town. They were ordered to return to the field; any departure would be construed as desertion. Around the bivouac fires the drinking and talking went on. After midnight Mr. Brackenridge rode through camp inquiring for the location of the Pittsburgh battalion; this was to assure all hearers that the Pittsburghers were actually present. A man challenged him, demanding to know why Kirkpatrick had been allowed to escape. The question was confusing, as Kirkpatrick had been banished on rebel instructions; others stepped in to offer the startled lawyer a drink and a hint to move on. When Mr. Brackenridge approached John Hamilton's leaderless battalion, the rowdy Daniel Hamilton was voluble in shouting out his belief in the sincerity of the lawyer, of whom he was making a kind of pet. But Daniel complained to the lawyer that Senator James Ross had been trying to talk people out of going to Pittsburgh.

"Damn the fellow!" was Mr. Brackenridge's instant rejoinder. His pitch was getting perfect. He rallied Daniel and the rest to march on Pittsburgh, but near the damned fort, not to the damned fort, showing what could be done without actually doing it, exhibiting discipline and doing no damage to people or property! . . . The battalion seemed to respond well to his presentation of a mere parade as an event of valor. The lawyer was becoming convinced that direct attempts at persuasion like Senator Ross's could never succeed. He thought his own tactics would.

The next morning, it all started again: drinking, manic parading, shooting; new units were arriving as well. At last Major General David Bradford called a meeting of battalion leaders in the woods beyond the field. Men crowded around to hear the plan. Mr. Brackenridge and James Ross joined the leadership committee, which began by reviewing the cases of the treasonous letter writers. David Bradford announced that he wanted to include Isaac Craig in the banishments. Mr. Brackenridge argued that, while the man was of course an idiot—again he drew laughs with the story of Craig's cravenness in taking down the excise sign—Craig should be allowed to stay in town, since he was quartermaster of the fort. The refusal of Presley Neville and others to leave town was discussed. The Pittsburghers proposed to ensure their departure but asked for eight days to let them get ready. The rebel committee grudgingly agreed to a grace period. This was getting really boring. Some riflemen sitting on a log called out to Bradford that if the committee didn't come up with a plan of action soon, they'd do something on their own. Bradford quickly announced a march on Pittsburgh.

Mr. Brackenridge concurred. "By all means!" he exhorted them: let the men march through town, turn before reaching the fort, drink some whiskey, compliments of the people of Pittsburgh, cross the river, and leave. That would show the government what the Forks militias were made of. Senator James Ross looked at the lawyer. "The veil is getting too thin," Ross warned him quietly. Yet the committee was breaking up, and a march, not an attack, did now seem to be the plan.

As battalion leaders went to muster their men, Mr. Brackenridge found himself nose to nose with Benjamin Parkinson. Parkinson had indeed seen through the veil and was enraged by the insult. "Give us whiskey?" Parkinson asked. He was grinding his teeth in fury. The lawyer tried to explain, but Parkinson gave him a warning: "We don't go there for your whiskey."

On the field, rebel militias were forming ranks, and their shouts about looting, plunder, and burning weren't reassuring. A group of Pittsburghers was rushing ahead, some to the fort, to ask Major Butler not to engage the rebels, some to get barrels of whiskey, close the taverns, and gather boats for ferrying the rebels out of town after the party.

Drums were beating. Mr. Brackenridge himself rode at the head of the march from Braddock's Field. Troops stretched in tight companies behind him for two and a half miles. He took the Monongahela road, deliberately away from the fort on the Allegheny, led the troops north into town and down Market Street toward the point, then executed a sudden left back toward the river, wheeling the whole army out onto another plain just east of town, where it was formally greeted by the Pittsburgh committee of twenty-one and assorted townspeople. Whiskey, water, and food were served to the troops by Pittsburgh's women. David Bradford set up his headquarters in the shade of a tree and seemed to revel in what he called a glorious revolution without bloodshed. As the summer afternoon went on, some rebels wandered the streets, bullying people they met and banging on tavern doors demanding whiskey, but the idea of reducing the town to ashes seemed to be dissipating. The hosts politely offered the footsoldiers ferry rides across the river in boats. Mounted troops were shown to the best fording point. By nighttime, there were fewer than two hundred rebels left in town.

Those remaining had a plan, however. Some who had already crossed the river would torch barns, owned by Major Kirkpatrick, on the high south ridge; at that signal, the rebels still in town would burn first Kirkpatrick's townhouse and then the homes and offices of the letter writers Day, Gibson, Brison, and Presley Neville. Since any fire on that scale would spread to the entire village, this was too much for some in the Pittsburgh committee. Wilkins, Jr., hearing of the plan, called for defense of the town; Mr. Brackenridge, so close to having dispelled the threat of destruction, begged Wilkins and the others to stick to the plan and show nothing but passivity. The lawyer was sure that overt resistance would bring the rebels back to finish Pittsburgh. Only rebel leaders could stop the town from burning. He ran to the arsonists to beg them to tear down the Kirkpatrick house, not burn it. And indeed David Bradford's partner James Marshall, arriving at Kirkpatrick's house, opposed the burning. The bereaved Andrew McFarlane opposed it too. He had no desire to destroy property, he said: if he and Kirkpatrick ever met, one of them would die. Leaders turned the gang away from the house. David Hamilton, the gloomy rebel moderate, took a boat across the river to see if he could stop the burning of Kirkpatrick's farm buildings there. Mr. Brackenridge crossed the river with David to order all ferryboats back to Pittsburgh, impeding any rebel return.

Ferrying alone back to town, he saw again the great signal of failure. The southern sky jumped with light. Major Kirkpatrick's barns were burning.

But the rebels had left the point. No fire was sweeping through town. Morning brought the exhausted citizens only further suspense. Rumor had it that men were waiting nearby to come back to carry out the burning. Word came too that rebel troops, passing Robert Johnson's house the night before, had threatened to shoot Johnson's wife. In the country, it was said, David Bradford was triumphant, and anyone who hadn't been at Braddock's Field was apologetic and disgraced.

As the committee of twenty-one assembled that evening to consider further contingencies, yet another crisis developed. Major Kirkpatrick was still in town. He hadn't really left; he was at the fort. Should rebels learn of Kirkpatrick's presence, they'd take revenge on the town. The committee ordered Presley Neville and Isaac Craig seized and sent down to rebel headquarters in Washington as a forfeit for Kirkpatrick. Craig, hearing he was being sought, fled to the fort, but Presley sent word that he'd turn himself in, and soon he sauntered into the committee room, smoking a cigar. He announced with a smirk that Major Kirkpatrick was willing to leave town if given a protective escort. The committee of twenty-one eagerly assigned a man the job.

Over at the fort, townspeople—not rebels—were gathering. Enraged by Kirkpatrick's willingness to sacrifice the town to rebel vengeance, they surrounded the fort in hopes of shooting Kirkpatrick or turning him over to the rebels. Moderates were wondering how to handle this new source of mob violence when rain again intervened. Darkness had fallen, and in a downpour, the assigned escort rode up to the fort leading a fresh horse with full saddlebags. He managed to slip past the wet and angry crowd at the gates, and soon he slipped out again, this time with Kirkpatrick riding beside him. A shot was fired after the two men, but they were gone in the night.

The rebels were almost ready to declare victory. As the town was purged, in the countryside Tom the Tinker blotted out all remaining traces of federal authority. A few hundred armed militiamen returned to the home of Philip Reagan, where Benjamin Wells's son John had failed to operate the Westmoreland County excise office. Reagan was taken into the woods and given a trial, which the assembled rebels called a court-martial. The verdict was guilty, the sentence tar and feathering, but the sentence was commuted. Instead, Reagan was forced to hand over his papers as a deputy, share whiskey with the rebels, and pledge his commitment to the rebel cause. Then the militia paraded Reagan through the villages. Crossing the Youghiogheny, the triumphant cadre approached Benjamin Wells's home to the beat of a drum. Nobody was there, but the house was full of plate, pewter, and featherbeds. The rebels stacked three beds in the middle of a room as kindling; lighting that, they threw bedclothes on top, and amid flames and smoke they smashed all crockery and kicked the cookware and pewter into the fire. By morning the house had been leveled to a hot, black pile, studded with melted pewter and potmetal. Reagan escaped that night, but in the morning, as Benjamin and John Wells returned to their flattened home, the rebels apprehended them and rode them away, again showing the prisoners to people on the road. At a mill owned by the father of one of the landless rebels, the Wellses too were tried by court-martial. The sentence was tar and feathering; it was commuted. The Wellses were made to resign their commissions, drink with the rebels, and declare fealty to the cause. They were released without a home and with only the clothes they wore. They had no offices or papers. They'd drunk spirits from the common pot and joined in the pledge of allegiance. To Tom the Tinker they no longer existed, as individuals or as officials.

With his family franchise and all its subsidiaries expunged from the Forks, Benjamin Wells expunged his person too, leaving his family with neighbors and heading for Philadelphia by way of Winchester, Virginia, to give new evidence, in which he would name Herman Husband an instigator of this new mood of regulation. Philip Reagan fled the Forks too, as did John Webster, the collector for Bedford County. Webster had been taken prisoner, held overnight, and forced to watch his haystacks and stables burn. After tearing up and treading on his papers, he found himself standing on a stump, giving three huzzas for Tom the Tinker, drinking toasts as rebels cheered around him.

The situation was more desperate now, moderates thought, than it had been before Braddock's Field. The blackface attacks had been frightening, but this was revolution almost accomplished. The village on the point had so far been spared, indeed saved, moderates believed, by their ploys, risky and distressing as those ploys were. Yet moderates were under attack from many sides. To embattled members of the Neville Connection still in town, the committee was a rebel instrument; Pittsburgh was controlled by the insurgency. To the townspeople, the committee had risked the burning of the town by helping Kirkpatrick escape rebel rage. To the rebels, Sodom hadn't yet committed itself to the cause of the new west and might still need to be purified by fire. Flustered, exhausted, with nowhere to hide, moderates kept hoping for calm, but the grand western congress, called by David Bradford and the Mingo church rebels, was still scheduled for August 14. Its agenda was to define a new relationship between the western country and the government of the United States. Five counties of Pennsylvania, as well as Ohio County in Virginia, were sending delegates.

Mr. Brackenridge kept being stunned by displays of irrationality. Some of the remaining Neville Connection had left town within the agreed-upon eight-day period, but Presley Neville was being obstinate. First Presley met with the committee of twenty-one and demanded a passport and an escort out of town. The committee gave him a pair of passports, one to get him through rebel territory, the other to explain his situation to the federal and state governments. But Presley hung around for days and then met with Mr. Brackenridge—whom he now insisted on treating as the rebel warlord—to demand that his status be reviewed, as an official order of business, at the upcoming regionwide congress. Presley wanted his banishment formally repealed.

Mr. Brackenridge couldn't believe it. Disasters multiplied while people contested fine points of nonexistent laws and the official resolutions of kangaroo assemblies. Again the lawyer explained the reality to Presley, this time with asperity: the young man's own person and property would be far safer if he simply removed himself for a time and let Mr. Brackenridge and others work for resolution. Presley did at last agree to leave, but grudgingly. He believed Mr. Brackenridge was forcing him out, and he planned a triumphant return.

Wanting to stay in town seemed absurd to the lawyer, who had been dreaming about running since before Braddock's Field. He was still a target for assassination and had never believed in displays of courage. With Wilkins, Jr., he'd discussed not only good destinations but also good excuses, as flight would be deemed treason by rebels patrolling the roads. Wilkins favored going up the Allegheny, into the deep woods, on the pretext of surveying. The lawyer dreamed only of Philadelphia.

Now he had an idea. The town should appoint him to travel to the president and explain Pittsburgh's situation. But Wilkins, Jr., objected. He'd come to believe that all moderates had a duty to stay and work for peace; more important, he didn't want to be left alone, the last reasonable man in town. Stuck, Mr. Brackenridge hoped to stay away from the upcoming six-county congress. His experience at the Mingo church told him that he and other prominent men would be called on to speak, to propose resolutions, and to stand up and vote, committing themselves to treason or risking assassination. He suggested to fellow moderates that the most prominent among them try to keep out of the congress. But they prevailed on him. Senator James Ross, Wilkinses Jr. and Sr., and Albert Gallatin all believed the best known of the moderates had a duty to get elected to the congress as delegates. They must capture the congress. They must try, one more time, to bring about submission and beg the government for amnesty.

So Mr. Brackenridge was elected a delegate from Pittsburgh. But he also decided to write personally to Tench Coxe, Secretary Hamilton's chief deputy, to explain the sensitivity of the moderates' situation at the Forks and beg for the understanding and forbearance of the federal government. As he began writing, he realized that the rebels were not above reading people's mail. So he employed his literary talents in writing for two audiences. For rebel readers, he couched his pleas for governmental understanding in what he hoped the rebels would mistake for fist-shaking rhetoric. It remained part of his strategy for peace to perform his best imitation, whenever rebels might be around, of a firebrand radical.

Neither moderates nor radicals could have predicted the event that, at the August 14 congress, turned the insurrection in a new direction. The congress was held at Parkinson's Ferry, hardly a neutral place: On a wide bend of the Monongahela River, well to the south of the village on the point, it had been named for a ferry, tavern, and store run by the brother of Benjamin Parkinson of the association; it was too close, geographically and emotionally, to Mingo Creek for moderates' comfort. The congress came to order high on a bluff, where a field full of stumps and fallen trees overlooked the river and hills. The size of the crowd made the outdoor setting necessary. From all townships in five Pennsylvania counties, and from Ohio County in Virginia, came 226 delegates, supported and monitored by 250 armed men, who acted as a kind of gallery.

The delegates were almost all radicals, menacingly supported by the gallery, which talked only of war. Herman Husband himself was present as a delegate from Bedford. As on the eve of the Battle of Alamance thirty years earlier, Husband was now counseling peace. Yet the people were talking less of the repeal of the excise tax than of a complete restructuring of society along the lines of Husband's sermons. They seemed more than ready to stare down every horn of the Beast to get it. Liberty poles announced that the whole area was in defiance of government. Some slogans on poles attacked the excise, but others called for something far more radical: equal taxation. Some promised death to cowards and traitors; some revived the all-purpose image of independence, a snake, now cut in segments representing the separate counties, warning, "Don't Tread on Me."

The western country had its own flag now too. Six stripes, alternating red and white, stood for the unified six counties of western Pennsylvania and northwestern Virginia. In conversations with spectators and delegates, it became clear to Mr. Brackenridge that people saw the whiskey tax only as a symbol. They wanted repeal, but they were also talking about a redistribution of wealth, especially of land, with rules for access to land and rewards for improvement. As the flag flew above the high bluff on the river, the moderates' task seemed impossible.

Then the congress was brought up short. On the morning of the fifteenth, the delegates received a message that came, amazing all assembled, from representatives of the president of the United States. Even more amazing, these representatives were in a house only four miles away. They'd just arrived; they'd been traveling hard and fast for days, hoping to forestall the worst.

The United States hadn't sent an army. It was just what Mr. Brackenridge and the moderates had been hoping for. George Washington was offering to negotiate for peace with the people of the western country.

CHAPTER NINE

Talking

The president had been nursing pain and frustration at Mount Vernon, victim of the injury he'd sustained on horseback at the Potomac's lower falls, when Marshal Lenox had begun serving writs on noncomplying distillers in Pennsylvania. When the shooting started on William Miller's farm, Washington, still in pain, had been back at work for about a week. It was not until ten days later, on July 25, that Henry Knox received word from Isaac Craig of the burning of Bower Hill. In the next few days, the administration received reports of the robbing of the U.S. mail, the march on Braddock's Field, the expulsion of the Neville Connection, and the scheduling of the Parkinson's Ferry congress.

The burning of Bower Hill was more than enough. The day that news arrived, Washington resumed what he and Hamilton had launched in the spring. Process of law in western Pennsylvania, the president said, had broken down. He called an emergency cabinet meeting to consider ways of using federal force to subdue the western counties. Timing the process service for June had been effective: Congress had closed its session right after passing the new excise-enforcement law, and with Congress in recess, the president had personal discretion to create the largest possible force. To invoke his powers under the Militia Act he needed only the certification of a justice of the Supreme Court that law enforcement had truly failed at the Forks.

Hamilton began gathering documentation for James Wilson, now a court justice, an old fellow nationalist in the confederation

Congress, and old ally of Robert Morris in the Pennsylvania assembly. It was Wilson who had almost single-handedly revised the radical Pennsylvania constitution in favor of creditors. Always desperately in debt, he was still an investor in increasingly irrational land and industrial schemes; he'd always been unabashed in connecting the need for federal strength with the importance of paying creditor interest. He required some hastily assembled documentation of the breakdown of law in the west, but on August 4, having made no independent investigation, Wilson certified the call for troops.

Thomas Mifflin, governor of Pennsylvania, posed a problem. An ally of the Jeffersonian opposition, Mifflin was an old states-rights man and had been a personal enemy of Washington since the early days of the revolution. Mifflin and the administration were in the midst of a clash over federal and state jurisdiction in Presque Isle, on Lake Erie, and Mifflin's subordinates had gotten in the habit of writing passionately challenging letters to the president. The governor had long been adept at handing out favors and appointments on all sides, using patronage to blur lines between opposing parties: a hard-drinking, glad-handing clubhouse politician, he'd been unscatheable for years in general elections, and the Washington administration badly needed a show of his wholehearted support to stifle political opposition to using troops. On August 2, the president and his cabinet met with Mifflin and other Pennsylvania officials. The meeting did not go smoothly.

The president asked Mifflin, as a show of cooperation, to call out the Pennsylvania militia against the rebels—a quick, preliminary measure, Washington told Mifflin, not dependent on Supreme Court certification. The Pennsylvania authorities objected. While federal enforcement might have failed, they said, the state's hadn't: noncompliance with the excise law was a federal, not a state, crime, so opportunity for state enforcement had arisen only with the attack on General Neville's home, which might involve both state and federal charges. As no state enforcement had yet been tried, calling out the militia would be as illegal as anything the rebels were doing. The Pennsylvanians went further: should the president require the governor to call out the militia, jurisdictional tensions would be such that Mifflin would have to take up the issue with his legislature before complying.

To the cabinet, this position was infuriating. When the Pennsylvanians cited the opinion of District Judge Addison that force would only promote resistance at the Forks, Hamilton replied that Addison's opinion showed that justice in the western counties was run by the insurgency. Acrimony intensified. The minutes broke off. A daunting conflict was shaping up between two executive branches over the legitimacy of using military power against the citizenry.

On the federal side, the most complete argument for the legitimacy—indeed, necessity—of sending troops to western Pennsylvania came, not surprisingly, from Alexander Hamilton, in an official report made on August 5 at the president's request, in which Hamilton summed up his long-standing views. He placed rebel violence in a military, not a criminal, light, focusing on the area's populace as a whole, not on individual attackers. He reminded Washington that Clymer had discovered at the Forks something far worse than mere opposition to excise: hatred of the United States had long been brewing there. He cited the two Pittsburgh conventions, where complaints had gone far beyond excise. Local law enforcement's failure either to arrest the Wellses' attackers or to call out the militia to defend Bower Hill were further examples of the regional quality of the insurrection. Mincing with his usual onrush of delicacy around the desire to smash with force (here he called it "what is in such cases the ultimate resort"), Hamilton noted that all milder means—sending Clymer, serving the writs—had now been tried without success.

The report was a triumph for being indisputable, in a context of crisis that Hamilton had hoped to create. He cited a resolution of the second antiexcise convention at Pittsburgh, which called for using "all legal means to obstruct the execution of the law." How can there be legal means, Hamilton asked—unanswerably—of obstructing the execution of a law? In a republic, the people vote for legislators. The legal means of repealing a law is to vote for new legislators. Noncompliance is bad enough, but obstruction of the federal law is by every definition destructive of the republic.

The report was unanswerable in a more profound way as well. Nobody would have agreed more heartily than the rebels themselves that they were engaged not in committing crimes, nor in opposing mere excise, but in a regionwide mobilization against the government by people loyal first and foremost to local leaders, disciplined by passion for their cause, or, where passion was lacking, by coercion. The people's movement described itself just as Hamilton did: a collective and univocal entity.

As a delegate to the Constitutional Convention, James Madison, then Hamilton's collaborator, had based his argument for replacing the confederation of states with a national government on a hypothetical situation, which was now arising in fact at the Forks. Suppose Congress were ever called upon, Madison had asked, to maintain order within one of the states. In a confederation, that conflict must occur between the central Congress and the member state. But in a national government, which acts on individuals, not on states, the conflict occurs between the government and the rioters as individuals. Military force can never be applied to citizens collectively without ceasing to be punishment and becoming war; citizens treated in that way will seize the opportunity to dissolve all compacts by which they might have been bound; union itself will dissolve. But when a government insists on treating each citizen as an individual, and treating insurgents, however numerous, however organized, and however they describe themselves, as criminals, not as a regional entity, union can survive even the most egregious crimes against it.

Others thought otherwise. Both the rebels and the high federalists believed that the people of western Pennsylvania, committed and subjected en masse to armed rebellion, could be recommitted and resubjected to the United States only en masse and by armed force. The federal government was embracing what Alexander

Hamilton and Tom the Tinker, disputing theorists of finance, had always believed it must. It would occupy a region, suspend civil liberties, and use military force to police the citizenry.

As debate went on between the state of Pennsylvania and the Washington administration over the legitimacy of calling out the militia against citizens, the cabinet split too, over the question of whether to send troops immediately or seek ways of avoiding such a drastic step. Edmund Randolph urged not only delay but also negotiation with the rebels. It was Randolph who, at the Constitutional Convention, had argued so strenuously for creating a national power to put down insurgencies. Yet the real strength of government, he now urged Washington, lies not in coercion but in the affection of the people. If the rebels would not agree to abide by the law, then they must be prosecuted as criminals, not suppressed as part of a populace; only if courts failed to prosecute could troops legally be used. Randolph was sure Judge Wilson had irresponsibly rubber-stamped the operation, and he asked Washington, with great eloquence and passion, to send a peace commission west in a sincere spirit of reconciliation.

Hamilton and Knox were arguing for moving immediately, with an overwhelming force of at least twelve thousand men, bigger than any American army to date, more than had beaten the British at Yorktown. Their high-federalist ally Attorney General Bradford, however, joined Randolph in arguing for negotiation. Yet Bradford's theory of negotiation was entirely different from Randolph's. In Bradford's view, negotiations could serve as a means of achieving political cover while readying troops for military action. The question of delay was somewhat academic anyway: Troops would need time to mobilize. Negotiations would meanwhile fail, revealing rebels as intractable. Sympathies of people throughout the nation would swing toward the president, forestalling militias in other western regions from acting in concert with the Forks; Mifflin and the political opposition would be silenced. Then the troops could move with impunity.

On August 6, Washington took what appeared to be a middle course between Hamilton's urgency for action and Randolph's plea for reconciliation, assigning Bradford to lead a presidential commission, including both federal and state commissioners, to negotiate with the rebels. The other federal commissioners would be Washington's friend and soon-to-be land agent Senator James Ross, already on the ground in Washington County, and Justice Jasper Yeates of the Pennsylvania Supreme Court. (State commissioners had already been appointed by Mifflin.) While Randolph still placed fervent hopes in the peace plan, Hamilton—though preferring to have troops positioned in the Appalachians before beginning negotiations—had worked with Bradford on serving the writs; he remained confident that an army would, in the end, march. Isaac Craig had sent word of the expulsion of Lenox and Neville, the muster at Braddock's Field, and the march on Pittsburgh. Major Kirkpatrick had written twice to the president; other federalists had been writing east, and the term "civil war" had been used. Hamilton responded to news of Braddock's Field by telling Craig it was highly satisfactory to get this sort of intelligence on rebel movements; he assured Craig that government would not be found wanting. Then: "And can there be any doubt of the sufficiency of its means?" He instructed Craig to flee with his family to Fort Fayette, should the worst happen. He underlined that instruction.

On August 7, the federal peace commissioners started west. The same day, Henry Knox sent orders to the governors of Pennsylvania, New Jersey, Maryland, and Virginia to call out a total of thirteen thousand militiamen and hold them ready to march. Washington issued a new proclamation, required by the Militia Law Act before the president could move troops, ordering insurgents to disperse and threatening military suppression if they did not. And the next day, two refugees from Pittsburgh arrived in Philadelphia.

General Neville and Marshal Lenox, exhausted and bedraggled after three weeks of hard overland travel, had stories to tell. They'd disembarked in Wheeling, Virginia, and sending their escorts back up to Fort Fayette, had continued alone down to Marietta in the Ohio territory, and had then hired two guides. Traveling east across rough country, they'd stayed in Virginia until well past the Alleghenies.

General Neville was eager to lend his aid to the military operation and looking forward to returning to Pittsburgh.

Even while traveling toward the Ohio, Attorney General Bradford found ways to pursue the real goal of negotiation by sending Edmund Randolph a steady stream of reports on rebel intractability. Bradford spent the first night in Lancaster, where he joined fellow commissioner Jasper Yeates; there they encountered General Neville and Marshal Lenox, still a day west of Philadelphia, who advised Bradford that there was no point in negotiating. The area was lost to rebel control, they said; the commission might as well turn back. Bradford assured them that his mission was to leave insurgents with no excuses and keep other states from coming to the Forks' aid when an army marched, and he sent an express rider back to Randolph—who was eagerly honchoing, in Philadelphia, the peace mission in which he still placed high hopes—with a report of the negative impressions of Lenox and Neville.

Bradford and Yeates gathered and sent home more negative impressions as they went west. A handbill had been brought from Pittsburgh, one of those distributed at Braddock's Field, showing that prominent men were now insurgents too. Farther west, news had it that a proclamation issued by Governor Mifflin had been read at the Forks only for the purpose of exposing it to sarcastic comment; in some places it had been torn up, with magistrates joining in. In Bedford, Bradford learned that the west was actually declaring its independence. At Greensburg, very near Pittsburgh now, he and Yeates met the banished Presley Neville, whose view was as dark as his father's—especially regarding Hugh Henry Brackenridge.

Some of these encounters suggested that things might not be as bad as they seemed. The prominent men on the handbill, it emerged in conversation at yet another tavern, were really anti-insurgents. Still, Bradford emphasized for Randolph, a frightening number of people had marched on Pittsburgh.

While Bradford, from the road, made an official record of the unlikeliness of his errand's success, Hamilton was taking control of the military buildup. Henry Knox had been worrying over some precarious land investments in Maine. Hamilton encouraged Knox to go and check personally on his land; Washington gave Knox permission to leave; Hamilton stepped with alacrity into the job of secretary of war. On August 14, Governor Thomas Lee of Maryland called out his state's militia. On the sixteenth, Governor Henry Lee of Virginia called out his. Governor Mifflin, despite his dissent, had already called out the Pennsylvania militia; New Jersey was signed up as well. The governors were responding to Knox's orders, but it was the author of the whiskey tax who now coordinated the military effort to enforce it.

Bradford and Yeates were having to travel fast if they wanted to confront the rebels at the Parkinson's Ferry congress on the fourteenth. They slept as little as possible and made up to forty miles a day; approaching the eastern front of the Alleghenies they put on even greater speed and arrived late on the night of the fourteenth at a house on the banks of the Youghiogheny, only four miles from Parkinson's Ferry. So exhausted they could barely write, they sent a note to Senator James Ross, the third commissioner, to say they were no good for immediate business but would come to Parkinson's Ferry the next day.

What the presidential commissioners saw when they arrived at Parkinson's Ferry astonished them. A huge gathering of people, mostly armed, was dispersing down the high bluff and along the riverfront. The six-striped flag was flying. William Bradford dashed off a note to Randolph reporting the presence of the flag. He also reported the burning of the stables and hay of the Bedford tax man John Webster, who had been made to hand over his papers, stand on a stump, and toast Tom the Tinker.

At the congress, tension between insurgents and moderates had reached a high pitch. Herman Husband might be counseling peace, but the militias he'd inspired were ready to fight the United States. For moderates, therefore, the arrival of these commissioners from the president offered providential hope, after weeks of terror and tension, that at the last minute the situation might be salvaged.

Mr. Brackenridge assured the rebels that the commission was so unimportant that it didn't much matter who met with it; many rebels now believed he was on their side anyway, and the lawyer got himself elected by the congress's standing committee of sixty to serve on a small committee of the conference to negotiate with the federal commissioners. On this committee were the radicals David Bradford and James Marshall, but so was the moderate Gallatin; Senator James Ross, the moderate from Washington County, was on the presidential commission itself. An understanding might be reached.

Moderates still had a difficult task. They'd not only have to arrive at an agreement with the commission but also sell any such agreement to the mass of delegates and militias. Still, they thought they'd lucked into a good chance to avoid either armed secession or military suppression.

William Bradford and his federal commissioners had a different plan. Already determinedly pessimistic about peace, they found further grounds for pessimism in the secessionist mood of Parkinson's Ferry, as well as in a rowdy crowd erecting a liberty pole outside the window of the tavern in Pittsburgh where they'd settled to await the Parkinson's Ferry conference committee. The first meeting with the committee was scheduled for the twentieth. The state commissioners hadn't yet arrived. Yet on the seventeenth, the federal commissioners wrote to Randolph to report that there was no prospect of enforcing the law without using what they called, with greater bluntness than most in the administration, the physical strength of the nation. William Bradford also wrote to the president unofficially. In the personal letter, he argued that delay in sending troops risked running into the paralyzing winter months. He warned Washington that rebels would only further arm themselves and bring in sympathizers from other states.

Bradford's letter to Washington had an even more important purpose, which neither Bradford nor the president would have wanted to reveal to Edmund Randolph. Under the relative safety of his guise as a negotiator, Bradford had been gathering an impressive amount of military intelligence. Ammunition was happily lacking here, he told Washington privately, as were bayonets, but every man had at least one working rifle, and there were eleven barrels of powder and five hundred stone of arms in the town of Washington. The army in Fort Fayette had cannon for defense, but militiamen at Fort Le Beouf up on Lake Erie had been recruited mainly from the Forks and might come to join the rebels; they could command Fort Fayette from the hills. A goal of the negotiations, Bradford said, must be to drive a wedge between moderates and radicals. By holding out hope to moderates, the negotiations might weaken the radicals' control over the region and make invasion easier.

Bradford's private letter, reaching Philadelphia on the twenty-third, along with the official commission report urging military action, had been preceded, around August 15, by Mr. Brackenridge's letter to Hamilton's deputy Tench Coxe. The lawyer's decision to write for two audiences at once—the government, begging forbearance and understanding at the Forks, and the rebel militias, who might rob the mail, and must see Mr. Brackenridge as committed to the cause—had some unintended consequences.

Pray for delay, Mr. Brackenridge urged Coxe, for if a federal force were sent west, people in the midlands wouldn't let it pass. The funding system, the lawyer just couldn't refrain from noting, in what was supposed to be a plea for conciliation—and to the treasury—was detested and abhorred by all intelligent people, as well as by the yeomanry of America; it would bring people together against the army. A growling, lurking discontent, Mr. Brackenridge said, would soon burst and discover itself everywhere. The rebels had even talked of making overtures to the British. Wait till Congress reopened in the fall, he begged; then the westerners' grievances could be addressed, and the excise suspended, as he took the liberty of noting he'd recommended two years earlier. Having worked himself into a terrified and terrifying lather, he closed by insisting that the real fear wasn't that the federal army would march to the Forks. The real fear was that the insurgents would march east, cross the Susquehanna, and take Philadelphia.

This extraordinary communication, which was passed quickly around the administration, seemed to say that unless Congress acceded to rebel demands in the next session, not only armed secession but an actual attack on the nation's capital would soon follow. Such was the effect of Mr. Brackenridge's prose that when the official commission report arrived, urging force, along with Bradford's private report to the president on the Forks' defense capabilities, nobody except possibly Edmund Randolph expected or even hoped to receive better news about rebel attitudes.

An eight-hour cabinet meeting on August 24 became a war council, with Hamilton in high gear as secretaries both of war and treasury. Randolph's hopes for a happy outcome were broken. The peace commission itself was now urging force. Randolph had no choice but to support Hamilton, who was scribbling notes on militia numbers and supply chains and sketching out plans with Washington for moving fifteen thousand men. Hamilton began ordering arms and supplies and sending word to Henry Lee of Virginia, who would serve under Washington as commander of the whole force.

Absolute secrecy was critical to these mobilizations. The rebel negotiating committee in Pittsburgh, Governor Mifflin, the U.S. Congress, and the public at large must not learn that before completing—or even beginning—peace negotiations, the administration was planning an invasion. Writing to Henry Lee, Hamilton told the governor not only to keep his orders secret but to postdate them.

Hamilton got busy in another area as well: stirring up public sentiment. As "Tully," he addressed a series of newspaper articles to "the virtuous and enlightened citizens of a new and happy country!"

Addressing the people directly as "you," he presented the western counties of Pennsylvania as having nullified "your" will. Tully scoffed at the traditional complaints of western settlers, confident that "you" would never be so gullible as to believe any human suffering existed beyond the Alleghenies, where "a scene of unparalleled prosperity upbraids the ingratitude and madness of those who are endeavoring to cloud the bright face of our political horizon, and to mar the happiest lot that beneficent Heaven ever indulged to undeserving mortals."

This tone proved effective in confirming the new mood of patriotism that had followed the year of instability of 1793. Many people around the country expressed hatred for the rebels and wondered why the president hadn't already moved against them.

Finally, Hamilton wrapped up the administration's ongoing struggle with Governor Mifflin. Mifflin's administration was continuing its practice of sending long, heated letters to the administration, and this month's batch had defended and explained the governor's reluctance, on both legal and political grounds, to call out his militia; Mifflin also tacitly challenged the legitimacy of Judge Wilson's certification and even the president's right to create a federal militia. Writing for Randolph, who was fast becoming irrelevant, Hamilton now launched the kind of attack in which he took the greatest pleasure. Excessive politeness emphasized the enjoyment he took not in persuasion but in decimation. One of Mifflin's most passionate arguments had been that the militia could disperse an insurgency but not occupy a region, nor hunt and arrest suspects. To Mifflin and many others, a militia's authority was immediate and situational, dissipating as soon as a riot was put down. Real police work and prosecution were reserved, by law, for local, state, and federal officers; empowering an army to enforce laws was itself illegal, Mifflin believed.

Hamilton was pleased to demonstrate, at exhaustive length, that the Militia Law Act, as well as certain parts of the Constitution itself, had been constructed for the very purpose of allowing troops to police citizens. The militia could "enforce the law," "cause the laws to be duly executed," and "suppress combinations," all of which must mean, Hamilton said, that the militia can also break up meetings and assemblies that exist simply for the purpose of non-compliance with the law, when such meetings are supported by violence that baffles ordinary law enforcement. He was talking now not only about attackers of Bower Hill but also about delegates at meetings and signers of petitions. His letter gave off a white heat.

The conference committee from Parkinson's Ferry, with its hopeful moderates, came to Pittsburgh on August 20 to meet with the federal commissioners, who had been joined at last by Mifflin's two state appointees. Mr. Brackenridge had already been to see the commissioners; he and Attorney General Bradford had been friends at Princeton. The lawyer felt he could explain the real situation to the commissioners before negotiations officially began. What emerged during his attempted prenegotiation shook him.

Most of his fellow moderates at the Forks, whether they found him brilliant or annoying or both, understood his tactic of feigned support for rebellion. He'd continued to play the role at Parkinson's Ferry, when moderates managed to get a committee appointed to tone down David Bradford's and James Marshall's proposals for armed regional defense. That committee consisted of the three most intellectually sophisticated men at the Forks—Herman Husband, Hugh Henry Brackenridge, and Albert Gallatin—who came together for the first time and utterly bewildered one another. Mr. Brackenridge tried to entertain Gallatin by drawing Husband out on the Book of Ezekiel, but Gallatin was impatient with the lawyer's frivolity. "He laughs alone," Gallatin said darkly of Brackenridge, with prescience. Gallatin openly advocated compliance with the law and suspected the lawyer of rebel complicity, but Senator James Ross had a hurried discussion with Gallatin, and Gallatin and Mr. Brackenridge did arrive at an understanding.

Now, arriving to talk to the commission, the lawyer found Isaac Craig already there, telling the tale of the expulsions of members of the Neville Connection. Mr. Brackenridge had to break into Craig's narrative, reminding Craig that banishees had been sent away only on the insistence of rebels who threatened to burn the town. Craig left, saying nothing, and Mr. Brackenridge turned to his classmate, the attorney general, and made an outright plea. "I am not an insurgent," he said. "That is a matter for future consideration" is all the attorney general would say. He'd been forwarded Mr. Brackenridge's letter to Tench Coxe.

Mr. Brackenridge spent a worried night. If the army did come, he now saw, he was a marked man. For the first time, he gave serious consideration to the rebel cause and its chances of success. The Forks could invite Spain all the way up the Mississippi to the headwaters of the Ohio at Pittsburgh, invite the British to keep their forts, make alliances with the Indians. Marksmen could meet the eastern army in the mountain passes and hold off attack. But even if successful, this plan would never work for long. First would come misery, then poverty. Still, those might be better, Mr. Brackenridge was thinking, than being maligned, disgraced, possibly assassinated by the very people he'd been exhausting himself trying to help.

The next morning, he saw Senator James Ross and told him that the rebel cause was gaining new appeal. Senator Ross didn't take this as a joke. He reminded the lawyer that the chance for amnesty, which all moderates had been looking for, had come by luck to the Forks. Moderates must seize the chance and stick to the plan.

Of course Mr. Brackenridge agreed. The rest of the committee arrived, and in a private house in Pittsburgh, negotiations opened. The federal commissioners threatened the entry of troops into the area and implied strongly, but only implied, that military incursion could be avoided if total submission were demonstrated by all people in the region. Repeal of the excise law was out of the question, but the government might be willing to hear federal tax cases in local courts, as permitted by the new law. The two groups then retired to separate houses. Over the next few days, in a series of elaborately worded written exchanges, the commission and the committee arrived at a deal that gave the moderates hope.

The president would refrain from commencing new prosecutions for treason, or any other crime against the United States committed in the fourth excise survey, until July of the next year. After that date, if the laws were obeyed, he would give a blanket pardon for all such crimes committed to date, aside from those committed by people already under indictment.

In turn, members of the entire Parkinson's Ferry committee of sixty must unanimously declare their determination to submit to the laws of the United States and to refrain from obstructing the operation of the excise law. They must formally renounce violence against U.S. officers and complying citizens. These declarations must be voted on by the committee of sixty, and the vote count reported: unanimity was important.

Most important, though, would be a full-scale popular referendum, conducted throughout the western counties, in which every township also voted its willingness to support the law. The commissioners never put in writing any promise that, in the event that such universal compliance were achieved, federal troops would not come. They only said that, if these terms were accepted by the standing committee of sixty, troops would be held back at least until the regionwide referendum had taken place. In another shrewd maneuver, they specifically did not include the Virginia delegation to Parkinson's Ferry in the deal. The Virginians, responding to their exclusion with precisely the panic that Attorney General Bradford was hoping for, began begging for inclusion.

Moderates were falling over themselves with eagerness to bring things to what they imagined would be a peaceful conclusion. The negotiating committee agreed not only to present the president's terms to the committee of sixty but also to take the extreme personal risk of openly recommending that the terms be accepted. On the twenty-third of August, negotiations with the federal commission concluded.

That day William Bradford wrote east again—unofficially again, and this time to Hamilton—to say that there was now reason to hope the army would have an easier time than he'd first predicted. He continued to emphasize the negative: the more he saw in western Pennsylvania, he said, the more he felt that the government should avoid a contest until it could field a regular army, not just a big militia, and that an occupying force would need to stay in the region to protect tax officers.

On August 28, with great trepidation, Mr. Brackenridge and the rest of the negotiating committee reconvened with the Parkinson's Ferry standing committee of sixty to report on the negotiations with the federal commission. This gathering was held not at Parkinson's Ferry but in the town of Brownsville, where the Redstone enters the Monongahela, and where in 1791 the first meeting of genteel local leaders had met in a tavern to discuss problems of excise unrest. Now the movement was no small, self-selected group of professional politicians; it couldn't have met in a tavern. The committee of sixty convened under a pavilion of boards hastily constructed to give shade from the blazing late-summer sun. Armed and sweating, men gathered around as a gallery. The first order of business— showing how far the rebels were from handing authority back to the federal and state governments—was to try a man who had made the mistake of calling the Parkinson's Ferry congress a scrub congress. Seventy men had seized the man and were accusing him of speaking ill of constituted authorities, common-law sedition, punishable at the very least by banishment and house burning. Mr. Brackenridge, resorting to shtick, got the accusers and the standing committee laughing and the punishment reduced to forcing the man to buy whiskey and being called a scrub himself.

Mr. Brackenridge had transported, by hired rider, one hundred printed copies of the conference committee's report recommending submission. Copies were handed out, and the report was read aloud. Muttering and protest began almost immediately. The people had seen themselves as being asked to *give* an amnesty to tax collectors, compliers, and the banished Neville Connection—not to beg an amnesty of the president. Repeal of the tax law had become the symbol of regional autonomy: that no repeal or even suspension of the law had been discussed outraged the gallery. The conference committee seemed to the people to have given up everything and gained nothing. There was talk of the committee's having been bribed.

Moderates, desperate now, managed to get an adjournment that delayed a vote on the resolutions until the next day. William Findley, Mr. Brackenridge's political enemy but fellow moderate, had arrived, and Findley's loyalty to the west was considered irreproachable by the people; moderates hoped he could help. The next day, no moderate wanted to be first to address the standing committee and the gallery, but Albert Gallatin finally agreed to do so. In a cogent speech, he made all the obvious arguments in favor of submitting to the law and against any foolish attempts at armed secession.

When Mr. Brackenridge spoke, he did, at last, play it straight. Not only did he back up all of Gallatin's arguments, he also told the rebels that this was it. If they didn't accept these hard-won resolutions and avail themselves of the safety of the amnesty, he was out, and this speech would be his last advice to them. Fully exposed for the first time, he sat down.

David Bradford, speaking next, urged the rebels to fight any invading army. When Bradford had finished, the committee of sixty—now looking only for safety—voted to hold no vote on the deal. But that meant rejection of all the president's terms, tantamount to an immediate declaration of and preparation for war; moderates who had just spoken in favor of submission were sure to be arrested as traitors. Gallatin made one last move, for which Mr. Brackenridge, rarely impressed by others' presence of mind, gave him great credit. The committee of sixty should have an internal vote, Gallatin proposed, just to take its own temperature, not for the commissioners, no standing up to be counted, a secret ballot. Such was the tension that men of the standing committee thought even their handwriting would be too revealing. Sixty slips of paper were handed out, each with "yea" and "nay" written on them. Each committeeman tore off the vote he wanted to cast and threw it in a hat, chewing on the other vote until it was unrecognizable.

When the vote was counted, the armed gallery in the sun was

shocked. Though the margin was slim—34–23—the standing committee had voted in favor of submission to the federal government.

David Bradford's face darkened. He left hurriedly. The gallery was muttering. The committee of sixty, divided now, and ever more tense, called a break and met again in the afternoon, diminished by the departure of radicals and the entire gallery. Armed men were hanging in knots around the town and fields, plotting revenge against the traitors, especially Mr. Brackenridge, who had fooled them with displays of loyalty and then sold them out to the commission. The standing committee quickly adopted a resolution approving the conference-committee report. Yet it tried to appease enraged radicals by appointing a new conference committee to seek a better deal with the commission.

From the point of view of William Bradford and the federal commissioners, all this complexity was absurd. There was no deal now. One of the main terms had been the standing committee's making a convincing show of unanimous submission. Yet fully two-fifths of the Parkinson's Ferry committee, as the commissioners read the vote, preferred civil war. Even more preposterous was the idea that better terms could be reached by some new conference committee.

Indeed, the very turmoil of the Brownsville meeting signaled that William Bradford had achieved his goals with almost perfect success. What had been a disciplined, regionwide movement against government was fatally divided. Moderates, more fearful now of the president than of Tom the Tinker, had been flushed out and exposed by the negotiations; they were vulnerable to violence, and a federal army was needed if only to protect them.

The commissioners therefore responded to the new negotiating committee with icy dismay. They announced that, given disastrous results at Brownsville, the federal militia—which they reminded the committee was fifteen thousand strong, with fifteen hundred Virginia sharpshooters—could be held back only until the referendum was held, which they now set for September 11 and refused to make any later.

The president clearly could not now accept, the commission said, a majority referendum for submission, township by township. The army, when it arrived, would need to know the name of each loyal U.S. citizen, in order to prevent confounding the loyal with the treasonous. The fate of males eighteen and older would depend on their signing, on September 11, and not a day later, an oath of submission to federal law. Those who signed on time, did not resist the troops in any way, and complied with the law in the future could count on an amnesty for past crimes. Anyone else, regardless of anything he'd done or not done during the insurgency, would be fair game for arrest by the troops. Leaving Senator Ross in Washington County to manage the oath signing, Bradford and Yeates started back for Philadelphia, their mission complete.

Further justifications for action were appearing. Rebellion seemed to be spreading east of the mountains even as it was falling apart at the Forks. Around the time of Bower Hill, pole raisings, blackface attacks, and burnings in effigy had started in Virginia, Pennsylvania, and Maryland—but it was when the state governors, answering the president's call for troops, began raising militias to suppress the Forks rebels, and draft resistance began springing up east of the mountains, that disaffection began to feel rampant. In Cumberland County, Virginia, two townships held a meeting that began by protesting the draft and ended by embracing and even surpassing the vision of Herman Husband: unless land is divided equally among the people, said the Cumberland protestors, there can be no true republican government. The governor of Maryland learned that rebels were planning to seize the armory at Frederick's Town and called out seven hundred men from seaboard militias to garrison the armory and protect it. The Maryland rebels were only ninety men, and they were turned down when they tried to buy flint and powder. The militias overwhelmed them; twenty rebels were arrested. Still, federal troops were needed now just to police eastern regions while marching west.

The seaboard cities, meanwhile, filled with patriotic fervor. The writings of "Tully" and other federalists had done their work. Eastern newspapers railed against the insurgency; the officer classes in city militias were gung ho to march for glory. The opposition party could take no credible position. More than one opposition paper avidly supported sending troops.

William Bradford, arriving home from his mission, was delighted to discover in Philadelphia what he called a federal and military spirit. Writing to his fellow commissioner Yeates, he noted with relish that such was the popularity of military suppression that even the Philadelphia democratic society had been forced to pretend to support it. Bradford expressed confidence that what he called the new revolutionary spirit—he underlined "new"—would soon be suppressed.

To Mr. Brackenridge, September 11, 1794, though an awful day for the Forks, gave new grounds for optimism. "I do solemnly promise henceforth to submit to the laws of the United States; that I will not, directly or indirectly, oppose the execution of the acts for raising a revenue on distilled spirits and stills; and that I will support, as far as the law requires, the civil authority in affording the protection due to all officers and other citizens." Such was the language of submission dictated by the presidential commission. Men eighteen and older, from Pittsburgh and Washington, from dozens of scattered settlements, from riverside industries and isolated cabins, came to their township meeting places and election-district polling places to assure themselves of amnesty. After the proposition was read aloud, each man answered yea or nay, and then, with either a justice of the peace or two members of the Parkinson's Ferry standing committee presiding, signed his name under a written version. People signed in fear of federal troops, but they feared signing too: Tom the Tinker was working hard to shut down the polls. He was feeling sorry for himself. Poor Tom, he wrote in the *Gazette,* having managed to get the country unified, had thought he could retire, but learning that the leaders were traitors, he was being forced to resume activities. Tom was giving fair warning. His hammer was up, his ladle hot, and he couldn't waste his time traveling the country without using them. Nonetheless, long strings of names filled the "yea" columns of final returns, page after page, with only blankness under "nay."

Rumors of violence flew all day. Senator James Ross was urged not to leave Washington with the returns: plans were afoot to waylay people carrying returns and burn out everyone who had signed. Mr. Brackenridge heard that rebels at Mingo Creek were determined to shoot anyone who tried to sign the oath; he saddled up and rode for a meeting at Mingo church to see if he could help. He spent the day running around the Mingo Creek area, and at one point he encountered Benjamin Parkinson and Andrew McFarlane, the two men he'd feared most at Braddock's Field. Yet Parkinson said he was recommending submission, and McFarlane and the lawyer, after a moment of tense silence, gruffly agreed that these were difficult times.

If two top rebels were signing the oath, Mr. Brackenridge thought, the amnesty might work; the troops might stay home; peace really might prevail. Yet Parkinson and McFarlane told him they were now under threat too, and Mr. Brackenridge, deciding not to attend the violent meeting at the church, started home. His way took him past the home of John Holcroft. The lawyer had not met Holcroft, who had led the first attack on Bower Hill and was believed to be the author of Tom the Tinker's notes. Mr. Brackenridge had passed the house, with trepidation, when he met a stranger who seemed to know him. This was Holcroft himself. Even he was considering signing the oath, he told the lawyer.

Mr. Brackenridge arrived in Pittsburgh in the evening. His polling place was closed. He was too late to sign. He signed the next morning, believing he ought to give personal support for what he'd recommended.

When the returns were tallied, James Ross sent a report to his fellow commissioners Bradford and Yeates, who were to report to Washington and the cabinet. While there were pages and pages of "yea"s, and an utter absence of any nay vote in any township, the commissioners cited what they called credible information that some towns still had a majority for resistance. Authority at the Forks, they advised one more time, now purely for eastern public-relations purposes, should be aided by military force.

That force was ready at last. The next day, troops from New Jersey, Maryland, Pennsylvania, and Virginia began marching west. The right wing, from the northern states, was to muster at Carlisle, in central Pennsylvania. The southern left wing would muster at Fort Cumberland in Maryland. The picture Hamilton had conjured two years earlier, when he'd imagined the plot thickening, the application of force appearing to be unavoidable, and the president's repairing in person to the scene of commotion, had been amplified. For Hamilton was going too.

He'd advised Washington that it seemed proper for the author of the tax to accompany troops that were prosecuting it. The president's giving the secretary of the treasury a high place in directing such an invasion took even some supporters aback. Nevertheless, on September 30, Washington and Hamilton stepped into a presidential coach and rode together down Market Street, leaving Philadelphia to join the army at Carlisle.

Washington was returning to scenes of his youth. Hamilton was going to the place he'd long been subduing in his mind.

CHAPTER TEN

The General Goes West

Two weeks later, Congressman William Findley, emissary from terrified residents of the Forks of the Ohio, stood before the president, hoping to persuade him to turn the army back. With Findley was David Redick, another Forks moderate. It was October 9. The commander in chief was sitting in pain in his quarters in Carlisle, Pennsylvania, east of the mountains, where forces from New Jersey and Pennsylvania were mustering.

The Parkinson's Ferry congress had met again and made a unanimous resolution of submission. Findley hoped it wasn't too late.

Carlisle was a town Washington approved of. Laid out on a grid, it had a broad main street flanked by raised, well-swept sidewalks and houses of brick and stone. The western end of town gave a distant view, miles across a rolling, fertile piedmont, of the nearest and least forbidding of what were many long ridges that the army must soon climb. Then, leaving the Atlantic watershed behind, the men would descend through twisting, gigantically wooded clefts and enter a turned-around world, walled off from respectable Carlisle, where rivers flowed backward toward little-known places. The president had committed himself to sending troops on that journey. In the room where he now sat—he had quarters in the home of a prominent local federalist—Secretary Hamilton hovered beside him, and Governor Mifflin, commander of Pennsylvania troops, had joined them to hear out Findley and Redick.

Findley was now the Forks moderates' main spokesman. He'd taken over from Mr. Brackenridge, who was in deep trouble. Officers and troops up and down the lines had learned to curse the hated name of Brackenridge, and they gleefully predicted he'd be hanged—skewered, some said—as soon as the army arrived at the Ohio. Thanks to a campaign conducted by General and Presley Neville (they were traveling with the army now, returning exiles, advising Hamilton on high-value insurgents), and to his own, inadvertently inflammatory letter to the Treasury Department, and to his failure to sign the oath on time, Hugh Henry Brackenridge was on the administration's list of top rebel leaders.

Findley, ever the politician, had kept up collegial communications with Attorney General Bradford even while remaining aloof from negotiations between the commission and the committee; he was appearing at Carlisle not only as emissary from a cowed region but also as a loyal-opposition member of the House, concerned about the fate of his constituents. In Congress, Findley had loudly opposed not merely Hamilton's finance plan but Hamilton's influence, and the influence of any executive department, on processes that he considered strictly the province of the House. He was furious at finding Alexander Hamilton on this expedition at all. The secretary of the treasury, never officially appointed or confirmed by the Senate to any such position, should not be taking charge of a massive military operation to enforce his own policies on the citizenry. The Nevilles were falsely calling Findley a rebel leader too; his name, he'd heard, was on their list. With Hamilton contriving to be always at the president's elbow, any appeal to Washington's fabled judiciousness, Findley feared, would fail. His own future might also become grim.

Still, he had a mission. He was to reassure the president that calm prevailed beyond the mountains and that bringing the army was unnecessary. After the September 11 referendum and the mobilization of thirteen thousand troops, Forks radicals were demoralized and moderates bold. Liberty poles might be going up east of the mountains, but in the radical stronghold of Washington, a liberty pole had been cut down. Tom the Tinker would have made such an act impossible to contemplate only a month earlier. Some of the rebels had started down the Ohio, fearing capture by the army and hoping for refuge in the wilds of Kentucky and beyond. The town committee of Pittsburgh, which had expelled members of the Neville Connection during those strange days and nights of summer, repealed the expulsions, declaring all rebellion at an end. It was becoming clear that the army might be arriving unopposed. Senator James Ross crowed that the commission's negotiations had cut off the rebellion's many heads.

Law-abiding Forks settlers therefore had a new thing to fear: the avenging force of government. The standing committee had unanimously voted for submission, and Findley and Redick left the Forks in the first week of October to plead with the president.

Washington and Hamilton, meanwhile, had been traveling to Carlisle from Philadelphia. The two men rode often inside the carriage. The president's crimped back kept him from mounting up, unless ceremonially necessary, though the carriage too jarred his injury and wore him down. A cavalry unit, learning early in the trip that the president was nearby, got excited by the idea of providing him with a gaudy escort, and since there was no way to refuse such an offer directly, the carriage had to detour a long, tedious way around Germantown to avoid them.

Washington hoped to avoid tiring salutes and ceremonies. Yet they could be useful to the public-relations aspects of the trip, which were an important part of its purpose. The artillery discharged fifteen guns as he entered Harrisburg, where he reviewed troops, entertained officers with wine, and addressed cheering townspeople. Leaving Harrisburg early the next morning, troops crossed the cold, shallow Susquehanna in boats, but Washington drove his own carriage over the river.

Mostly, however, he noted the qualities of the roads, towns, farms, and industries. He was passing westward for the first time since the 1780s, when, briefly free of public duties, he'd been the victorious commander in pursuit of land, canals, and opportunities. Beauty of countryside was never a theme of the diaries in which Washington jotted notes on the minutiae of development. He got out to inspect a competing canal company's locks and found them impressive. He considered the various styles of farming in eastern Pennsylvania, the layouts of towns, the numbers of mills. Even as this plan to march westward had come together, and Senator James Ross had been serving as a commissioner to the rebels, Washington had been sending Ross further thoughts on selling off land.

He was also deeply engaged in the organizational challenges of the military effort. Converging on Carlisle, and on Fort Cumberland, Maryland, from many points east, were artillery units with cannon, mortars, and the light cannon known as grasshoppers; mounted guards; ranks and ranks of footsoldiers; various quartermaster corps; wagons heavy with ammunition; wagons with forges for making balls; wagons with tents, cookware, officers' clothing, blankets, and personal supplies; and state governors' staffs and entourages with their own arms, horses, wagons, and effects. All of these men and supplies were traveling from parts of four states, on differing schedules, under varying conditions, in a hodgepodge of units. They needed to be mixed and matched, camped, fed, deployed, and moved into an alien and hostile area, ready for a pitched battle that might not occur. Cobbled together and cumbersome, this was the nation's first army of significant size. It was entering terrain unknown to it, preparing to engage what its leaders considered a strange and unpredictable people.

Washington had always excelled at military administration, and Hamilton was back in his revolutionary role as the chief of staff, enjoying a new one as secretary of war. In his diary, Washington reverted to the old staff term, "family." Hamilton wrote to state militia commanders to set logistics, to War Department subordinates to harass them about lackadaisical supply, to subordinates in the Treasury Department to cope with army contractors. He worried about canteens, cooking kettles, rounds of cartridges, woolen jackets, pairs of shoes, and artillery field pieces. With carte blanche from Washington to serve as an extension of the president, he opened all correspondence; originated, wrote, and personally signed crucial orders; and served as the president's link with Governor Lee, who not only commanded Virginia's forces but technically was second only to Washington in commanding the operation. Washington deemed his fellow Virginian a genius lacking in judgment. Hamilton was happy to ensure that Lee caused no slip-ups.

The citizen army that Washington and Hamilton were moving west had two classes. Officers came from the ranks of the creditor aristocracy in the seaboard cities. These were young volunteers, hyped on the patriotism of Hamilton's writings as "Tully" and other exhortations, eager for low-risk glory. Gorgeously uniformed, mounted, and armed, they hoped to associate themselves in the public mind with the leaner, more truly endangered army that was finally engaging the native tribes farther west; they called the western rabble they were out to punish "white Indians" and saw themselves as avengers of union. Yet they'd volunteered under certain conditions. Their ranks must be high. Their brigade colors must be exciting and appropriate. Their commanders must not be certain people they didn't like. State governors spent precious hours trying to salve acrimony among young men over personal snubs and outraged dress sense. When preferences could not be satisfied, many adventurers refused, at the last minute, to participate, and those who did serve brought extreme personal touchiness, along with happy dreams of vengeance, to the western march.

The men these cavaliers were supposed to be commanding were mainly militia draftees. Because better-off draftees hired substitutes to serve in their places, the ranks were crowded with the poorest laborers and landless workers, recent immigrants and subsistence farmers. They had no uniforms. Their clothing couldn't keep out autumn dampness and chill. To Hamilton's frustration, the supply process was chronically sluggish, and desperately needed tents, overalls, and jackets, even blankets, were scarce. The men slept in cold fields, sometimes in tents but always on the ground, usually without straw for insulation. Drinking water could be bad, food paltry. Officers stayed in warm taverns and homes, where they spent their plentiful coin on extra food and drink. At times they were lavishly fed and entertained by hosts who could proffer fine wines and the charms of piano-playing daughters. Out in the camps, men drank whiskey and fired newly issued muskets for fun. Drunk on wine in brick houses, officers didn't focus on orders not to waste powder.

Mornings began with floggings. Draft evasion had been rampant, with militiamen simply running and hiding. Once pressed into service, men deserted incorrigibly, embarrassing state governors and undermining the mission's political spin: this was supposed to be a patriotic citizen army, reporting eagerly for duty to suppress ambitious traitors. Despite the governors' repeated calls for troops, filling draft quotas had been almost impossible. The mission required forced marches of up to twenty-five miles a day. Rumors circulated among the troops that they were actually being sent to reinforce the Indian war. The men malingered; they organized mass refusals to follow orders. Much time was spent dispatching parties to hunt deserters, who were then beaten by festively dressed commanders before ranks of surly men.

Some of the footsoldiers—especially those from New Jersey—did seem to harbor as much hatred for westerners as their officers did. New Jerseyans had been aroused by a sardonic article, published anonymously in many seaboard papers in September, slighting the entire militia as "your watermelon army from the Jersey shore," whose puny efforts would be no match for westerners. The piece was attributed by the troops to the hated Brackenridge. In response, New Jersey's Governor Howell whipped up a romantic song, "Dash to the Mountains, Jersey Blue." It had lines like "Unstain'd with crimes, unus'd to fear/ In deep array our youths appear" and "Push home your steel, you'll soon re-view/ Your native plains, brave Jersey Blue." Howell's troops were the rowdiest and least disciplined, with the highest proportion of geared-up volunteers prone to plundering.

Footsoldiers from the other three states, if less personally irked by the rebels, felt resentment for the mission and had hopes mainly for plunder too. They were all hungry and cold. While families cowered in farmhouses, freelancing soldiers crashed drunk through fields of just-ripened crops, tearing down fences for firewood, slaughtering chickens and pigs, building fires, and sleeping where they fell.

Troops were supposed to be rounding up, along the way, suspects in eastern liberty-pole raisings. One pumped-up officer, hunting men who had raised a pole at Carlisle, accidentally pistol-shot an innocent boy who had an illness that kept him from standing when ordered to. The ball lodged in the boy's groin; death came with agony. Some officers and men drinking at a tavern were greeted by a local drunk, who gave huzzas for the whiskey rebels. The soldiers tried to ignore him, but he followed them into a back room, cursing out the army and mocking its mission. A captain ordered a private to arrest the man, who grabbed at the private's bayonet. In the struggle the private accidentally stabbed the man, who died praising the rebels. When President Washington joined the troops at Carlisle on October 4, accompanied by Secretary Hamilton and a small escort of mounted scouts, bells rang and artillery shook the ground, but the people of Carlisle, subjected to occupation by hordes of unruly soldiers, and now to killing, stayed quiet.

Washington had Hamilton write Governor Mifflin to express poignant regret for the two civilian deaths. The perpetrators were arrested and tried in civilian courts—though the incidents were clearly accidents, and a judge released both men. Washington announced to the governors and their generals that he wanted officers to start exercising control over the men and themselves. He remained fixed on the idea that protest and outright rebellion were twin expressions of self-created democratic societies, which must be eradicated. Yet it also remained a precious principle, he directed Hamilton to tell Governor Mifflin, that those enforcing the law not themselves break it, or even seem to break it.

Mifflin wasn't the best recipient of advice. He got falling-down drunk one night in Carlisle and ordered the Philadelphia Light Horse to fire on all comers; the Horse happily responded by shooting up units of the Jersey militia; Mifflin had to issue a formal apology. Proud horse units were forever vying with one another. As the president first entered camp at Carlisle, the Jersey and Pennsylvania cavalries tried to ride each other off the road to be first to salute him. When the president officially reviewed the troops, the solemnity and straightness of his bearing, the acres of glinting steel surrounding his augustness, were covered in the national and international press, as intended; he also attended church services, during which a Presbyterian minister preached subservience to the government. Yet when William Findley and David Redick arrived in town, five days after the president, it seemed to them that barely restrained pandemonium reigned in both town and camp.

What Findley encountered in Carlisle made him more concerned than ever for the Forks. The two civilian killings had been at the very least avoidable, he thought, but even worse was the seeming eagerness of officers and men to commit deliberate and indiscriminate butchery as soon as they got over the mountains. The keeper of a tavern begged Findley and Redick, for their own safety, not to proceed to Carlisle, where soldiers swaggered about declaring themselves ready to murder anyone from the west. Ideas like skewering Mr. Brackenridge seemed to Findley to be coming from the top down—yet the men seemed restrained from utter abandon only by the toughness and clarity of Washington himself.

Findley blamed Hamilton and the Nevilles. The scene reminded him of the Forks region itself, when under the thumb of rebel militias. Yet this army seemed thirstier for blood, more intent on murder, less disciplined. Rebel militias had been trying to take over the legitimate government. These soldiers were even more frightening: they *were* the legitimate government.

Washington and Hamilton interviewed Findley and Redick and found the news from the west heartening. These emissaries, along with their constituents, were clearly scared; apparently the army was unlikely to meet any real opposition. Though receiving them with irreproachable politeness, Washington suggested that in the future, citizens might want to be more cautious about inflaming others with antigovernment talk. He reminded Findley of the effort and expense involved in preparing military expeditions; momentum was moving this army; it was too late for assurances, no matter how sincere, to stop it. At times Hamilton stepped in to cross-examine his political opponent, whose name he'd already placed on a list for possible arrest. How, specifically, could Findley be sure that submission would prevail in Washington County? In Allegheny County? In Fayette?

The fact was, Washington said, that atonement of some sort would have to be made by the entire region. Yet the troops would be law-abiding, the president promised. They would establish peace, not prosecute, judge, sentence, or execute; those functions would be reserved for civil authorities. He said that imposing discipline on the army had been his main project since arriving at Carlisle, and he'd been successful, he believed. He also reminded Findley that citizens at the Forks who had signed the September 11 submission would, as promised, be under the amnesty, safe from harm no matter what they'd done.

Washington also said—as if in passing, and disconcertingly to Findley and Redick—that with Congress about to begin its session, and much pressing business at the capital, he might turn back and send the army on to the Forks without him. Findley vehemently hoped not. If troops must come to the Forks, he badly wanted the president there too. He believed that Washington was doing his best to enforce restraint among the officers and troops; he believed that the president would abide by the amnesty and use troops only to secure peace, not to punish. But Findley had long suspected Hamilton of inciting this rebellion solely for the purpose of quelling it with brutal force, which the soldiers outside in the streets were looking forward to indulging. During this very discussion, Findley witnessed Hamilton's role as busy second in command, reading letters and dispatching messengers even while managing never to leave the president's side. Hoping fervently that Washington, not Hamilton, would be the one to control this operation, Findley repeatedly urged the president to come all the way.

Findley bitterly resented the concept of regional, not individual, atonement. Yet he didn't blame Washington. He blamed Hamilton.

Redick left Carlisle for the west, placing all hope on the
Pittsburgh of the one man they thought could protect
m what they saw as the vengeful fury of his own treasury
secretary.

Washington began seeing troops off from Carlisle on the morning
of October 10. The order of march included Jerseyans and Pennsylvanians in mounted legions, many units of footsoldiers, artillery
pieces, the whole line bracketed front and rear by horse guards.
When errors prevented baggage wagons for the Jersey Horse from
arriving, and part of the legion had to wait for the next day to leave,
Washington angrily scolded the officers in charge. He was on his
way to Fort Cumberland to mobilize the southern wing. He planned
on rejoining this northern wing in a few days, farther west, before
it pushed into rebel territory. Then, if all seemed well, he'd return to
Philadelphia and leave the regional atonement of the Forks to
others.

He traveled southward to Cumberland by back roads, to avoid
ceremony. The progress of real estate development in the area
mingled with some powerful memories. He was conscious that this
was the last time he would view scenes he'd helped change forever.
In the 1750s, Washington had made Fort Cumberland his main
advance point for the Virginia militia's desperate efforts against the
French and Indians. It had been impossible, then, to imagine a
president of a United States. Now, at Fort Cumberland, 3,200
men stood in a double line while Washington rode between them
in pomp. The valley road on which he left had been cut from the
wilderness, under his command, almost forty years earlier.

When he rejoined the northern wing, it had progressed to the
steep little town of Bedford. Lee's Maryland and Virginia troops
were moving west now too; the wings were to converge at the
Youghiogheny on the far side of the mountains. Troops in Bedford
were amazed. The scarcity of houses seemed eerie. The narrowness
of passes did too. Towering rocks and ancient pines hung over the
road and dimmed even the midday sun. The people seemed, to offi-

cers and men alike, grotesquely poor, weird, and hard to understand. This was the eastern edge of rebel territory. Bedford County had sent delegates to the Parkinson's Ferry congress; Herman Husband, who lived nearby, was high on Washington's and Hamilton's list for arrest and removal to Philadelphia.

On the evening of October 18, Washington paraded three thousand troops in Bedford. Metal clanked up the steep dirt street as the mountain people watched in silence. Dragoons shouted orders. Ranks sluggishly responded. At the county courthouse the army lit a patriotic transparency, a traditional holiday dazzlement, sometimes accompanied by fireworks, and rarely seen in Bedford: This one announced the triumph of President Washington himself in large text illuminated by candles. On the reverse it read, "Woe to Anarchy."

Yet even as his transparency lit the rebellion's frontier, the president was preparing to go home. On the twentieth, Alexander Hamilton, writing for the president, sent Henry Lee orders for command of all forces. The next morning, the president started east.

Days and nights of cold, steady rain accompanied Alexander Hamilton, General Lee, and thousands of troops down the Alleghenies' western slopes in two huge wings, folding on the Youghiogheny. Horses broke down; wheels strained against mud; wagons tipped and capsized. Men slogging ankle-deep, already fighting diarrhea and fever, were drenched and shivering. Tents were still scarce, and now even officers slept in what they considered filthy, lice-ridden hovels. Ascents and descents seemed endlessly steep and tortuous, the valleys deep and narrow. As word came down the line that no glorious battles were likely to justify all this effort, officers grew testy.

Hamilton did receive written instructions from his eastward-traveling president. It was critical, the president told Hamilton, from an ever-growing distance, that the army maintain the highest standards of legality as it entered the western country. Pillage especially must be stopped. High in the mountains, though, troops were miles ahead of their supplies, with no food or blankets and only frayed clothing. Some wore flaps of ruined shoes; many chose to negotiate the rocky ground, no matter how sharp or frigid, in bare feet. Washington's standing order, imposed at Carlisle, had been to flog any man caught stealing. Officers carried out that order mercilessly, even while soldiers had no choice but to run amok in narrow valleys and on steep hillsides, snatching from isolated farms all the scarce grain, cows, eggs, and chickens they could find.

Hamilton resolved this dissonance between orders and reality. He made theft legal. The quartermaster corps, he announced, would impress civilian property along the way. Now families watched helplessly as bayonet-wielding soldiers—no longer freelancing thieves but officials, authorized by the president—commandeered hard-won winter supplies of grain, meat, firewood, and blankets on behalf of the government of the United States. A steady, freezing rain meant the arrival of winter. Families whose sustenance was carted away faced grim months ahead.

For the army, though, impressment worked. By the end of the first week in November, troops were being deployed, more or less comfortably, throughout the Forks region, and officers were comparing their journey to Hannibal's crossing of the Alps.

Hamilton stayed away from Pittsburgh at first, moving among temporary headquarters in Washington, Uniontown, and the various camps. Lee set up his headquarters between the Youghiogheny and the Monongahela. The two communicated by express rider. Lee announced the presence of the army to the people in a proclamation describing the extremes of restraint that President Washington, fatherlike, had gone to, how disappointed their father was to have been forced to bring an army. Everyone in the area, Lee suggested, ought to sign new oaths of allegiance, which soldiers would soon be visiting them to administer.

Hamilton orchestrated the larger purpose. As he put it in a letter to Washington, the area did give the impression of being in a state of submission, and that state would be all the stronger, he predicted, for what was about to happen. Normal process of law would have required turning arrested suspects over to the civil judiciary for indictment and trial, but as Hamilton had established in his August 5 report and his letter to Governor Mifflin, the situation wasn't normal. If not exactly war, it resembled war. The whole population had been defined as insurgent. The very presence of federal troops made the Forks a kind of battlefield, even if no shots were fired. Rules for capturing and interrogating prisoners of war weren't governed by the Bill of Rights. Circumstances at the Forks, as Hamilton, Washington, and Lee defined them, justified a new and impromptu blend of military inquest and civil prosecution.

A federal judge, Richard Peters, had accompanied the army, along with U.S. Attorney William Rawle, to coordinate civil process with the military authority, but the judge was to be instructed by the military arm, not the other way round, and he was expected to be cooperative; the president had informed Henry Lee of that, above Hamilton's signature, in the general orders. As Hamilton reminded Washington in a letter, the judicial branch would, of course, be permitted to take charge of suspects, as due process required—but only after the executive branch had finished investigating suspects' potential value as examples. With these goals in mind, Hamilton and Lee began making arrests.

The first arrests had actually been made a month earlier. Herman Husband, top man with David Bradford on the administration's list, was captured at his farmhouse, along with a few others. When Washington had gone to Fort Cumberland to review the southern troops, leaving Hamilton in charge of operations at Bedford, Judge Peters had authorized troops to arrest Husband and a few associates. Despite his eagerness to see Husband behind bars, Washington, on learning of the arrest, was confused by its precipitousness. He expressed concern—well placed, as it turned out—that other important suspects would take alarm at the news and flee. Hamilton did his best to give Washington the impression that high-value insurgents could still be readily arrested, but he'd taken no chances with Husband.

Husband had been in jail before. He met this new arrest with equanimity. The arrival of a federal army was no surprise to him. It was a horn of the Beast; he'd seen it coming. He was marched down out of mountains he'd walked so often, forced to travel in the wrong direction, toward the greedy kingdoms of the east. After the hardest kind of overland march, Husband arrived at the Philadelphia jail late in October. Old and frail, amid nasty conditions that tended to weaken prisoners, Husband remained undaunted.

By the time Hamilton and Lee began making mass arrests at the Forks, it seemed to Forks moderates that more than two thousand men had fled the area; almost anybody who had committed an act of terror, and wasn't within the amnesty, had gone down the Ohio or into the countryside. Daniel Hamilton was gone, as was the craven Alexander Fulton who had been made to sign the Braddock's Field orders. Most important, David Bradford had escaped down the Ohio and had been seen on the Mississippi. Anyone left in the area was either innocent of rebel violence, or legally protected by the amnesty, or both.

Nevertheless, in the middle of the cold night of November 13, what Husband had envisioned as a horn gored and tossed the people. A synchronized effort throughout the region—focused most vociferously on Washington and Allegheny counties—brought soldiers to the doors of slumbering families. To prevent suspects from taking alarm, the effort involved no warrants. General Lee and U.S. Attorney Rawle had recommended that course of action, and Hamilton offered further legal support: Treason has different rules, he reminded Washington in a letter; any law-abiding man, according to common law, may on his own authority apprehend a traitor.

The Dreadful Night, as Forks lore would call it, involved three lists compiled by Hamilton, the Nevilles, and U.S. Attorney Rawle. On the first list were people within the amnesty. On the second were those suspected of committing treason; these should be arrested. On the third were material witnesses, also to be brought in. Yet Lee's orders also empowered each general to arrest, at that general's own discretion, anyone whom that general suspected was guilty, whether or not the name was on the lists. Offenses for which these new, unlisted suspects could be arrested weren't limited to such things as attacks on collectors and on Bower Hill, expelling the Nevilles from Pittsburgh, or robbing the mail; generals were given discretion to arrest people on suspicion of having marched to Braddock's Field, served at a Parkinson's Ferry meeting, raised a liberty pole, or, in the case of local officials, having failed to prevent rebellious activity.

And since the first list, with names of people protected by the amnesty, wasn't included with Lee's orders—it could be supplied, Lee said, if requested, but the generals weren't to wait for it—almost every adult male was fair game for capture. That most of those arrested would have to be turned loose later was not an issue for the Dreadful Night. Lee qualified the discretion he was granting his generals by instructing them to arrest only real offenders, and prominent people or those especially violent. But since each general passed the orders, along with the empowerments and discretions, down to lower officers to execute, the Dreadful Night was carried out by cavaliers delighted, after pent-up weeks of travel, to be given extraordinary powers over the widest range of potential suspects, on grounds not limited to acts of terror or treason.

The operation went exactly as would have been expected. Hundreds of Forks residents, within and without the amnesty, were yanked from bed at bayonet point in the cold. Footsoldiers prodded the startled prisoners, close to naked and some barefoot, out of cabins into new-fallen snow while mounted officers barked commands and told furious wives and crying children that the men were being taken to be hanged. Supposed witnesses were treated as suspects; local magistrates were rousted too. All were run through the snow in chains, toward various lockups in town jails, stables, and cattle pens, to await interrogation by Hamilton, Lee, Rawle, the Nevilles, and their subordinates.

General Anthony "Blackbeard" White, of the New Jersey militia, was well known for mental instability. Having been prevented from getting the militia command he wanted, he'd made it to

Carlisle by tagging along with a horse guard; since then he'd managed to get control of a small corps. It was Blackbeard White whom Lee selected to handle prisoners arrested at Mingo Creek, where so many rebel actions had originated, and where Alexander Hamilton hoped to get the most valuable intelligence. Forty Mingo Creek prisoners were brought to a dark log structure, where White was waiting for them. He had them tied back to back in pairs and forced into sitting positions in the icy mud of the tavern cellar. The building he'd selected was new: chinks between the logs were undaubed, the cellar floorless. White ordered the guards to build a fire for themselves, but to keep prisoners away from warmth, at the end of the cellar. He then met with the tavernkeeper who operated the place. On pain of death, the general said, these prisoners were to get no food or drink.

For more than two days, White starved and dehydrated his shivering, exhausted captives, steadily cursing and castigating them, glorying in their helplessness and describing their imminent hanging. Even White's troops became concerned about the captives, who seemed barely alive when White finally decided to move them out. He quick-marched them twelve miles through bad weather to the town of Washington, where in physical and emotional collapse, they were held in jail, without charge, ready for questioning by the military.

Ensuing interrogations resulted, not surprisingly, in the eventual release of most prisoners. In the days after the Dreadful Night, mass arrests went on anyway: the brutality of the arrests and the torment of detention served the purpose of discouraging citizens of the Forks—and everywhere else—not only from engaging in resistance but also from forming societies and organizations. The world was watching. The ultimate goal, superseding any individual prosecution, was national unity. When Judge Peters did take charge of prisoners whom the military hadn't simply sent home, the speed and scale of arrests forced him to review an extraordinary number of cases very quickly. Women mobbed his court to plead for their husbands, sometimes padding their dresses to appear pregnant, seeming to weep pitifully. Peters released many detainees; some he turned over to the state courts to prosecute for minor crimes. But Hamilton and Lee had made clear to Peters that, regardless of evidence, a reasonable number of insurgents must be taken to Philadelphia. Grand juries were dispensed with, per battlefield conditions. With pumped-up officers cursing him furiously whenever he turned anyone loose, the judge feared the army would revolt. He held a number of men for removal to Philadelphia despite what he viewed as lack of evidence against them.

Moved from jails and holding pens to the lockup at Fort Fayette, there to await removal to Philadelphia, the chosen prisoners were escorted by horse guards, the most trim and gleaming of the eastern urbanites. Even in Philadelphia the Philadelphia Horse was striking; its gorgeousness here was breathtakingly strange. Uniformed in smooth blue broadcloth, riding huge bay horses so perfectly matched and powerful they could have pulled coaches, these well-bred scions of a distant city moved along bare fields and through russet woods in a line of pairs, silver-decorated bridles and stirrups glinting. They rode with swords held aloft and pointing upward to reflect the sun.

Between each pair came a pair of prisoners bound for the fort's lockup. However defiant, they were starved and cold, atop horses of every shape, color, and condition, on bare backs and threadbare blankets, men as varied in size, shape, and condition as their mounts. People watched in astonishment as the column undulated half a mile through wet leaves and tall pines: badly mismatched pairs of mortals between sets of blue-silver centaurs, all beneath a sawtooth edge of steel.

William Findley was sorrier than ever that the president had failed to accompany the troops. So great was Findley's desire for Washington's controlling presence that, before the army had arrived, he'd traveled eastward one last time, hoping to give the president even greater assurances of utter submission, but he'd found Washington no longer with the army. Now, just as he'd expected, Hamilton and

Lee seemed to take it on themselves to unleash dragoons and show the Forks no mercy.

Yet the real dissonance between what the president expected and what Hamilton was doing was invisible to Findley. Other observers also believed that had Washington been present, he wouldn't have authorized such things as mass arrests on no evidence. Had he been present, he couldn't have, but Washington had returned untarnished to the seat of government and left in charge his treasury secretary, of whose tendencies nobody was more keenly aware than he, and whom almost nobody else considered an appropriate leader for the expedition. Findley might yearn for a firm, guiding beneficence that would have saved the Forks from degradation. But the president and Hamilton exchanged letters about the arrests. Washington was in perfect harmony, both explicitly and tacitly, with Hamilton's execution.

It was with regard to the purpose behind that execution that Hamilton was taking a course plausibly resembling, but really the reverse of, the one expected by the president. Washington was hardly squeamish about frightening people with roundups and shaking information out of them, and his official orders had subordinated the civil to the military authority. But he thought the purpose of doing so was to get intelligence on the conniving few who had, he was sure, led ignorant people astray. He wanted to indict French-inspired opposition politicians, public officers betraying their country for twisted ambition. Hamilton had promised Washington a long list of such suspects, many of them merely attendees at the Pittsburgh conventions—he'd even named Judge Addison. Yet the decisions that Hamilton was making on the ground were predicated on his own keener understanding of the rebellion's real origins. It would have been useful and satisfying to hang a David Bradford. But Hamilton was out to remove the heart of the people's movement he'd been struggling with for more than a decade, not to prosecute individuals. William Findley, when trying to persuade Washington to turn the army back, had argued that only the very poor and the landless were still insurgent. To Hamilton, that news didn't make heavy enforcement any less necessary; quite the contrary. Throughout the arrests and prosecutions, ordinary rural men—their names might appear only on militia lists—became the subjects of Hamilton's example. Only Herman Husband, who could be seen both as the authentic voice of ordinary people's resistance and as a rich, prominent rabble-rouser, fulfilled both Hamilton's and Washington's profiles. Hence Hamilton's precipitous move to arrest him.

In his reports, Hamilton somewhat halfheartedly reassured Washington that the big men might still be prosecuted. But he knew that Benjamin Parkinson, John Holcroft, and Alexander Fulton were in hiding, as were many others. And of course there had never been a basis for arresting people like Judge Addison. What Hamilton's reports to Washington began presenting most energetically was the need to maintain, for the foreseeable future, a military presence to police the region.

Hamilton did spend time prompting detainees to manufacture evidence against two prominent men: William Findley and Albert Gallatin. They were Hamilton's bitterest western enemies in Congress. They'd both opposed the tax, the finance plan as a whole, and Hamilton's influence in the administration. Nobody had been more obviously committed than they to calming rebel hostility, though Gallatin was more vulnerable; he'd signed the second, inflammatory Pittsburgh petition. Yet Hamilton saw a chance to identify each of them as the very sort of leader whom Washington believed this expedition had been intended to prosecute. To that end, John Powers, a local moderate, who was hosting General Lee's headquarters near the confluence of the Youghiogheny and the Monongahela, was summoned to one of Hamilton's temporary headquarters. Powers appeared promptly, wondering how he could be of service. When Hamilton quizzed him on the role Albert Gallatin had played in the rebellion, Powers had little information to give. Hamilton expressed disappointment and asked whether memory would be improved by Powers's taking an hour or so in another room. Powers, confused, agreed; then, finding himself thrust at bayonet point into a room full of imprisoned suspects, he understood. He sat there, heart pounding amid the silent, shabby prisoners. The door was guarded by a soldier with a gun. Nobody moved.

An hour later, he was ushered back into Hamilton's office. Still polite, Hamilton asked whether Powers had remembered anything, and Powers, frightened, said he hadn't. Hamilton changed. The questioning had been a test, he announced; he already had the evidence he needed on Gallatin. Powers's refusal to help only showed rebel sympathy. Hamilton called for the guard, and this time it wasn't a test. John Powers was taken to the lockup at Fort Fayette. His offers of posting bail were declined, as were his demands to know the charge against him. He wasn't charged, but he stayed in jail until after Hamilton, having failed to find any grounds for arresting Gallatin, had left the area.

Hamilton took a similar approach when John Hamilton, colonel of the Mingo Creek militia and high sheriff of Washington County, decided to turn himself in. Hearing that he was to be arrested, John had time to escape down the river. Yet he chose to suffer interrogation and fight prosecution in court. He thought he had a case. He'd refused to join in the attack on Bower Hill. He'd tried to countermand the order to march on Braddock's Field. He'd been working for moderation ever since. He didn't realize that trials weren't foremost in Alexander Hamilton's plan. John Hamilton was just prominent enough at the Forks to make a fine example, yet unlike Findley and Gallatin, not so well known in the eastern world that evidence would be needed for imprisoning him indefinitely. Hamilton wrote to Washington. While it wasn't clear that anything could be proved against John Hamilton, he said, the man was in every other respect an admirable subject.

John Hamilton met with Judge Peters and asked to hear any charges against him. Peters put him off, claiming other business; witnesses were meanwhile brought, one by one, before Peters, Rawle, and Alexander Hamilton and told to testify that John Hamilton had sent his regiment to Bower Hill. He hadn't, and when the detainees declined to say he had, they were told that their

own amnesties would be revoked and they'd be arrested themselves. Each witness was then passed, for a more assertive rendition
of that threat, first to the irate General Neville—now serving at the
Forks as a unique blend of prosecutor and plaintiff—and finally to
an especially intimidating Philadelphia Light Horse officer. Still,
none would testify falsely.

Orders went out anyway, and John Hamilton was arrested while
waiting to see Judge Peters. He demanded repeatedly to know the
charge. He announced again and again that he would submit to
Peters for examination. He was sent, with no hearing, to the fort at
Pittsburgh, where he awaited removal to Philadelphia with other
prisoners.

Mr. Brackenridge, high on the list, should have been used to feeling horrible anxiety, given his many months of living under rebel
threat, but his current situation surpassed anything he'd known even
at the height of rebellion. Members of the Neville Connection, who
had started the "skewering" campaign while traveling with the
army, assured Alexander Hamilton that Brackenridge had been
playing a double game all along and was the chief rebel leader. Even
David Bradford, they said, had been a pawn of mastermind Brackenridge. The Nevilles persistently depicted Brackenridge, Findley,
and Gallatin as brothers in a treasonous junta. Brackenridge was far
more evidently culpable than the other two and had little political
support. Really, he was the perfect subject for hanging.

The Nevilles manufactured documentary evidence too. Before
David Bradford's flight, Isaac Craig asked Bradford to contradict in
writing Mr. Brackenridge's claim of having argued, at Braddock's
Field, against Craig's expulsion from Pittsburgh. The Nevilles
added facts to the file. Brackenridge had advised against calling out
the militia to protect Bower Hill; he'd told Presley and other exiles
that they'd be better off out of Pittsburgh; most damning of all, he'd
addressed the meeting at the Mingo Creek church, where David
Bradford had called upon the people of the western country to over-
throw the government. The Nevilles didn't mention that Presley had

pressured Mr. Brackenridge, as a personal favor, to attend that meeting.

Hamilton had no problem crediting these characterizations. Mr. Brackenridge's letter to the treasury had seemed to threaten an attack on Philadelphia even as it castigated the plan of national finance. In 1792, Brackenridge had written the *National Gazette* article urging repeal of the whiskey tax. As the best-educated, best-known person at the Forks, with a modest national reputation to boot, Brackenridge would make an ideal example, just the kind of self-interested opposition politician President Washington was looking for. The lawyer was fair game too, having been a day late in signing the submission that guaranteed amnesty. The only potential problem, Hamilton wrote to Washington, was that the commissioners had legitimized the lawyer by dealing with him during the negotiation phase.

Mr. Brackenridge was incredulous. People brought him stories every day of what the Nevilles were saying. While he'd disparaged the Neville Connection for years, he'd also worked tirelessly to prevent disasters from befalling Isaac Craig and Presley; he'd helped save Kirkpatrick's house and get Kirkpatrick himself safely out of town. Somehow it was he—he wasn't sure he could bear it—who had been singled out as a target for vengeance from the nation he'd hoped to devote his talents to glorifying and expanding. He could not credit Presley or General Neville, or even Craig or Kirkpatrick, despite their faults, with so vociferously desiring his utter downfall and death. His terrified musings focused on John Woods, the Nevilles' lawyer and family counselor, now helping General Neville identify and interrogate suspects. Mr. Brackenridge deduced that Woods was leading the campaign to kill and defame him.

He flailed wildly over what to do, for everything he'd done so far had gone wrong. When the army had been mustering east of the mountains, he'd written another letter, this time to President Washington, but there had seemed no point in sending it: Findley's partner, Redick, back from the interview at Carlisle, told Brackenridge that the president, when told Brackenridge wasn't a rebel, had maintained stony silence. Sickened by news that the troops planned to execute him, Brackenridge next decided to take his case straight to the soldiers. He published handbills explaining his conduct; he gave them to Findley and Redick to take on their second trip, for distribution to officers and men. Militia commanders responded with impatience or weak assurances of safety, and when Redick passed the handbills out to the troops, a new chapter was added to the story of the scoundrel Brackenridge's shamelessness: now the traitor was polluting the pure, avenging army of union.

As troops drew near the Forks, Mr. Brackenridge thought constantly of running, this time not from Tom the Tinker but from the government. He could go down the Mississippi, like David Bradford. There were the Spanish, or the British. Desperation kept pushing his imaginings toward Indians, up in the great wilderness across the Allegheny. He'd disdained their ways, but he might have a chance with them. He'd defended the drunk Mamachtaga, "Trees Blown Around by a Storm," who refused to tell self-serving lies in the courtroom and had been abandoned, in the end, even by his own tribe. Mr. Brackenridge knew a hunter who could take him into the woods. . . .

Yet when the exiled Nevilles returned to Pittsburgh, with a flashy escort from their ancestral Virginia, Mr. Brackenridge was still in town. He'd made up his mind to die on his own hearth. Decision didn't calm his anguish. He watched the conquering army ride past his house and thought the soldiers looked up at his window and laughed. The grand entrance inspired festivities appropriate to the restoration of a military and commercial dynasty. As the Nevilles led what appeared to be their personal army down the muddy streets, flags flew, horns squawked, and cannon shook the ground. Pittsburgh's social round instantly rebloomed. Eastern officers would soon be amazed to find such deluxe balls and teas in the wilderness.

Mr. Brackenridge, gazing on the happy return, felt his own assassination near, and that very night a contingent of soldiers came to his house, making clear their intention to execute him.

General and Presley Neville appeared too, running from Presley's townhouse down the street. They placed themselves between the troops and the door. The Nevilles harangued the men. Brackenridge, they said, had stood his ground. He hadn't run. Now it was time for the judiciary to deal with him. He must not be assassinated.

As the troops dispersed, Mr. Brackenridge saw that the Nevilles had a better idea than murder. They were saving him for the utter disgrace of trial and hanging. Interrogators were said to be releasing suspects—some of them guilty—who agreed to manufacture evidence against Gallatin, Findley, and Brackenridge. While mental habit forced him to note the irony—he could barely be civil to Findley—mental habit could no longer console him. Under constant barrages of panic and indignation, his sense of self was teetering.

Being realistic hadn't been realistic. Waiting with mounting horror for arrest and interrogation, the death he feared now was one brought on by madness.

Then things got worse. The quartermaster corps selected Mr. Brackenridge's house, as the biggest in town, for the Pittsburgh headquarters of General Lee, who was moving up from the Youghiogheny. As dragoons stomped in, the lawyer moved his family to a single room. He determined not to leave it until arrested. The awful thing was that Henry Lee and Hugh Henry Brackenridge had been at Princeton together. The upperclassman Brackenridge had tutored young Lee. Now the lawyer, forced to welcome Lee into the house, could barely shake hands with the general. Lee seemed embarrassed too. It must be awkward, Brackenridge reflected, to take the cold hand of one who had once seemed promising, now disgraced as a traitor, soon to be a corpse.

At night he lay fully clothed on a couch in the crowded room. Arrests usually came at night; he wanted to be ready. Between tense naps he read Plutarch's *Lives*. Once he'd hoped to inspire a national culture that might give the United States its own Plutarch. Returning now to the story of Solon, Athenian democracy's lawgiver, Mr. Brackenridge began to wonder, for the first time, just what he'd been doing these past months. Under Solon's law, a moderate may not remain neutral during a civil war. Neutrality, in fact, is punishable by death; moderates are forced to take a side, for moderation, Solon believed, must be dispersed throughout the ranks of each extreme to lessen civil conflict. This had been Brackenridge's own plan: infect rebel extremists with his own moderation. His motive, he reflected, had been laudable. His actions, however, had been hazardous, and he hadn't been able to see how hazardous till now. Solon's had been a small republic. The United States was too big, Pittsburgh too remote from the seat of government. Solon's moderates, Mr. Brackenridge thought, would have known one another, could have explained themselves. They would have understood one another.

Finally the Neville counselor John Woods, having compiled much evidence against Brackenridge, turned up the pièce de résistance. This was a letter, containing evidence, Woods announced, that made successful prosecution certain. General Neville and Woods were so excited that they took time out from interrogating and threatening prisoners to show the letter to Alexander Hamilton. Subordinates and others gathered in Hamilton's office to peruse a document that might condemn to death Pittsburgh's best-known, most eccentric citizen.

Senator James Ross came in too, worried. He'd been trying to counter the Nevilles' anti-Brackenridge campaign. As the president's friend and an ardent federalist, he'd been arguing with Hamilton for Brackenridge's reputation and life. But Ross knew that if this letter turned out to be what the Nevilles said it was, his case was weak.

The letter had been written by Brackenridge, Woods explained, to the chief insurgent David Bradford, and it proved the existence of a conspiratorial relationship between the two. Ross had been claiming for days that there had been no written intercourse between Brackenridge and Bradford. But this note, Woods said, reflected frequent, ongoing communication between them and showed a shared commitment to carrying out the insurgency. It had been written in

August; in it, Brackenridge asked Bradford—in a way that does imply a steady collaboration—to send new copies of some papers, which Brackenridge had mislaid, and which were essential to carrying forth "the business."

Neville and Woods waited eagerly as Hamilton read the note. Certainly it disproved Ross's idea that the two suspects hadn't communicated. "What do you make of this?" Hamilton challenged Ross. "Is that not"—he made the senator look at the letter—"the handwriting of Brackenridge?"

Ross knew Brackenridge's handwriting, which was famously terrible. He read the letter carefully. After a moment Ross said, "It is the handwriting." The Nevilles prepared to pounce, but after a moment Ross went on. "There is only one small matter," he said. "It is addressed to *William* Bradford, Attorney General of the United States."

Hamilton, visibly startled, looked again. General Neville seemed slowly to freeze. Brackenridge had indeed addressed the letter not to the chief insurgent, now fugitive, David Bradford, but unmistakably to William Bradford, leader of the presidential commission. This innocuous thing must have passed between them during the peace negotiations. Neville and Woods had brought Hamilton something that damned not Mr. Brackenridge but themselves, and potentially the entire operation, for hastiness and overreaching.

It was worse than nothing. Proceeding against Brackenridge on the basis of this evidence would have caused Hamilton—and the president—political disaster.

For the first time since May, when he'd begun taking steps that brought an army to the Forks of the Ohio, Alexander Hamilton took a long pause. He gazed at Neville and Woods, who stood as if mortified. Apparently they'd thought they could use the secretary of the treasury of the United States—for that matter, encourage bringing to the Forks a highly controversial, thirteen-thousand-man federal militia—to pursue what amounted to a vapid local vendetta. The silence grew oppressive. General Neville, onlookers thought, might not ever speak again. Hamilton did at last say something: "Gentlemen." But only monosyllables followed. "You are too fast," he said. "This will not do."

When Mr. Brackenridge was finally served a subpoena to appear for questioning, he was relieved only to have been spared being hustled out of his home by soldiers. The day before he was to turn himself in, he dined with General Lee, who had insisted on the lawyer's joining the officers' mess in Brackenridge's house. The meal felt to Mr. Brackenridge like the last eaten by a condemned man. Shaky and exhausted, he surrendered himself the next morning. Alexander Hamilton and Hugh Henry Brackenridge sat face-to-face.

Unexpectedly, Hamilton's mood was hard to assess. The secretary seemed to think Brackenridge would and should be hanged and also seemed, somehow, to regret thinking it. The lawyer humbly asked permission to narrate his story from the beginning. Hamilton agreed. Mr. Brackenridge began speaking. Hamilton began writing. The narration went on for many hours. At one point Hamilton stopped writing. Brackenridge had just been describing David Bradford's stepping forth as a leader when the people had demanded it—meaning that Bradford had at first been pushed forward, and had only later made rebel leadership his own. The lawyer was exhibiting a tendency, Hamilton said, to excuse major participants, and this tendency was unwise. Mr. Brackenridge wasn't under the amnesty. He was vulnerable to arrest. His story, Hamilton advised him, would determine his fate.

This surprised Mr. Brackenridge. Hamilton seemed to be offering him a way out. Perhaps to avoid arrest, he had only to implicate others. He knew of Hamilton's desire for evidence against Findley and Gallatin. A door to safety had been thrown wide. So with his next statement the enervated lawyer felt that he handed over his life. "I am not within the amnesty," he acknowledged. "And I am sensible of the extent of the power of the government. But were the narrative to begin again, I would not change a single word."

He resumed the tale, and after he'd told of Presley Neville's asking him, as a personal favor, to attend the Mingo church meeting, and of Presley's promising to vouch for his reluctance to go to that meeting, Hamilton again stopped writing. He wanted to adjourn for the midday dinner break. Lee was sending messages to Brackenridge to come home and dine again at the general's table, but the lawyer was near the edge of sanity and could only wait. Hamilton, meanwhile, was having what Mr. Brackenridge later realized was a tense lunchtime discussion with Presley Neville, during which Hamilton sharply quizzed Presley, for the first time, on circumstances surrounding the lawyer's attending the Mingo church meeting. And in the afternoon session, Hamilton began by saying that Mr. Brackenridge's actions seemed to have been grossly mischaracterized. The remark offered more hope than Mr. Brackenridge had been able to feel in a long time.

Yet Hamilton soon grew testy again. The lawyer was describing his speech at the Mingo Creek church. Hamilton had been given to understand that the speech supported rebellion and mocked the government. Mr. Brackenridge suggested they get affidavits from those he'd asked to join him as witnesses at that meeting. Hamilton's inner turmoil only seemed to increase. Then came the story of Brackenridge's pretending, at Braddock's Field, to support the rebellion in order to keep Pittsburgh from burning. This idea seemed to stagger Hamilton, and Brackenridge was mildly emboldened, venturing a similarity between his own conduct at Braddock's Field and that of King Richard II before a mob of 100,000 at Blackheath. Hamilton was listening.

The day ended abruptly when Hamilton complained of an aching chest. Brackenridge's spirits fizzled. He hoped the secretary's pain was caused by sympathy for the prisoner, though he believed it was caused by too much writing, and feared Hamilton had decided, if regretfully, that an arrest must be made that evening. Again fully clothed, Mr. Brackenridge passed a watchful night. The next morning, finding himself not arrested, he returned for more questioning, and by now Hamilton had made up his mind. When the lawyer finished dictating, Hamilton was actually smiling. The famous charm, rarely glimpsed by residents of the Forks, was on him as he assured Mr. Brackenridge that not a single doubt was left about the lawyer's conduct, which had indeed been horribly misrepresented. General Lee would be informed of the situation. There was no need, Hamilton said, even for an interview with Judge Peters.

As Brackenridge stared at him, Hamilton said, "Had we listened to some people, I do not know what we might have done."

When Mr. Brackenridge was asked to sign each page of his statement, he found he could barely work his fingers.

On Christmas morning, 1794, twenty thousand Philadelphians mobbed the broad, cobbled streets of their city to see the defeated whiskey rebels brought in from the west. At eleven-thirty, troopers mustered the rebels before the Black Horse Tavern in preparation for the parade.

If the people were expecting a big show, they had reason to be disappointed. Thousands had marched on Braddock's Field. There were twenty prisoners, and General Blackbeard White himself had been given the job of escorting them from the Forks. Already skinny, pale, and exhausted by questioning and imprisonment when leaving Fort Fayette on November 25, they'd spent a month crossing mountains forbidding enough in summer, locked now in winter. Each prisoner had walked, alone now, between a pair of mounted troopers. Days, they pulled each foot from snow and ice and put it in front of the other. Light on bare branches faded quickly. When the sun set behind them, they slept in frozen barns or cellars. The troopers kept swords drawn, ready to fend off any attempt at rescue. General White had ordered the beheading of anyone attempting escape: heads, he'd announced hopefully, would be displayed in the city.

John Hamilton, the most prominent among them, had never been questioned. Neither indictments nor verdicts had been needed to bring about this phase of what became, as prisoners prepared to be marched through the city, an example in the most literal sense.

Before the Black Horse the prisoners were given white slips of paper and ordered to place them on their hats as cockades. This was General White's idea: the few, thin rebels must be identifiable amid expectant crowds. Parades had become common lately. The city was celebrating, with days of pealing churchbells and booming salutes, the return of each army unit from the west. The president himself had been seen to emerge from his house and watch, with what seemed to onlookers inexpressible pleasure, as a returning regiment rode past.

The troopers arranged their prisoners in the usual order of march and drove them, the slips of brightness on their heads, through streets of shouting crowds. The rebels made a pitiful impression. The route was long and circuitous. Led at last into the Philadelphia city jail, they found Herman Husband and the others who had been arrested in October. To welcome new arrivals, orders were not to feed them and to give them no light.

CHAPTER ELEVEN

That So-Called
Whiskey Rebellion

Only Herman Husband didn't get home. District Attorney Rawle and Attorney General Bradford couldn't persuade grand juries even to indict some of the prisoners who had been marched over the mountains and paraded as victory prizes; actually convicting anyone in that first group, as well as others brought in later, proved nearly impossible.

It wasn't that Philadelphia juries were nullifying in protest. As Judge Peters had predicted, there simply wasn't any evidence against most of the men who had been selected for removal and trial. Despite Peters's concerns, none of the twenty men brought in that Christmas was released for lack of evidence. Charges weren't revealed to prisoners in advance of hearings. The judges explicitly instructed juries to return indictments and guilty verdicts. But there were just too many mistaken identities, too few witnesses, too much confused and inconclusive testimony. When certain high-value suspects did turn themselves in, they were offered deals to testify against their less well-known followers. Since normal law enforcement strategy was to get low-level criminals to testify against higher-level ones, Philadelphia juries disdained the prosecution and discredited the testimony.

The prosecution strategy confounded the administration's critics too. It seemed as if Hamilton and Attorney General Bradford were incompetently ignoring guiltier parties, who would have made good examples, and foolishly tormenting the innocent while failing to convict them.

But successful prosecution had never been the way Hamilton expected to drive his point where he wanted it driven. He'd hoped to hang Findley and Gallatin, and he'd tried to substitute Brackenridge, but the real subject of his operation had remained the whole people of the Forks, not prominent individuals pressed into leadership. Holding large numbers of lesser-known people in Philadelphia for long periods of confusion and fear, and then sending them home, extended the policy Hamilton and Lee had imposed on the entire Forks in the fall. Hamilton had started this fight in the confederation Congress in the 1780s. The idea was to destroy the will of an enemy that, though stubborn, had in the end been no match for the energy and scope of the national government.

Only twelve cases went to trial, and in the end only two rebels were convicted. These were Philip Wigle, who had beaten up Benjamin Wells and been among the cadre that burned Wells's house after Braddock's Field; and a John Mitchell, widely considered simple, whom David Bradford had sent to rob the mail. A landless miller's son and a subsistence farmer of dwindling property were hardly the arrogant, French-inspired politicos whom Washington had described, in an address to Congress, as having led the ignorant people of the Forks into treason. The administration was still enjoying renewed popularity. Hanging what appeared to be two sad cases might have raised questions about the real purpose of the operation.

Washington evinced the mercifulness that, with the crisis over, and easterners sated, most people hoped to see. He pardoned the condemned men.

By then, prisoners had been forced, despite lack of evidence, to wait for months in Philadelphia. Some stayed in rooming houses on bail; others couldn't post or hadn't been granted bail and lay in the city jail. Witnesses came slowly from the Forks. Trials didn't even start till May of 1795. It would be 1796 before everyone was released, to make his way, however he might, home to the Forks of the Ohio.

The example went on there too. An occupying force of fifteen hundred remained camped in the town of Washington. Lee had issued a general pardon; loyalty oaths had been collected; stills were registered. Judge Addison was deputized to work with the army on bringing in remaining suspects. The Neville Connection resumed its entrepreneurial endeavors, and General Neville resumed enforcing the excise law. The Wells family, happy to be back in the collections business, helped out. The amazing sight, that hot summer of 1794, on the bluff at Parkinson's Ferry, when for two days a new flag had flown over a western congress, wouldn't recur around Pittsburgh. Radicals' hopes for the American Revolution were over.

Yet the whiskey tax remained hard to collect. There were occasional disruptions of court proceedings and occasional threats, but mainly there was sneakiness and recalcitrance, smuggling and moonshining. The authority that established itself at last in the western country was not challenged. It was eluded.

"The Whiskey Rebellion": this was Alexander Hamilton's term for what people at the Forks had been doing. With it Hamilton scored a final victory over the rebels, permanently reducing their struggle to one over a beloved local drink. Hamilton did retire from the cabinet early in 1795. The experience of suppressing the rebellion had revived some old dreams. His hopes for empire were not exclusively commercial; the martial called out to him with increasing urgency, and at the end of the 1790s he commanded the United States Army, only technically second to the infirm Washington, who had been called out of retirement to put a beloved face on a possible war with France. In official charge, at last, of American military power, Hamilton badly wanted that war to happen. Preparations for it were swelling the army; he wanted to make the force permanent and fill it with his own sense of order. But the supply process became infuriatingly chaotic, as usual, and when war didn't come, and the army shrank almost to nothing, Hamilton's disappointment raged. He'd imagined marching troops south, preemptively invading Spanish Florida before it could be taken by the French, not stopping there, driving onward, into South America. He mused too about bringing his army into Virginia and putting that state, as he phrased it, to the test.

Yet he had some jubilant moments during and after the suppression of the Whiskey Rebellion, and when in high spirits, he could be surprisingly frank about the useful part insurrection had played in realizing his vision for the country. The rebellion (he didn't say its suppression) had strengthened the government, he was happy to boast. The rebellion solidified the country, he said, and it made national finance flourish.

In Washington's stated opinion, suppressing the Whiskey Rebellion had drawn from the American people the support for law and government that marked their highest character. Washington also noted that the operation worked out well for him personally. With commercial distilling newly profitable, he added whiskey making to his endeavors at Mount Vernon. He continued to fret over his western lands: letters to his lazy land agent included orders to deliver files and papers to Presley Neville and Senator James Ross, his new agents. When the president had been on his way to Carlisle in the fall of '94, he'd received satisfying news of decisive victory over the far western Indians. British and Indian power in the northwest was effectively ended. The far west was truly opened. With the suppression of the rebellion, his land in the west, which he'd been annoyed about having to sell cheap, increased in value by about 50 percent.

Edmund Randolph found himself having a nightmare from which he never awakened when, one morning in August of 1795, he arrived at the president's house for a meeting that had already been mysteriously postponed. With Washington were Hamilton's successor in the cabinet, Oliver Wolcott, and Knox's successor, Timothy Pickering, third-string functionaries of high federalism, which Hamilton, from outside government, was making the monolithic philosophy of the executive branch. Randolph had become the last surviving member of the first-term cabinet.

Washington mystified Randolph by asking him to wait outside. When ushered in, Randolph was surprised to be presented with a paper that the president asked him to read and explain. It was a dispatch from the French minister to authorities in Paris, analyzing the U.S. government's conduct in the Whiskey Rebellion. The minister cited Randolph as his source not only of privileged information but also of a portrait of Washington as a puppet—frontman for the monarchist ambitions of Hamilton and other federalists, who had incited the rebellion in order to exercise absolute power over the American people and punish political enemies in government. Randolph had also solicited a bribe from the French government, the dispatch said.

Washington invited Pickering and Wolcott to interrogate Randolph. Recovering himself, Randolph declined to be questioned under these circumstances; he left the room; he tendered in writing his resignation as secretary of state. He did have a relationship with the French minister. He'd been probed for information; he may have been less than discreet. But he was anguished over the accusation of disloyalty to the United States—and especially to Washington—and he was correct in thinking that it was Pickering and Wolcott who had accused him of treason.

Randolph wrote Washington a letter. Seeking public vindication, he also printed it as a pamphlet. But the appeal was impossible. Randolph could only beg Washington to recall the times when Randolph had been a trusted counselor, plead with Washington to remember that sometimes Washington didn't remember things. Torturing events again and again, the pamphlet ran to more than one hundred pages, an impenetrable thicket behind which a man stood screaming. Randolph, as Washington's former confidant, knew all the signs: the president just wanted him gone now. It didn't matter what Randolph had done, or not done, or what Randolph might say about it now. Knowing that writing could never penetrate Washington's feelings drove Randolph forward instead of suggesting he stop.

When Washington received the published pamphlet he threw it

on the floor, beleaguered. Randolph didn't achieve any vindication from the public either, in part because the letter, protesting too much, made him look at once foolish and guilty, but mainly because it wasn't the vindication of the public he needed.

In the election of 1800, the Jeffersonians came to power and the whiskey tax was repealed. President Jefferson's treasury secretary was Albert Gallatin. The new regime was good for some other former rebels too—or at least for those branded rebels who were actually moderates. Having escaped down the Mississippi, David Bradford never came back to live in western Pennsylvania; he spent the rest of his life on a plantation in Bayou Sara, in what under Jefferson became the Louisiana territory of the United States. William Findley, however, served in Congress until 1817. Though hated by the Morris and Hamilton federalists, he'd never been especially beloved by the Jefferson-Madison opposition. Earlier in his career, Findley had suggested, in debate in the Pennsylvania assembly, that Madison to the contrary, interest can be a political good, if acknowledged. Findley thought it more honest for representatives—not really high-minded public servants, reluctant for power, but professional politicians—to admit to representing not disinterested judgment but interested constituencies. Mentally living in the coming age of Jackson gave him, during the federalist era, an embattled energy, which paid off during the Jefferson administration in credibility and power.

Mr. Brackenridge, however, vindicated by Alexander Hamilton, wasn't vindicated by the army, and his terror and outrage went on. He tried to clear his name, but he also refused to keep a low profile; he represented settlers in damage suits against occupying officers. Then General Neville, hiring additional legal help for prosecuting local distillers, thought having a reputed rebel on the team might move juries the government's way. He offered Mr. Brackenridge the job. Mr. Brackenridge, true to erratic form, accepted.

With time, he became known less for irony than for irascibility.

By the end of the decade, he was a leader of the Pittsburgh Jeffersonian party, but even as he watched Findley and Gallatin win elections, the voters continued to view him with suspicion, and he never again held elected office. When the Jeffersonians took power in Pennsylvania, Brackenridge was appointed a justice of the state supreme court and moved east to Carlisle. By then he had a reputation for steady drinking. He was known for charging juries with his bare feet propped on the bar of justice. A tavernkeeper in Canonsburg who had inspired his wrath was confronted by the sight of Judge Brackenridge stomping into the crowded tavern, damning the tavernkeeper fifteen times, and then, overwhelmed by fury, ripping off his own clothes and standing near-naked before the startled crowd, fuming. He took to chastising even the Jeffersonians for political sins, but his judgeship was for life, and he died in office.

He often sought refuge in new chapters of *Modern Chivalry*. It had no plot, so it needed no ending, and the characters' idiotic ploys went on and on.

Herman Husband was indicted and tried not for treason but for sedition. A conviction might have seemed easy to get: there had been depositions from Benjamin Wells and Philip Reagan laying the blame for rebellion on Husband's writings and sermons, which could easily be read as urging violent revolution against the federal government. Yet at Parkinson's Ferry, where the prosecution focused its questioning, nobody had heard Husband preach violence. He'd advised peace. The jury quickly found Husband not guilty. He was released on May 12, 1795, and collapsed on the way out of Philadelphia. He could go no farther than a tavern just outside town.

Emmy was with him; his eldest son, John, who hadn't seen his father since Husband's southern trip fourteen years earlier, came from North Carolina. Pneumonia had settled in Husband's old lungs, weakened from the long walk over the mountains. He lay slowly failing in the tavern. On June 19, he died. Emmy and John buried him nearby. His grave site is not known.

On the night of his arrest, lying in the Bedford jail, Husband had known he was leaving, perhaps forever, the wild country to which he'd brought settlement, civilization, and trouble. That night, hoping to reassure Emmy, he hastily wrote her a letter. "A prison seems the safest place for one of my age," he wrote, adding wryly, though without irony, "and profession." That profession was prophecy. Husband saw another world in America. The beauty of the vision left him, in the end, with nowhere to turn. Nonviolence both sustained and failed him. The abomination of desolation couldn't be extinguished, he thought, without a last battle for the American soul.

Someone's barn goes up in flames on a moonless night. Ink runs down an official document soaked in alcohol. A lonely victim jogs, panting and pursued, down a dirt track. Hoisted up a pole, a homemade flag hangs over men who wander through smoke, guns pointing at nothing in particular, firing again and again. Those are not things Herman Husband saw in the Whiskey Rebellion. He wrote, that night in the Bedford jail, to his family, but he had spiritual descendants too. "Make yourselves easy about me," Husband urged from behind cold iron. "For I am so rejoiced that at times, old as I am, I can scarcely keep from dancing and singing, for which I cannot account."

NOTES

Following the general essay below, brief chapter essays provide sources and, where possibly useful, discussion of key events and ideas. Full citations are given in "Sources"—which I've limited to listing only the works mentioned here.

I don't give references for readily acquired, noncontroversial information drawn from many cited sources. Alexander Hamilton was born on a Caribbean island. Every biography says so, in words more or less to that effect; I don't try to prove or give credit for it. I cite sources for facts not generally known and from which I've drawn ideas and analyses. I also point out discrepancies in the record; explain, when I depart from other interpretations, my bases for doing so; and suggest further reading.

There is much to know about the Whiskey Rebellion that does not appear in this book. Where I'm sending you, I've been; I hope these essays will aid students of the rebellion in their own digging and sorting.

WRITERS ON THE WHISKEY REBELLION

So many of the rebellion's actors were also writers, whose accounts played roles in the drama itself, that the historiography of the rebellion begins with the rebellion in progress. The earliest attempt at a comprehensive overview is Alexander Hamilton's official "Report on Opposition to Internal Duties," August 5, 1794. Many events in the report had been described, immediately after their happening, in letters to superiors and friends from the tax inspector John Neville and the quartermaster Isaac Craig, as well as by victims of attacks who gave depositions. Other contemporaneous accounts include statements made by rebel participants and journals kept by soldiers sent to suppress the rebellion. Claims on Congress made by the tax collector Benjamin Wells are a rich source of eyewitness accounts. A long letter from the participant Alexander Fulton to President Washington relates some key events from an unusual perspective. Letters from the presidential commissioners to the cabinet narrate events of fall 1794 on a day-to-day basis.

Those eyewitness accounts vary in purpose, emphasis, and tone and differ on brute fact. When participants began publishing, dispute became overt. William Findley's *History of the Insurrection* replies indignantly to

Hamilton's report, making fine distinctions meant largely to show that there really was no organized rebellion at all. (The man who started the fire at Bower Hill wasn't acting on orders, for example; the book contains dozens of similar remarks.) Findley was the first to accuse Hamilton publicly and cogently of having deliberately provoked the rebellion in order to create an excuse for suppressing it, a strategy Findley calls "a refinement in cruelty." While often ponderous and self-contradictory, the book is especially good on the suppression. Findley is also interesting as an early exponent of a frontier republicanism that would become common in rhetoric of the Jackson era.

Hugh Henry Brackenridge's *Incidents of the Insurrection* was intended to clear its author's name: Brackenridge had been accused of being a rebel leader. Brackenridge's book includes letters and depositions from participants; his narrative covers his own actions on a day-to-day and even minute-to-minute basis; his work has therefore always been invaluable for later writers. The modern Whiskey Rebellion scholars discussed below rely at times on Brackenridge yet are careful to give context for his points of view. The importance of Brackenridge's account to this book is probably obvious.

In the next generation, arguing over the rebellion became a sport in the Pittsburgh area. Neville Craig, a son of Isaac Craig and grandson of John Neville, published his *History of Pittsburgh* in 1851, glorifying his genitors' actions in the rebellion and attacking Brackenridge as instigator; in 1859, Brackenridge's son Henry Marie responded with *History of the Western Insurrection in Western Pennsylvania,* largely restating his father's position and attacking Neville Craig, Nevilles in general, and their friends. (Craig in turn published *Exposure of a Few of the Many Misstatements in H. M. Brackenridge's History of the Whiskey Insurrection.*) The younger Brackenridge does glorify the elder Brackenridge as an embattled republican sage; still, his book is intelligently and compellingly written and includes important primary material. Publishing while north-south sectional conflict was coming to crisis, H. M. Brackenridge was the first writer to place what were then half-century-old events in a later political context. Craig's book is highly derivative of the Hildreth work mentioned below.

For a time, professional historians and biographers battled over the rebellion's meaning too. Early critics of federalism took Findley's point of view, minimizing rebel violence, describing rebels as loyal, and sympathizing with rebel plight; in the other camp, Richard Hildreth, in his *History of the United States* (1849), epitomized a tradition, begun by John Marshall in his *Life of George Washington,* of presenting the rebels as wild Scots-Irish drunks, geared up by treasonous antifederalist leaders, and Hamilton and Washington as patient saviors regretfully forced, after perhaps too many shows of leniency, to act.

According to Thomas Slaughter (whose work is discussed below), by the end of the nineteenth century the Civil War had pushed the rebellion off the screen for many readers of history. In the twentieth century, it seems to me, textbook writers, federal-era overviewers, and Hamilton and Washington biographers—writers, that is, not specializing in the rebellion yet forced to acknowledge its existence—have tended to ignore its implications and misunderstand its causes and effects. To many otherwise well-informed readers of American history, the rebellion is now remembered, if at all, as a sidebar about a dustup.

Of recent works not devoted to the rebellion, the fairest and most detailed discussion of the subject appears in Chapter Ten of Elkins and McKitrick's *The Age of Federalism,* the essential synthesis—at once magisterial and page-turning—of the politics of the period. Still, Elkins and McKitrick are more interested in delineating the role of the democratic societies than in tracing other, to me more salient, influences on the rebellion. Recent, widely read biographies of Alexander Hamilton by Richard Brookhiser and Ron Chernow, who rely on *The Age of Federalism* for many matters, largely ignore its analysis of the rebellion, typifying a long line of popular Hamilton biographers—including Broadus Mitchell and John C. Miller—in glossing over the primary record and presenting the rebellion largely as Hamilton hoped it would be presented.

Thus the few modern, full-length works devoted solely to the rebellion have great value. Leland Baldwin's long-out-of-print *Whiskey Rebels,* published in 1939 and lightly revised in 1968, is the only full-length work (before this one) written in a narrative style for nonspecialist readers while relying on close attention to the full primary and secondary record. Limited by the unavailability in its day of certain important sources, marred by patronizing attitudes toward aspects of its subject, Baldwin's work nevertheless succeeds as a lively and accurate chronological history, a sturdy raft from which to delve in darker waters.

Thomas Slaughter's *The Whiskey Rebellion,* published in 1986, is the only academic work on the rebellion in print; Dorothy Fennell's *From Rebelliousness to Insurrection* (1981) and Terry Bouton's *Tying Up the Revolution* (1996) are unpublished doctoral dissertations. All three studies are crucial. Slaughter descries a key east-west sectional conflict too often overlooked by historians in favor of north-south division; he grounds the rebellion in a long tradition of excise protest, radical republicanism, and regional strife, focusing on what he sees as an overreaction by Hamilton, Washington, and other "friends of order" largely to meetings, assemblies, and petitions. While my departures from Slaughter—especially from his emphasis on the importance of country-party and republican ideology—are noted in some of the chapter essays below, his text and notes remain the major academic apparatus through which a personal understanding of the rebellion can be developed. Slaughter's explorations of Washington's western land speculations are especially valuable, as is his exhaustive primary research on the federal militia that suppressed the rebellion.

Dorothy Fennell's original and highly informative dissertation, which Slaughter also cites, is a work of progressive history, focusing on social and economic issues to which the rebels were responding and placing the rebellion in a context of abrupt local shifts in labor and production. Relying in part on Robert Eugene Harper's dissertation, *The Class Structure of Western Pennsylvania,* Fennell studies property ownership and other economic factors, persuasively defining the victims of rebel attacks as those monopolizing local trade. She closely analyzes the economics of distilling; she places blackface attacks in a long history of economic and social regulation. Three other aspects of Fennell's work have particular importance: her discovery of the Benjamin Wells Claims as a detailed primary record; her identification of a moment in 1794 when the rebellion shifted from traditional blackface attacks to undisguised, organized militia action; and her discussion of Herman Husband as an underacknowledged inspiration for that shift.

Terry Bouton marshals, with provocative and illuminating effect, the economic and financial matters—federal, state, and local—that for him make the rebellion not a discrete event but the climax of a series of actions, ongoing in western Pennsylvania from at least as early as the mid-1780s, related to paper and land-bank finance as mechanisms of populism, as well as to the efforts of Robert Morris, in both the confederation Congress and the Pennsylvania assembly, to crush popular finance and promote the interests of bondholders at all costs. Reviving and developing *The Power of the Purse,* the benchmark work of E. J. Ferguson on the domestic debt, Bouton is working toward a new understanding of founding finance, a subject many historians and biographers (especially those of its author, Hamilton) decline to lead their readers realistically through. Bouton relies at times on Fennell—and follows her on Husband—but he also criticizes tendencies he sees in fellow progressives to romanticize the agrarian. He presents the rebels not as dismayed by the shift to a mercantile and industrial economy but as frustrated by state and federal policies that blocked their benefiting from that shift.

Bouton's and Fennell's analyses have been critically important to this book. Yet as I hope my narrative shows, I depart from a tendency I discern, especially in the work of Bouton, but also in that of recent progressive historians in general, to read local regulations like the Whiskey Rebellion—usurpation of the judiciary; armed intimidation of dissenters by self-appointed representatives of the people—as epitomizing the best in popular sovereignty. My thinking on this issue benefits from Garry Wills's study of American distrust of sophisticated government, *A Necessary*

Evil; my departure from the progressives persists in the face of their well-taken point (also made by the rebels themselves) that such extralegal and illegal regulatory tactics had been essential to achieving American independence and producing the Washington administration.

With the three major scholarly studies must be ranked chapters on the Whiskey Rebellion in Richard Kohn's *Eagle and Sword*, on the early development of the United States military establishment, which deal closely with the Washington administration's decisions and tactics in suppressing the rebellion. James Patrick McClure's monumental, unpublished dissertation, *The Ends of the American Earth*, covers white settlement in the Upper Ohio Valley to 1795; only in McClure's exhaustively documented chapters on the rebellion did I find scholarly support for my own sense of the chronology implied by the taxman William Faulkner's deposition of 1792, the watershed represented by the second Pittsburgh convention, and the real nature of various militia-based organizations at the Forks of the Ohio.

Another important work is Wythe Holt's major essay "The Whiskey Rebellion of 1794" (part of a larger, forthcoming work), which focuses on legal issues in the interrogations and trials of the rebels. Holt's use of trial testimony and Judge William Paterson's papers is essential to understanding issues touched on only lightly in this book. Holt attacks Slaughter's approach as ideologically wishy-washy, following Fennell on Herman Husband and joining Bouton and other progressives in presenting rebel tactics as admirably evincing working-class democracy in action.

Other writers who have dealt in various ways with the Whiskey Rebellion: Stephen Boyd, who edited *The Whiskey Rebellion: Past and Present Perspectives* (with an important historiography by Slaughter); Mary Tachau, whose "The Whiskey Rebellion in Kentucky" covers tax resistance beyond the Forks of the Ohio; and Roger Gould, whose essay "Patron-Client Ties, State Centralization, and the Whiskey Rebellion" must rank among the most deliberately dry essays ever written, yet arrives at some startling and credible conclusions, beyond the scope of this work and calling for further thought. Gould deploys statistics to demonstrate that prominent participants in the rebellion were elites with state rather than federal connections.

Among many works of Pennsylvania history, Russell Ferguson's evocatively written *Early Western Pennsylvania Politics*, published in 1938, focuses with great effectiveness on personalities who acted during the rebellion. Norma W. Hartman's cited article clarifies the identity of Oliver Miller, killed in the first Bower Hill attack; Hartman's work is also presented in Mary Pat Swanger's summary of the rebellion; both writers are members of Oliver Miller Homestead Associates, of Pittsburgh, which possesses much interesting information about the rebellion in the context of local history and genealogy. Among many local histories, Boyd Crumrine's *History of*

Washington County, published in 1882, serves as a good guide to biographies and genealogies of many principal players.

Scattered works of related interest include Henry McCook's *The Latimers,* a novel published in 1897 and set during the rebellion, drawing in part on local tradition; another fictional treatment appears in *Tree of Liberty* by Elizabeth Page. A book by the local historian C. M. Ewing, *The Causes of That So Called Whiskey Insurrection of 1794,* written in 1930, attacks Alexander Hamilton with compelling irascibility and no attempt at impartiality. The guidebooks by Helene Smith and Jerry Clouse are useful for locating rebellion sites.

Essays below delve into specific sources and ideas for each chapter.

PROLOGUE: THE PRESIDENT, THE WEST, AND THE REBELLION

Washington and the presidency. Major sources for the centrality of Washington's personality to the idea of a U.S. presidency are Wills's *Cincinattus* and Elkins and McKitrick's first chapter. The president's clothing, hair products, and other personal matters are detailed in Paul Leicester Ford.

Washington's aging. Flexner, in his volume 4, describes the memory loss; in volume 3 he discusses Washington's sensation of rapid aging and concern that he wouldn't be fit for a second term. Randolph, an eyewitness (with an ax to grind), describes the president as complaining daily of not trusting his own memory. See also conflicts over memory between Washington and Hamilton in Chapter Seven.

Mount Vernon, the Federal City, and the journey of spring '94. Flexner raises Washington's childlessness in the context of dynastic ambitions of plantation owners. All cited secondary sources on Washington give detailed information on Mount Vernon's operations and its economic and agricultural challenges; I follow Smith's Chapter Ten for Washington's frettings in the spring of '94. "Transmutation toward gold": from Washington's *Writings,* quoted by Ford. For more on Washington's relationship to the Federal City see Elkins and McKitrick, Chapter Four. Descriptions of presidential carriages, travel arrangements, etc., are drawn from the notes of Tobias Lear, in Decatur. Many works on Washington recount the injury of June 1794, the return to the capital, and the dinner with the Indians; Smith cites John Quincy Adams on Washington's sharing the peace pipe.

Washington and the west. The subject is covered in all cited Washington biographies. Knollenberg's Chapter Fourteen details Washington's efforts, often shady, to engross western land. Of dedicated studies, Cook focuses on Washington's western lands, Sakolski on the land bubble as a whole. Slaughter devotes an important chapter to Washington's western interests in the context of the Whiskey Rebellion and notes, with many biographers,

Washington's desire to keep the Mississippi closed. For a lively exploration of Washington's Potomac projects, see Achenbach.

CHAPTER ONE: OVER THE MOUNTAINS

Hugh Henry Brackenridge. Marder and Newlin are the standard biographers—Marder following Newlin closely. In *After the Revolution,* Ellis gives valuable information and insight regarding the seriousness and scope of Brackenridge's literary ambitions. Most important to my appreciation of Brackenridge are his own works, often hastily written yet always full of personality and verve. For Brackenridge on Indians, see *Narrative of a Late Expedition,* and "Thoughts on the Present Indian War" in *Gazette Publications,* which also has much of Brackenridge's political writing, as well as the many modes of his poetry and drama not touched on here.

Settlement and growth at the Forks of the Ohio. For topography, see especially Russell Ferguson's first chapter. McClure exhaustively details the role of the British Army and its departure; Indian relations and white-Indian violence; the border war; settlement patterns; treaties; and new-state movements. Regarding population statistics, McClure notes that the federal census of 1790 gives a misleading number of 376 for Pittsburgh—when in fact the area that for most people composed the town had about one thousand people by 1790. Before McClure, the Bucks were the major source on headwaters settlement; their work is more readily available than McClure's. Fennell uses primary sources to tell the story of the "blacks" and describes competing provincial authorities as leading to skepticism about all authority. Some other writers make more than I do of the influence of Scots-Irish culture on the attitudes of the whiskey rebels—but for the importance of that culture to Appalachian life, see David Hackett Fischer's benchmark study. Slaughter is especially effective in linking the Pennsylvania new-state movement with those of Watauga and Franklin; he also cites contemporaneous observers on children playing near corpses. Findley discusses Indians' revolutionary-period depredations of white settlements.

The Johnson tar and feathering. The primary source is Neville's informal cover note to Clymer of 9/15/1791, in the Wolcott Papers, introducing Johnson, who apparently carried the more formal letter to Clymer in Philadelphia and gave testimony there. The front page of the note, describing the attackers' garb, was not microfilmed and must be read in the original. Johnson's amiability and simplicity are mentioned by Alexander Addison in a letter to Governor Mifflin, 5/12/1794, *Pennsylvania Archives.* Washington County resolutions of 8/23/91 appear in a copy of the *Pittsburgh Gazette,* enclosed by Neville in his letter to Clymer of 9/8/91, in the Wolcott Papers. Fennell's Chapters Four and Five give detail on the tar and featherers as a class; she describes certain rebels' situations individually, including Daniel Hamilton's. The *Beers Commemorative Biographical Record,* seeming to follow Crumrine, covers the many Washington County Hamiltons.

The Green Tree meeting. In *Incidents,* Brackenridge describes the meeting and, secondhand, the earlier, nondelegated Brownsville meeting; he frequently evinces his disdain for Woods, sardonically calling him "my brother of the bar." It is my belief that Woods, as the Nevilles' lawyer, attended the meeting only to report on it; Neville's letter to Clymer of 9/8/1791, in the Wolcott Papers, refers to Neville's having been "informed" (incorrectly, in this case, thus probably deliberately) that the meeting's demands were radical. Newlin is the source for Brackenridge's relationship with David Bradford. Fennell focuses on the elite status of the Green Tree attendees; it is her idea that the tar and feathering of the night before was intended to send the delegates a message (Baldwin, on the other hand, calls the attack "desultory"). Resolutions of the Green Tree meeting: *Pennsylvania Archives.*

Brackenridge and Husband. Brackenridge describes the meeting in *Incidents*; Schoepf also visited Husband's farm and had similar if less sardonic impressions. For more on Husband, see Chapter Five.

CHAPTER TWO: THE CURSE OF PULP

Excise protest. Inspired by Fennell and Bouton, I view rebel objections to the tax as having less to do with antiexcise traditions than with particular mechanisms Hamilton built into the tax. But Slaughter places the rebellion in a long tradition of protest against excise, exploring riots going back to the fifteenth century and the crisis of the Walpole era; following Bailyn's seminal work on the subject, he also invokes the connection of British country-party politics and American colonial and independence politics. Readers interested in British country- and court-party traditions and their relationship to American politics should see, along with Bailyn and Slaughter, Black and Kramnick; for Walpole's excise crisis, see Langford. Walpole's influence on Hamilton is suggestive in this context; Ha-Joon Chang traces that influence with regard to manufacturing and tariffs.

Hamilton's nose. Hamilton to Laurens, 4/1779 (no day given), Hamilton's *Papers.* Concocting a mock list of attributes that might prove attractive to a wife, Hamilton refers with self-mocking pride to the impressive length of his nose. Implications, evidently lewd, were blacked out of the original letter by Hamilton's son John Church Hamilton: see editor's note 2 on the letter.

The public debt and the war effort. Much of this chapter closely follows Bouton's analysis; I paraphrase Bouton's interpretation of the original floating and funding of the blue-chip tier and use his example of what a buyer was really getting with a thousand-dollar bond. The most complete understanding of state and federal debt instruments, currencies, requisitions, depreciation laws, taxation efforts, army buying procedures, and final-settlement accounting is that of E. J. Ferguson, on whom Bouton relies. One of Ferguson's most important conclusions is that the familiar distinction between patriotic "original holders" and crass "speculators"—rehashed in many works on the founding period—is largely a bogus one, at least regarding the blue-chip portion of the debt: Ferguson shows that the most attractive bonds moved very little, and that their original holders were also speculators, who like lower-scale speculators gambled, often irrationally, in all forms of public debt, both state and national. Bouton is unique in developing Ferguson's work with reference to the Whiskey Rebellion.

Robert Morris in the Congress. Nobody else has followed Morris's turbulent congressional career with the closeness of E. J. Ferguson, in both *The Power of the Purse* and the introduction and notes to Morris's *Papers.* Ferguson shows, I think conclusively, that Morris's nationalist agenda, in which Hamilton was a key congressional operative, was direct precursor to Hamilton's federalist finance program. But Syrett and Cooke, editors of Hamilton's *Papers,* explicitly disagree with those who emphasize the Morris influence on Hamilton (see their general note on "Report on the Public Credit," January 1790), pointing to Hamilton's independent development of ideas shared with Morris and Hamilton's reading of the economist Jacques Necker. Most of Hamilton's biographers, citing especially Necker and Hume as influences, pass lightly and uncritically over the relationship with Morris—though Mitchell calls the relationship an apprenticeship and Morris the one person from whom Hamilton would take correction in finance; Miller does go so far as to call Morris a war profiteer. Bouton is the eye-opening source on the opposition of Morris's agenda to that of the rural popular movement, hence of Morris's significance to Hamilton's activities during the Whiskey Rebellion. See also Hamilton's famous finance letter to Morris of 4/30/1781 in Hamilton's *Papers.* My description of the mercantile code and its effects distills Ferguson's.

Debtors, creditors, and founding-era economies. Much of the currency scholarship I cite is ultimately based on Brock, who refutes the common view that all colonial paper was wildly inflationary. E. J. Ferguson's first chapter is essential to understanding colonial currency; another important source is the readable and illuminating Grubb. Bouton equates the Whiskey Rebellion with the depressed American economy, debtor-creditor struggles, and populists' commitment to paper and land-bank finance, fleshing out the decades-long economic depression with special attention to rural Pennsylvania. Opinions of paper finance expressed by Robert Morris and other financiers are a subject in themselves: E. J. Ferguson and Hawke, among others, point to merchants' allegiance to paper throughout the colonial period; Bouton equates creditors' growing hatred of paper with an alliance to nationalist government and fear of state legislatures' popular-finance laws.

The popular movement. Elkins and McKitrick, though naturally more interested in official politics and the ideology of the democratic societies, are unusually fair to the popular movement. Hamilton, rejecting the finance philosophy of labor radicals, declined to acknowledge that they had a philosophy at all; that tactic has been borrowed by historians who view as anachronistic any attempt to take seriously economic radicalism in the eighteenth century. Progressive historians, for their part, often sentimentalize the movement's traditional tactics, which in English village life had most often been dedicated to maintaining rather than overturning social hierarchies. Readers who want to piece together the story of eighteenth-century labor radicalism and its impact in the 1770s on protests in Boston and Philadelphia, hence on American independence, should see Young, Nash, Foner, Zobel, and Countryman; Foner is my source for Adams's remark on the Pennsylvania constitution. Bouton serves as a chief guide to sources on this subject and as an important source himself; he is the most focused authority on road closings and other obstructive tactics in Pennsylvania, as well as for assembly battles of the 1780s between creditors and debtors. For more on the popular movement's tactics, its roots in village regulation, and Parliament's Black Act, see Thompson, whom Fennell also cites; for analyses of how those tactics emerged in revolutionary America, see especially Young, Pencak, and Shaw.

The Pennsylvania constitution. Key primary sources include Paine and the 1776 Pennsylvania constitution itself. Good sources for the political battles of revolutionary and postwar Pennsylvania include Lincoln, Selsam, Brunhouse, and Ryerson. Tinkcom argues that the radical constitution wasn't the disaster that some others claim it was. Hawke, a disarmingly fine writer and skeptical thinker, takes issue with the idea that rural Pennsylvanians felt any special resentment for eastern policies; his shrewd analysis is compelling, yet to me it can't withstand the petitions and statistics cited by Bouton, Selsam, and others.

The bondholder lobby and the impost. Bouton streamlines and focuses the story, which E. J. Ferguson supports in greater detail, of Morris's mounting desperation and his schemes regarding funding the war debt and the creation of the bondholder lobby; Bouton cites Morris's letters, especially to Ridley on 10/6/1782 and to Washington on 10/16/82, and his reports to Congress, especially of 7/29/82, all in Morris's *Papers*. While many writers on Hamilton discuss nationalists' hopes for the impost, few focus on the impost as a wedge for a full slate of federal taxes, including excise, or on the fact that for the Morris group in Congress, the primary purpose of federal taxation was not to pay and supply soldiers but to ensure regular interest payments to investors. For full exploration of those matters, see E. J. Ferguson.

The Newburgh crisis. The officer petition, the Newburgh addresses, the impost bills and votes, and Washington's letter to Congress are in *Journals of the American Congress* for late 1782 and early '83 (the petition and addresses are appended to Hamilton's committee report of 4/24/1783). The story is clearly and thoroughly detailed by Kohn, who describes its purpose as a threat, at least, of coup d'état, with Hamilton and the Morrises encouraging, for their own ends, Gates's dream of mutiny. Kohn presents his evidence for the Morris-Hamilton conspiracy—circumstantial yet logical and persuasive, especially in light of Hamilton's letters to Washington during and after the crisis—in footnote 19 for his *William and Mary Quarterly* article, not in his book. Kohn also describes the Society of the Cincinnati as a means of perpetuating the officer class as a force in politics. For a dissenting view, see Nelson, who argues that there was no real threat of coup from Gates (his article is followed by a rebuttal from Kohn). Morris's tactics in Congress during the crisis can be followed in E. J. Ferguson, who cites Madison's reference to the excitement caused by the officers' demands. For Hamilton's efforts to push the impost through Congress during the crisis, while keeping funds attached to bondholders, see his resolutions and opposition to motions proposed on 1/27/1783, 1/28/83, 1/29/83, 2/19/83, and 3/11/83, in his *Papers.*

Hamilton and Washington. In Hamilton's *Papers,* the revived relationship can be traced in letters of 3/12/1783, 3/17/83 (with Hamilton's crossed-out confession of having desired, however briefly, to produce a threat of coup), 3/24/83, 3/25/83, 3/31/83, 4/4/83 (with Hamilton's most complete confession), 4/15/83, 4/16/83 (with Washington's qualification of his remarks of 4/4), and 4/22/83. Most Hamilton biographers treat Hamilton's involvement in the crisis as naughty yet ultimately harmless dabbling for a worthy cause; all sources on Washington describe Washington's masterful quelling of the coup, which almost all describe as a failed attempt at worst. Bouton suggests that as a means of swelling the debt and its lobby, the crisis was a success, paving the way for Hamilton's programs of the 1790s. In that context, I note that while many writers admiringly cite Washington's famous reference to the army's being dangerous to play with, they ignore the implications of the remark, as Washington himself clarified them in his seldom-cited follow-up letter. Ambiguities in the Washington-Hamilton relationship, surfacing during the Newburgh crisis, went on to play an even more complicated part, I believe, in the Whiskey Rebellion and lead me to see Washington's role in the crisis more ambiguously than do Flexner, Freeman, et al.

Chapter Three: Spirits Distilled within the United States

Hamilton's finance program and the whiskey tax. Readers of American history are likely to have an impression of the whiskey tax as, if anything, the last detail in Hamilton's persuading Congress to fund a national debt and assume states' debts in it. The standard view is expressed by Slaughter: "Once assumption of state debts was agreed upon, a method of paying for them inevitably followed." (p. 19) In this chapter I flip the usual hierarchies—at the very least, I think, correctively—to subordinate funding and assumption to the excise tax. As Ferguson shows, especially in his Chapter Eight, Robert Morris viewed assumption not merely as something to be paid for by federal taxes, including internal taxes, but as a tactic for achieving such taxes and earmarking their proceeds to bondholders. Hamilton clearly had his eyes on the prize of excise at the outset of developing the finance plan: inexplicably to me, biographers make nothing of his writing and appending to the original report of 1790—not draft funding or assumption bills—but a long, fully developed draft import and excise tax bill, almost identical to the one passed in 1791. Brookhiser ignores excise completely, blurring it with the duties on luxury imports, thus managing to ascribe westerners' resentment of the whiskey tax to their love of whiskey drinking. Chernow too places objection to the tax largely in the context of frontiersmen's recreational consumption of alcohol. As discussed later in this chapter, Hamilton used the same argument. He at least was being disingenuous.

Hamilton as treasury secretary. Flexner describes Hamilton as seeing treasury as top job. Hamilton's letter to Morris: 4/30/1781, Hamilton's *Papers.* All biographers delve into the remarkable number of challenging tasks that confronted Hamilton when he took the job.

Populists, nationalists, and state governments. Foner discusses the post-war shift westward of the popular movement. All sources on the period cover Shays; Ferguson does so with unusual detail regarding tax-and-debt issues involved. For fights in the Pennsylvania assembly over Morris's bank, the radical plan for state debt, populist recalcitrance in western Pennsylvania and elsewhere, and the disastrous extent of foreclosure: Bouton, Brunhouse, Tinkcom, and Russell Ferguson. Brunhouse sees a paper emission in Pennsylvania as a major populist victory; Bouton sees it as too little, too late; most important for this story, bitter dissatisfaction on both creditor and debtor sides is borne out in most cited accounts of Pennsylvania politics of the period. Crist's biography of Robert White-hill is lively but not politically illuminating. Slaughter is the most compact and focused source for the western independence movements' grievances regarding Indian attacks and the Mississippi; he also notes (with many biographers) Washington's desire to keep the Mississippi closed until national unity could be established. Of Whiskey Rebellion scholars, Slaughter is alone in focusing closely on violence between Indians and whites, punctuating his narrative with compelling and painful descriptions of massacres. McClure offers much detail on Indian war techniques, populist meetings, and circulars connecting western Pennsylvania with Kentucky.

Finance and the constitutional convention. Most writers on the period cite the Shays Rebellion and the fear of economic leveling that it inspired as a cause of nationalist regrouping. Yet Chernow, quoting *The Federalist,* Number Six (where Hamilton refers to Daniel Shays as a "desperate debtor"), also describes Hamilton as sympathizing with Shays and suggests that federal assumption of state debts reflected Hamilton's desire to equalize burdens and relieve debtors' straits. While Hamilton was indeed critical of the aggressive debt-retirement schemes of Massachusetts, Chernow's seems an impossible reading when the quotation is placed in context of the whole essay: like other nationalists urging ratification, Hamilton presents Shays (using "desperate," I think, in its sense of "recklessly violent") as a type to be eradicated, not relieved. For Randolph's remarks at the opening of the convention, see Farrand (McHenry's notes are most to the point). Bouton, seeing the drive toward a national constitution as originating largely in creditor reaction to postwar populism, is supported by Ferguson, who views the failure of nationalism in the confederation Congress and the resulting crisis among creditors as important prods to the convention. Grubb is my inspiration for defining the constitutional prohibition against state currency as the decisive victory for Hamilton and the old Morris agenda. Antifederalism's shaky alliance with the popular movement is beyond the scope of this chapter; for a detailed discussion, see Bouton, who also covers, with Brunhouse and Tinkcom, the revision of the Pennsylvania constitution.

The impost triumphant. For the first Congress's impost bills, see *Statutes at Large*: "An Act for Laying a Duty on Goods . . ." 7/4/1789; "An Act to Regulate the Collection . . ." 7/31/89.

Funding, assumption, and the revenue bill. Tracking the excise proposal through Congress, I've drawn mainly on Hamilton's *Papers, Annals of Congress,* and *House Journal.* For Hamilton's March report, see *Papers,* 3/4/1790. For a comprehensive argument linking excise to assumption, see Fisher Ames's speech in *Annals,* 5/25/90; for preassumption votes on the watered-down version of the revenue bill, see *Annals,* 6/14/90, 6/18/90, 6/21/90. Madison's insistence on discriminating between "original holders" and "speculators" took over both the debates and much later discussion of the finance plan—misleadingly, as far as both Hamilton and many populists and republicans were concerned. (The staunchly republican Maclay expresses his frustration with discrimination; he thought the only republican thing to do with debt was extinguish it.) For lucid and informative discussion of the issue, see Elkins and McKitrick.

Speculation fever. All writers on the period talk about it, and many note Maclay's disgust over it, but E. J. Ferguson, providing detail on the goals of speculators and the machinations of Morris and associates during the debates, is again the indispensable source for understanding it. See also Elkins and McKitrick, who elucidate Madison's break with Hamilton largely in terms of the speculation frenzy.

Assumption of state debts and passage of the whiskey tax. For assumption, see *Statutes at Large,* "An Act Making Provision for the Debt of the United States," 8/4/1790; and "An Act Making Further Provision for the Payment of the Debt of the United States," 8/5/90. Ellis, in *Founding Brothers,* brings to life the dinner at which Jefferson oversaw deals on the capital and assumption; see also Elkins and McKitrick, as well as Mitchell's chapters on the debates. For Hamilton's arguments in favor of excise, see his report of 12/13/90, in his *Papers.* One of his arguments that I cite here—that the tax was on a luxury—he actually made in the original "Report" of January 1790 and revived when responding to antitax petitions in 1792. Slaughter cites Hamilton's allies Fisher Ames and Tench Coxe on the understanding among Hamiltonians that assumption could pass only if artificially separated from the funding mechanism—and that when passed, assumption would give Congress no choice but to pass the excise and new import duties.

Whiskey and the tax. "An Act Repealing, after the Last Day of June Next, the Duties Heretofore Laid upon Distilled Spirits Imported from Abroad, and Laying Others in their Stead, and Also upon Spirits Distilled within the United States and for Appropriating the Same," 3/3/1792, *Statutes at Large.* It is Bouton's thesis that in the eighteenth century ordinary people in the countryside had a far more cogent understanding of finance than most people have today. Instructions for whiskey making can be found in Smiley and in Nixon and McKaw. Rorabaugh and Kellner have much detail on drinking and distilling in eighteenth- and nineteenth-century America. The reduction of grain to whiskey as a means of transport is cited by Baldwin, based in part on H. H. Brackenridge's "Thoughts on the Excise Law," also explicated in H. M. Brackenridge's opening chapter. I've relied largely on Fennell to develop an understanding of the rural distilling business, whiskey's use as currency, the relationship of the British government to large and small distilling, Hamilton's thinking regarding gallon and dollar numbers in the tax, and the concentration of distilling in the Monongahela area. Hamilton's ideas about government-encouraged industry are best explicated by Elkins and McKitrick, Chapter Seven; also see Slaughter, Chapter Eight, on Hamilton, the distilling business, and the whiskey tax.

Chapter Four: Herman Husband

Herman Husband and the Whiskey Rebellion. Jones's unpublished dissertation is the only full-scale scholarly biography of Husband. Lazenby's trade book, often fanciful and unsupported by scholarly apparatus, has been out of print for decades. Lazenby's correspondence with Husband descendants and her notes on Husband family lore, in the Darlington Library of the University of Pittsburgh, include copies of docket notices for Husband's arrests in North Carolina and letters from Emmy Husband. Other sources include Schoepf, H. H. Brackenridge in *Incidents,* and most important, the works of Husband that I've cited, especially his unpublished manuscript exegesis of the Book of Daniel, in the John Scull Archive.

Husband's role in the rebellion is important yet obscure. While Lazenby is committed to the notion that Husband was not involved, Julian Boyd's scathing review of Lazenby's book calls Husband a "powerful influence" on the rebellion. Jones discusses Husband's involvement but doesn't see Husband's late-career sermons as preaching violent insurrection. It is Fennell, in devoting a major chapter to Husband, and presenting his late work as urging outright insurrection, who links Husband's late sermons to the decisive shift in the rebellion from a series of blackface attacks to an unmasked, militia-organized insurrection.

I follow Fennell, as have Bouton and Holt; Holt also gives attention to the legal issues involved in Husband's being prosecuted for seditious speech. Evidence for Husband's leadership includes depositions by Benjamin Wells and Philip Reagan, since lost but referred to in a letter of 10/1/1794 from Hamilton's deputy Tench Coxe to William Rawle, in the Tench Coxe Letters, National Archives: Coxe mentions only Husband, Husband's associate Filson, and David Bradford (see later chapters) as leaders he recalls being named in that deposition. As further discussed in Chapter Ten, Washington and Hamilton, evidently responding to information given in depositions, and possibly also given by Neville and Marshal Lenox, placed Husband at the top of the list of high-value suspects. Hamilton risked the alarm and flight of David Bradford and others, and worried Washington on that account, by moving early on Husband; Husband was sent with the other Bedford suspects directly to Philadelphia. Washington refers only to Husband, Bradford, and a Mr. Guthrie as high-value suspects in a letter to Hamilton of 10/26/1794, and by name only to Husband in a letter to Hamilton of 10/31/94. Chapter Nine of Brackenridge's *Incidents* describes the hopes of many Parkinson's Ferry attendees as involving extreme restructuring of society, along the lines of Husband's late sermons (with which Brackenridge seems unfamiliar).

Still, Husband's appearance at Parkinson's Ferry is the sole direct evidence of his serving in a leadership role—and at that point he was working with Brackenridge and Gallatin to urge moderation. With Fennell, I connect the themes of the late sermons, especially specific references to citizen militias in *XIV Sermons on the Characters of Jacob's Fourteen Sons*, Sermon Seven, to the Mingo Creek Association's mobilizing those militias not only against promoters of the whiskey tax but also against anyone at the Forks who appeared to benefit from or comply with the national finance plan. Given Washington's and Hamilton's thinking about Husband, and the government's prosecuting him for sedition, it seems overwhelmingly likely that those sermons played a direct and important part in the radical activities of the Forks militias in the summer of 1794.

The Great Awakening and the American millennium. I am informed and inspired by Heimert in emphasizing the unifying effects of Whitefield's tours and the impact of postmillennial evangelicism on ideas about social justice in an independent America; Heimert also deemphasizes fire-and-brimstone preaching in the Awakening and presents rationalist ideas as serving the interests of the creditor class. Other sources, primary and secondary, for evangelical, apocalyptic, and related thinking include Edwards, Lowman, Newton, Williams, Tracy, and Niebuhr. Nash, in *The Urban Crucible*, Chapter Eight, is illuminating on Whitefield and his successors and makes strong connections between evangelicism and the popular movement. Noll describes the soldiers taking Whitefield's garments.

Early Quakers, ranting, other nonconformism. Rexroth is a good source on dissenting sects; Schama's volume 2 gives a lively overview; "English Dissenters" at exlibris.org is a deft and handy reference. Much Quaker writing of the seventeenth and eighteenth centuries condemns the taint of the "ranting spirit."

The North Carolina Regulation. I'm showing the regulation through the narrowest of prisms. Husband gives his idea of an impartial account in *A Fan for Fanning* . . . . For further reading, good sources include Kars and the concise "Commemorative Souvenir Program of the Bicentennial of the Battle of Alamance." In the exegesis of Daniel cited above, Husband describes his reaction to the Stamp Act protestors. It is Jones's speculation that before the Battle of Alamance, Husband involved himself in negotiations with provincial troops.

Husband in Pennsylvania. For Husband on sex, marriage, fidelity, and parenthood, see his interpretation of "The Song of Songs," following errata to *Sermon to the Bucks and Hinds of America*, in a collection of three publications at the library of the Historical Society of Western Pennsylvania. Husband's exact family situation in the Bedford area is unclear: Two of his elder sons left to return to North Carolina; other children lived with Husband and Emmy in the Glades. The Woods political ring is covered in Jones and Bouton. For Husband's surveying and mapping, including his descriptions of clothing himself and his horse and the size of fallen trees, see his undated letter to Governor Mifflin in the John Scull Archive. Husband sets out his monetary theories in *Proposals to Amend and Perfect*; he describes his vision of the Alleghenies and the New Jerusalem in *A Sermon to the Bucks and Hinds*; he expands on the Allegheny topography with reference to Daniel's visions in the unpublished manuscript cited above. The maps are referred to by Schoepf; one of Husband's hand-drawn maps is in his letter to Mifflin; see also his own plates to *Bucks and Hinds* and *Dialogue between an Assembly-Man and a Convention-Man*. Schoepf is the source for Husband's planning a trip to Canada (it's not certain that the trip was made).

Husband's constitution. Nothing in Husband's work is more open to interpretation than *Proposals to Amend and Perfect, A Sermon to the Bucks and Hinds,* and *XIV Sermons on the Characters of Jacob's Fourteen Sons,* where Husband sets out his not always internally consistent ideas about constitutional government. My interpretation is influenced by those of Jones and Fennell. That Husband was becoming frustrated after ratification of the U.S. Constitution can be seen in some of the inconsistencies: As Fennell notes, *To Amend and Perfect* and *Bucks and Hinds* are more limited in scope; *XIV Sermons* offers a larger and more ambitious plan, based in part on Husband's disappointment over the U.S. Constitution. My presentation of Husband as unique in prefiguring the modern welfare state combines Husband's constitutional writings with some of his other ideas, referred to elsewhere in this chapter.

Husband and the militias. Sermon Seven of *XIV Sermons* makes Husband's most explicit call to action against oppression and his most explicit connection between existing militia structures and the means of throwing off the yoke of tyranny. There is no direct evidence to show that Husband personally inspired the rebel takeover of local civic and military functions that I explore in the next chapter (Husband may also have been observing such activities and approving them). Yet as explained in the first note on this chapter, Wells's and Reagan's testimony, the intensity that Hamilton and Washington brought to capturing Husband, and Husband's prosecution for sedition suggest that the call for militia action in *XIV Sermons* and the emergence of the Mingo Creek Association, described in Chapter Six, were directly related.

CHAPTER FIVE: THE NEVILLE CONNECTION

Administration of the whiskey tax. In Hamilton's *Papers*: Washington to Hamilton, 3/15/1791; Hamilton's "Circular," 9/30/91.

The Nevilles. Background on John Neville comes from Felton, the

Craig-Neville Papers, Findley, Baldwin, and McClure. H. H. Brackenridge in *Incidents* and Henry Marie Brackenridge both give vivid pictures of Presley Neville and Kirkpatrick. Background on Craig is in the Craig-Neville Papers. The description of Bower Hill is based on Felton, Baldwin, and my observation of the parking lot on the mansion's former site. "Diversified commercial farm" is Fennell's term for Bower Hill; my description of the Neville Connection as an army-contracting operation, and as monopolizers of the whiskey trade, is also based largely on Fennell.

The military buildup. For the politics of the first U.S.-Indian war, leading to the Militia Act, see Kohn. Progress—or lack of it—in constructing Fort Fayette can be followed in Henry Knox's increasingly exasperated letters to quartermaster-entrepreneur Isaac Craig and Craig's evasively polite replies, in the Isaac Craig Papers and the Craig-Neville Papers. In *Incidents,* Brackenridge refers to Pitt's dismantling.

Attacks on collectors. The John Connor story is told by Findley, who claims that it was Neville's idea to send Connor to serve the warrants and accuses Neville of intending the service to be unsuccessful. The attack on Wilson is reported by Neville to Clymer in a letter of 11/17/1791, in the Wolcott Papers—in which Neville also calls for armed force.

Brackenridge in politics. My description of the Green Tree petition is based on resolutions of the meeting, *Pennsylvania Archives.* Brackenridge's backstory is drawn mainly from Newlin and Marder. For Madison's ideas about representation, I'm inspired by Wills, in *Explaining America,* Part Four. The story of Brackenridge's meeting Sabina Wolfe is told in most Brackenridge sources; the possible visual effect of Sabina's leaping the fence was suggested via e-mail by Barbara Bockrath, a living-history expert and secretary of the Oliver Miller Homestead Association. For Brackenridge's political writing, see his *Gazette Publications.*

Hamilton's response to complaints. For Brackenridge's argument against the whiskey tax, see "Thoughts on the Excise Law" in Marder's edition of *Incidents.* It is the insight of Elkins and McKitrick (p. 282) that the creative phase of Hamilton's career approached its eclipse in 1792. For Hamilton's response to the petitions, see his "Report on the Difficulties in the Execution of the Act Laying Duties on Distilled Spirits," 3/6/1792. I rely in part on Fennell's analyses of the effects on small distillers of Hamilton's proposed changes in the law and the workings of the commissary system; Fennell cites Albert Gallatin, as Jefferson's treasury secretary, for the ultimate reduction of real tax to a sixth of a cent. The commissary system would not take full effect immediately—but Hamilton's "Report on Opposition to Internal Duties," 8/5/94, makes clear that he saw new army-buying rules as part of the excise enforcement efforts of 1792.

The tax law of 1792. In *Statutes at Large*: "An Act Concerning the Duties on Spirits Distilled within the United States," 5/8/1792. Debate can be followed in *Annals of Congress,* 4/30/92; some congressmen saw the purpose of the new bill as making it easier for people to pay. Findley is the source for his own objections to the tax, the debate, and his feeling that he'd made an enemy of Hamilton.

Hamilton's eagerness to use force. As the next chapter shows in detail, in the fall of 1792, Hamilton was pushing Washington for a military solution; as early as that July, in response to complaints about noncompliance in North Carolina, Hamilton asked about the readiness of the Virginia militia to act against rioters in North Carolina; in that letter he says, "The thing must be brought to an issue; and will be" (*Papers,* 7/25/92). This was two years before rebel militias attacked Bower Hill and marched on Braddock's Field; tax resistance had involved only protest meetings, failure to register, and a few criminal acts. Hamilton was linking nationalist finance policy and the domestic use of military force as early as the Newburgh crisis of 1783; for his thoughts at the Constitutional Convention on the necessarily coercive role of government and arms, see Farrand, Yates's and Madison's notes, 6/18/87. Kohn is informative on tendencies toward militarism in Hamilton's career and explicit in describing Hamilton as pursuing as early as 1792 the use of military power to enforce the whiskey tax. In Chapter Five of *Founding Brothers,* Ellis connects Hamilton's late-career military ambitions with his behavior in suppressing the Whiskey Rebellion. For more on this issue, see Chapter Nine.

CHAPTER SIX: TOM THE TINKER

The Mingo Creek Association. I follow Fennell's description of the militias as offering the only official forum for public service and allowing ordinary people to achieve leadership. McClure's Chapter Nine is the best source for the development, activities, and roots of the association. While its charter and resolutions, including the duties it imposed on militia companies and the forming of an extralegal court, were not officially signed until 1794— copies are in the Rawle Papers—Faulkner's experience shows the group operating from the time of the Robert Johnson attack and growing throughout 1792. The association called itself by many names; for clarity, I use only one. The association can be confused with the more upscale and far less serious Washington County democratic society. While both Baldwin and Slaughter place the Mingo Creek group within the French-inspired national craze for democratic societies—Elkins and McKitrick do too, while also suggesting other antecedents—McClure's scholarship, which is uniquely thorough, supports my sense of the association's deeper background in the rural popular-finance movement of preceding decades. Bouton (especially in "A Road Closed") and Holt see the association as spearheading popular democracy by supplying an extralegal alternative to the official court system; Bouton points with admiration to the resulting drop-off in suits brought in the state court. But as this "court" was operated by a self-appointed body that deployed gang attacks while requiring would-be litigants to appeal to its own, extralegally elected judges, I see the situation differently. For skeptical and penetrating discussion of how the local, spontaneous political action often prized by progressives tends to treat the rights of minorities and dissenters, see Wills in *A Necessary Evil*.

Threats against William Faulkner. See Faulkner's undated deposition, taken on behalf of Clymer, in the Whiskey Rebellion Collection. The source for Faulkner's search for deserters comes from Hamilton's "Report on Opposition to Internal Duties" of 8/5/1794, evidently via Neville; Faulkner doesn't refer to that reason for his being in the countryside. Baldwin and Slaughter err in placing the threats later than the second convention and also, oddly, later than the actual ransacking of Faulkner's home; the depositions of Faulkner and others clarify the chronology; McClure's reading supports my own. While Hamilton's "Report" says that Faulkner's letter was published on the twenty-first, the letter was actually published on the twenty-fifth, as Slaughter notes. Findley, who must have it that the western country was peaceful until Clymer's visit, claims that Clymer took false testimony from Faulkner; that allegation isn't specific, and even if true, wouldn't invalidate Faulkner's entire story. The physical description of Parkinson is drawn from Findley and from Brackenridge in *Incidents*.

The second Pittsburgh convention. No useful documentation of the delegating process exists; H. M. Brackenridge states that the second convention was delegated but poorly organized, its representation unclear. Slaughter and Fennell, for differing reasons, see the second convention as resembling the first in remaining distinct from incidents of violence; neither writer looks closely at the significance of Faulkner's deposition. The chronology in the note above identifies second-convention attendees Parkinson and John Hamilton as leaders of the active Mingo Creek Association; the convention's newly radical demands and explicit strategy of organizing and regulating the broad community clearly reflect the influence of the association leaders. That the resolutions were followed by the fulfillment of preconvention threats against Faulkner further bears out the dominance of the association in the convention. Regarding Gallatin: I touch very lightly on him in this book, relying mainly on Brackenridge and Baldwin.

The Faulkner attacks. The sources are depositions given by Myers, Goudy, and other soldiers in Faulkner's command, and by Margaret Faulkner and Margaret Campbell, all in the Whiskey Rebellion Collection.

Hamilton and Washington on military suppression. For Hamilton's expectation of the failure of law enforcement, his urging military force, and his focus on the Forks as an example, see Hamilton's *Papers*: Hamilton to Washington, 9/1/1792; Hamilton to Coxe, 9/1/92; Hamilton to Jay, 9/3/92; Hamilton to Washington, 9/9/92; Randolph to Hamilton, 9/8/92. In Washington's *Writings*, see Washington to Hamilton, 9/7/92, 9/16/92, 9/17/92; and the Proclamation of 9/15/92.

Clymer's mission. The story can be partly constructed from the Addison-Clymer correspondence in the Wolcott Papers; Clymer's letters to Hamilton of September and October 1792 and Hamilton's letter to Coxe, 9/1/92, in Hamilton's *Papers*; and Findley. I largely follow Slaughter's entertaining account. In his letter to Hamilton of 10/10/92, Clymer describes the Forks as generally disaffected; on 9/28/92, before his discussion with Neville, his reported impression had been more moderate.

The Wells attacks. The major source is the Benjamin Wells Claims, a series of depositions and letters scattered about the House Records of the National Archives, comprising Benjamin Wells's claims against Congress for damages sustained during the rebellion, which Wells pursued for decades. Fennell appears to have first discovered the relevance of this archive to the rebellion; it contains eyewitness descriptions of attacks described in this chapter and in Chapter Nine. The November visit is described in a separate deposition of Wells apparently included by Neville in a letter to Clymer (though not clearly connected to a dated letter, at least in the microfilm version), in the Wolcott Papers.

Tom the Tinker. The raising of liberty poles, the sending and publishing of Tom's notes, the hanging of Neville in effigy, the barn burnings, and the still shootings are documented in all sources on the rebellion, largely synthesizing Brackenridge's *Incidents*, Neville's letters to Clymer, Gallatin's statement to U.S. Attorney Rawle in *Incidents*, and Hamilton's "Report on Opposition to Internal Duties" of 8/5/1794. Neville describes his fight with Long and precautionary measures at Bower Hill in a letter to Clymer of 3/21/94, in the Wolcott Papers.

CHAPTER SEVEN: THE HILLS GIVE LIGHT TO THE VALES

Washington, Hamilton, and Randolph. The flap can be traced in Hamilton's *Papers,* including editorial notes with Randolph's correspondence: Hamilton to Muhlenberg, 12/16/1793; Hamilton to the select committee, 3/24/94, 4/1/94; Baldwin to Hamilton, 3/29/94; the committee to Hamilton, 4/5/94; Hamilton to Washington, 3/24/94, 4/1/94, 4/8/94, 4/21/94, 4/23/94, 4/25/94; Randolph to Washington, 3/23/94, 4/1/94, 4/23/94; Madison to Jefferson, 3/26/94; Washington to Hamilton, 4/8/94; 4/22/94, 4/24/94; 4/27/94. For more on Randolph in the cabinet, see Elkins and McKitrick. It is the view of Flexner, among others, that after Jefferson's departure from the cabinet, Hamilton became especially dominant. In the cabinet's response to the memo referred to below, in the Tench Coxe Letters, William Bradford begins to emerge as a shrewd political player in Hamilton's camp, advising immediate restraint in the service of ultimate high-federalist success.

The Washington County democratic society. A copy of the remonstrance is in the Rawle Papers; a circular cabinet memo of 4/14/1794 discussing ways of responding to the remonstrance is in the Tench Coxe Letters. On the French influence and the craze for democratic societies, see Elkins and McKitrick—but McClure's Chapter Nine is the best source for key distinctions, which Elkins and McKitrick only partially make, between the Mingo Creek Association and the Washington County democratic society. (See also my notes to Chapter Six, above.) For an example of French fever in the west, see Brackenridge's "Caput" essay in the Marder edition of *Incidents*. All of Washington's biographers explore Washington's extreme disapprobation of the societies; for Washington's thoughts on the Washington County society in particular, see Washington to Randolph, 4/11/1794, in Washington's *Writings*.

Washington and the west. Slaughter has a groundbreaking chapter on this important subject. Knollenberg's Chapter Fourteen is concise on Washington's licit and illicit efforts to engross western land. For Washington's feelings about rent and sales and his relationship with his agent John Cannon, see in *Writings* his letters to Cannon of 4/13/1787, 6/25/90, 9/7/91, 4/19/92, 6/27/95; and to Presley Neville, 6/16/94. Cannon chaired the second Pittsburgh convention and signed the circular calling out the militia (described in the next chapter).

Hamilton's analysis of the resistance. It was reflexive among some elite politicians—amplified, perhaps, after ratification—to describe popular uprisings as caused by designing individuals, and to refrain from crediting the people themselves with genuine cause for dissatisfaction or with the ability to analyze and organize effectively. As discussed above, Hamilton did not explicitly give ordinary people credit for having either a finance philosophy or strong organizational abilities. But his actions and decisions, as narrated in this and later chapters; his knowledge of the Mingo Creek Association paperwork in Rawle's files; his history in the confederation Congress; and his general perspicacity indicate to me that despite publicly concurring in Washington's assumptions, Hamilton identified the energized, often anonymous militiamen at the Forks, not a few upscale politicians, as the real source of tax resistance. His activities at the Forks, described in Chapter Ten, bear this out.

The June 5 law and the May 31 docket. For an example of local outrage over suspects' being forced to stand trial far from their neighborhoods, see the lead article by "A Citizen" in the *Pittsburgh Gazette*, 12/10/1791, sent by Neville to Clymer, in the Wolcott Papers. Baldwin is the major source for the contents of the May docket; Slaughter discusses the invalid dates and William Bradford's statements about the purpose of serving writs, citing Bradford's letter to Boudinot of 8/1/94, in the Wallace Papers. Findley, believing Hamilton tampered with due process by deliberately having the writs served under the old law, lashes out against Hamilton; Hamiltonians like Mitchell and Miller decline to consider the issue seriously. Both Slaughter and Baldwin do raise the tampering issue but decline to make a judgment (Slaughter's notes are far more critical of Hamilton than his text). Baldwin seems to stack the deck against Hamilton, implying that easing trial rules was the main purpose of the new law and that Hamilton thus violated the law's major thrust; Brookhiser plays the same idea the other way, crediting Hamilton personally with having eased the trial rules and suggesting, with Miller, that the rebels responded to a concession with greater recalcitrance. In fact, the new law had mainly to do with tightening enforcement (see *Statutes at Large*, 6/5/94). Baldwin also misreads Hamilton's "Report" of 8/5/94 as suggesting that imminent easing of trial rules prompted rebels to act; in fact Hamilton refers in the "Report" only to the law's tightened enforcement.

But whether the May filing was technically illicit seems off the point. There can be little doubt that Hamilton deliberately had the writs filed to beat passage of the new law. Had he wished removed from these warrants what was widely considered the most onerous burden—which Congress was even then removing by law—he would have had it removed, either by not pressing Rawle to file warrants before the law changed on June 6 or by asking Rawle—in the almost impossibly unlikely event that warrants were filed without Hamilton's direct supervision—to bring them in line with the relaxed rules.

Shutting down tax offices. Primary sources for the Wells situation are in the Wells Claims; the John Lynn attack and Neville's frustration with federal inaction are documented in Neville's letters to Clymer of 6/13/1794 and 6/20/94, in the Wolcott Papers.

Serving the writs. For Brackenridge's meeting with Lenox: Brackenridge's *Incidents*. The description of serving writs is based on Lenox's September 1794 report to Hamilton, in both the Wolcott Papers and the *Pennsylvania Archives*. Background on Lenox is drawn from his obituary, "Another Revolutionary Hero Gone," and his resume in "Davis-Lenox House." Henry Marie Brackenridge refers to the use of scythes during the harvest.

The confrontation at the Miller farm. My sources are Lenox's report, cited above, and the statements of William Miller in Brackenridge's *Incidents*. Fennell gives a somewhat different version, based on Thomas Williams's deposition and Thomas Porter's trial testimony in the Neville Papers.

The first attack on Bower Hill. The attack occurred early in the morning of the sixteenth. For the election of leaders, the march, and the attack itself, the (conflicting) sources are Holcroft's statements to U.S. Attorney Rawle and William Miller's narrative, both in Brackenridge's *Incidents*; and Neville's letter to Tench Coxe, 7/18/1794, in "New Light on the Whiskey Insurrection." As Baldwin notes, irreducible discrepancies abound. Rebels wanted to minimize their defeat, Neville to maximize it. Neville says the posse numbered about one hundred, sixty with guns, the rest with sticks and stones; Holcroft mentions thirty-seven guns; Miller counts thirty men, fifteen with guns, of which six were working. The women's role in defending the house is described by a Craig descendant in a footnote to Neville's letter, based on the memory of Harriet Craig, the Nevilles' granddaughter. I use the generic term "guns" because no source is specific on how the general was armed. Both Holcroft and Miller claim retreat was called only after a horn from the house signaled the slaves to fire on the rebels from the rear; Neville says that while his slaves were trained for defense, they'd already gone to the fields; he did use the slaves the next day and had no compunction about acknowledging it. That the Oliver Miller who was killed during the attack was William Miller's teenaged nephew and not, as most writers on the subject have believed, William's father, is clarified by Hartman, who gives seemingly irrefutable support for the clarification.

The second attack. The meeting of Brackenridge and Presley Neville occurred on the seventeenth, the morning after the first attack; the second attack took place in the late afternoon of the seventeenth. For Brackenridge's activities through the end of this chapter, I rely on Brackenridge in *Incidents*. The statement to U.S. Attorney Rawle by the militiaman James Therr (according to McClure, a misprint for "Kerr," a suspect named later on Alexander Hamilton's list), in *Incidents*, is a primary source for rebel regrouping and planning. Baldwin believes that Benjamin Parkinson, like John Hamilton, declined to serve at Bower Hill; Fennell has followed that assertion; but as McClure notes, Therr/Kerr mentions Parkinson (by initials) as a member of the committee overseeing the attack, a description that better accords with Parkinson's earlier and later roles. The conditions under which Bradford, Marshall, and John Hamilton declined to serve are unclear: Hamilton seems likely to have been present at Couch's Fort; Bradford and Marshall are more likely to have simply not shown up. I've drawn information on the McFarlane brothers largely from Hassler, supported by Findley and Brackenridge. *Incidents* includes David Hamilton's statement to Rawle, with a version of the parleys with Kirkpatrick. Kirkpatrick gives his own point of view of the parleys, the attack, and his capture and escape, in a letter to Washington of 7/28/1794, Wolcott Papers. Neville's losses in the burning and mayhem are listed in *American State Papers*, "Claims," volume 1. Other key sources are Lenox's September report to Hamilton and Neville's letter to Coxe, cited above: Neville says the rebels shot the horses (the claims also list a cow and a breeding sow); Lenox is the source for his own and Presley Neville's treatment by and escape from the rebels.

Negotiations and escape. McFarlane's funeral took place on the eighteenth. Main sources for this section: Brackenridge's *Incidents*; Findley; Lenox's report to Hamilton, cited above; Craig to Knox, 7/25/1794, Isaac Craig Papers. The vessel in which Neville and Lenox escaped is called a small boat by Craig, a barge by Lenox.

Chapter Eight: A New Sodom

The Mingo church meeting. The meeting took place on the twenty-third. The main source is Brackenridge's *Incidents*, which presents depositions and vouchers from Pittsburghers who attended the meeting and from the rebel David Hamilton. Bouton, in "A Road Closed," explicates David Bradford's involvement in road closings; the radical Washington County resolutions of 1791, appointing Bradford a delegate to the Green Tree meeting, appear in a copy of the *Pittsburgh Gazette*, sent by Neville to Clymer, in the Wolcott Papers. Addison's letter to Brackenridge of 1/18/1795, *Pennsylvania Archives*, states that Bradford and Marshall discussed robbing the mail on the way to the meeting.

The robbing of the mail; the militia circulars. I've taken the story mainly from Alexander Fulton's long, self-justifying letter to Washington, in the Whiskey Rebellion Collection. Copies of the Bradford committee's circular, dated 7/28/1794, calling out the militias, as well as the countermand of 7/30/94, are in both the Yeates Papers and the Whiskey Rebellion Collection. Findley is the source for the Washington County courthouse meeting.

Braddock's Field. The march took place on August 1. In *Incidents*, Brackenridge covers the mood of Pittsburgh and the plans of the committee; the other key source for action before, during, and after the muster is the report of Wilkins, Sr., to Irvine, *Pennsylvania Archives*, where the town committee's resolutions also appear. Fennell's studies demonstrate the paucity of still owners at the muster. Discrepancies: As Baldwin points out, Wilkins estimates there were five thousand to six thousand men at Braddock's Field and is likely to have made the best count; he'd been an officer in the revolution and was counting while men were strung out on the march. Brackenridge estimates as many as seven thousand men on the field; according to him there was some coming and going, far more coming than going. Baldwin also gives Gallatin's estimate of fifteen hundred to two thousand, which seems uselessly low, a probable attempt to minimize the significance of the action.

The Wells and Webster attacks. Reagan's and the Wellses' abduction and trials and the destruction of Benjamin Wells's home are documented by Wells himself and by eyewitnesses John and Jeremiah Woodruff in the Wells Claims, HR 21A–G3.1. The Webster events are described by Findley.

The position of moderates. In *Incidents,* Brackenridge outlines his own and other moderates' thinking and describes being prevailed upon to serve at Parkinson's Ferry. Brackenridge's letter to Tench Coxe is in the Tench Coxe Papers, along with Coxe's response and an interesting further letter from Brackenridge, showing rising anxiety.

The Parkinson's Ferry congress. The flag is described by Brackenridge in *Incidents,* by Gallatin in his statement to U.S. Attorney Rawle in *Incidents,* and in the federal commissioners' letter to Randolph of 8/17/1794. Gideon, a vexillologist with a special interest in the rebellion and local history, reviews those references and cites other sources on the slogans and symbols flying from liberty poles, arguing persuasively that the flag now displayed at the Century Inn in Scenery Hill, Pennsylvania, widely regarded as having been flown by the Whiskey Rebels, is unlikely to have been a flag of the rebellion—and might have been a regimental flag of the suppressing federal army. For the broad, radical social agenda and commitment to secession and war held by many attendees of the congress, see Brackenridge in *Incidents.*

CHAPTER NINE: TALKING

The 7/25 cabinet meeting and Wilson's certification. Kohn notes that while there is no record of a cabinet meeting on the twenty-fifth, the meeting is evidenced in Randolph's letter to Washington of 8/5/1794; the editors of Hamilton's *Papers* agree that an undocumented meeting took place prior to the documented meeting of 8/2/94. Kohn cites William Bradford's letter of 8/1/94 to Elias Boudinot as evincing genuine suspense over Wilson's agreeing to certify, but Holt, noting that Wilson made no independent investigation, sees the certification as a rubber stamp; Randolph in his 8/5/94 letter to Washington sees it the same way.

The 8/2 meeting with Mifflin. See *American State Papers,* misc., volume 1, for minutes; there also see Mifflin to Washington, 8/12/1794, for Mifflin's recollection that Washington viewed the state militia as a "preliminary measure." Tinkcom is my source for Mifflin's personality and political career, as well as for state-federal disputes on Presque Isle.

Hamilton's report. "Report on Opposition to Internal Duties," 8/5/1794, Hamilton's *Papers.*

Madison, Hamilton, and force. See Farrand, Madison's notes, 5/31/1787. Kohn, whose interpretation inspires my discussion here, also cites Madison's remarks at the Virginia ratifying convention. In 1787, Hamilton and

Madison agreed that coercion—as the ultimate foundation of government, once law has failed—cannot operate effectively in a confederated system but requires national government, which thus requires at least a small regular army, to be used against rioters only when "the penal system and the courts, marshals, posse comitatus, militia" (Kohn, p. 76) have failed. Whether Hamilton ever concurred in Madison's underlying rationale for the principle is unclear to me. As early as the summer of 1792, Hamilton was defining such conflicts as existing between the national government and the whole people of a region; by early 1799 (see Chapter Eleven, below) he was imagining the federal government's attacking the state of Virginia, a condition of civil war that national government had once been intended to avoid. For Madison's own development from positions once shared with Hamilton, see especially Elkins and McKitrick.

The cabinet debate and the decision to negotiate. For Randolph's views on negotiation, see Randolph to Washington, 8/5/1794, Washington's *Papers*. For the Knox-Hamilton view, see Hamilton to Washington, 8/2/94, in Hamilton's *Papers*, and Knox to Washington, 8/4/94, in Washington's *Papers*. Holt bluntly calls the negotiations "sham"; Kohn lists the purposes of negotiation as dividing the rebels, gathering intelligence, and gaining time to prepare the public for invasion. But Kohn also says that federal negotiating may have been sincere until August 24. His own argument seems to suggest otherwise: as he pointedly notes, the commission wrote its most damning report, calling for military suppression, on August 17, before even starting negotiations, in which it acted as if holding off troops were still an option. Bradford's plan for the negotiations, which went into effect as early as August 6, when Washington appointed the commission, was never intended to avoid a military solution: for Bradford's correspondence and actions during this phase, see various notes on the commission, below. Craig's correspondence with Knox and Hamilton can be found in the Isaac Craig Papers; the letter I cite is from Hamilton on 8/23/94. Chernow cites, as evidence that Hamilton never wanted a military suppression, Hamilton's note to the commissioners of 8/8/94, in Hamilton's *Papers*—which does permit the commissioners to discuss with the rebels changes in the tax law and expresses the desire for peaceful resolution. Yet the note also passes on the suggestion of Neville that rebels show their submission by publicly asking Robert Johnson to resume his office, a suggestion that, had the commission made it, would have inspired the opposite of submission, as Neville and Hamilton knew. Much else in the primary record, for this and other chapters, reveals Hamilton's early and late eagerness to use force; see also my notes on Hamilton, Washington, and military force in Chapters Four and Six. Chernow's view, like that of many other Hamilton biographers, is the official one of the administration.

"Civil war." Gibson to Mifflin, 7/18/1794, *Pennsylvania Archives.*

Knox's orders. "Secretary of War to Governor Mifflin," 8/7/1794, *Pennsylvania Archives.*

Washington's proclamation. Washington's *Writings,* 8/7/1794.

The arrival of Neville and Lenox. Lenox's report, *Pennsylvania Archives.*

The commissioners on the road. The story is drawn from drafts of letters and other documents in the Yeates Papers and the Wallace Papers, Historical Society of Pennsylvania, and from Bradford's and the commission's letters, reports, and log in the Whiskey Rebellion Collection. Much of the commission's official reporting is also collected in the *Pennsylvania Archives* and *American State Papers,* misc., volume 1. Bradford is surprisingly blunt (in a letter of 8/8/1794, in the collection) in describing to Randolph his assurances to Neville and Lenox regarding the real purpose of the mission.

Knox's departure. It is Kohn's speculation that, as Washington and Hamilton did not see Knox as a quick administrator, Washington's response to Knox's request for leave to go to Maine—8/8/1794, in Washington's *Writings*—reflects a prior understanding; also that, in meetings about the rebellion, Hamilton encouraged Knox's desire to inspect lands personally.

Radicals and moderates at Parkinson's Ferry. As noted above, in *Incidents* Brackenridge gives his impression of the broad social agenda and commitment to secession and war held by many attendees. He also describes his interactions with Gallatin and Husband. Findley praises Gallatin as an openly moderating influence. Fennell describes the radical scope of what she terms the Parkinson Ferry "resolutions," although she bases her discussion on the report of the commissioners of 9/24/1794, *American State Papers,* misc., volume 1, which details the congress's socially radical demands as relayed by the committee. Fennell also discusses the Virginia militia units' drafting resolutions focusing on class issues and defining republican government as one that provides for the poor. For more on Virginia's involvement, see Barksdale and Lee.

The Commission in Pittsburgh. See the commission report of 8/17/1794, *Pennsylvania Archives,* and Bradford's private letter to Washington of the same date, in the Whiskey Rebellion Collection.

Brackenridge's letter. Brackenridge to Coxe, 8/8/1794, Tench Coxe Papers.

Postdating Lee's orders. Hamilton to Lee, 8/24/1794, Hamilton's *Papers.*

"Tully." Hamilton's *Papers,* 8/23/1794, 9/2/94.

Federal-state debate. The argument can be followed in *American State Papers,* misc., volume 1, August letters of Mifflin to Randolph and Randolph's replies. In the decisive letter of 8/30/1794, Hamilton is writing for Randolph: see Hamilton's *Papers.*

Brackenridge and the commission. Brackenridge's *Incidents.* For Gallatin's view of Brackenridge's tactics with the rebels, see Gallatin's statement to U.S. Attorney Rawle, also in *Incidents.*

The negotiations and the deal. American State Papers, misc., volume 1, commission report of 9/24/1794, with copies of correspondence between the commission and the committee. The complete original correspondence can be found in the Whiskey Rebellion Collection; draft versions are in the Yeates Papers and the Wallace Papers. The tactical benefit of ignoring the Virginia delegation is noted by Bradford to Hamilton, 8/23/94, in the collection; in a letter of 8/22/94, the committee makes clear its eagerness to comply and its belief that compliance will prevent military action. Given lags in east-west communication, the promise to hold back troops at least until after the referendum was academic at best: the commission's letter to the cabinet of the seventeenth, urging immediate military action, didn't arrive in Philadelphia until the twenty-third—accelerating military preparations on the twenty-fourth, the very day a deal for compliance was being struck with the rebels. When the cabinet received word that Bradford had promised to hold off troops until September 11, the effort to raise troops was under way; as Bradford knew, they couldn't have marched earlier than they did in any event.

The Brownsville meeting. Brackenridge's *Incidents;* letter from the commissioners to Randolph, 8/30/1794, Whiskey Rebellion Collection.

The spread of rebellion, patriotic fervor, and the oath signing. On the spread of rebellion, I follow Baldwin, Slaughter, and Fennell. Bradford's letter to Yeates on the new patriotism, 9/19/1794, is in the Tench Coxe Papers. Both Brackenridge and Findley describe the day of the referendum. Returns are in the Whiskey Rebellion Collection; letters to and from Ross regarding the returns are in the Wallace Papers.

The final commission report, 9/24/1794. American State Papers, misc., volume 1.

Hamilton's desire to accompany the troops. Hamilton to Washington, 9/19/1794 and 12/24/95, Hamilton's *Papers.*

CHAPTER TEN: THE GENERAL GOES WEST

Findley. Because he now enters the story as a participant, Findley is unusually compelling on the army at Carlisle, his mission from the Parkinson's Ferry congress, and his suspicions of Hamilton. For Findley as a moderating politician, see his letter to William Bradford, 9/16/1794, in the Wallace Papers.

Moderation at the Forks. Both Brackenridge's *Incidents* and Findley attest to the changed mood at the Forks. In *Pennsylvania Archives,* "Pittsburgh Resolves Relative to Proscriptions" rescinds the banishings; "Resolutions of the Pittsburgh Meeting," 9/27/1794, describes a general submission and the urgent need to communicate it to the government. Kohn quotes Ross on the commission's having cut off the rebellion's "hydra heads."

The Neville campaign against Brackenridge. Findley and Brackenridge, rarely in agreement, agree on Brackenridge's plight and its main source. The Nevilles' role with the army is described well by H. M. Brackenridge.

Washington, Hamilton, and the troops. According to Slaughter, the number of troops ultimately raised was almost thirteen thousand—though it also seems that there was an attempt to keep some men east of the mountains when it became clear that fighting would be minimal and supply a problem. For the president's impressions of the trip, see his diary dedicated to the expedition, Washington's *Papers,* "The Diaries of George Washington," volume 6. The journey west is very closely traced by Freeman. Flexner describes Washington as experiencing back pain. For Washington's continued focus on his lands in this period, see his letters to Ross, 8/1/1794 and 8/6/94, in *Writings.* Flexner describes Washington's skepticism about Lee's judgment; Hamilton expresses his own sense of Lee's need for supervision—supervision by Hamilton—in a letter to Washington of 12/24/95. The army's movements are brought to life by Paul Ford and by William Gould, two of Baldwin's main sources, also cited by Slaughter. Gould describes the review of troops, Washington's driving his own carriage, and the various corps and units. For an example of Hamilton's thoroughness in supervising supply, see Hamilton to Hodgdon, 9/30/1794, in Hamilton's *Papers.*

The two-class army. I closely follow Slaughter's exhaustively researched chapter on the "watermelon army." William Gould describes the bivouacs; Ford complains about drinking water and food. The claim that Howell wrote "Jersey Blue" appears in an addendum to William Gould.

Washington and Findley on discipline. See Hamilton to Mifflin, 10/10/1794, in Hamilton's *Papers.* Miller is my source for Mifflin's drunken exploit. Findley gives his eyewitness impressions of the scene at Carlisle. H. M. Brackenridge has a shrewder analysis than Findley's of the role of poor troop discipline in the operation yet—like Findley—refuses to place responsibility with the president, blaming Hamilton alone.

Washington's meeting with Findley. Washington's diary cited in the fourth note for this chapter describes the meeting, as does Findley. Findley's impression that Hamilton was running things is borne out by the memory of a messenger quoted by John Church Hamilton, cited by Chernow: According to the messenger, Washington tended to be aloof, talking mainly about roads and distances; Hamilton was "the master spirit." In *Vindication,* Randolph refers to an unfortunate impression that the president needed to have Hamilton always at his elbow.

Washington's decision to return east. Washington to Randolph, 10/9/1794 and 10/16/94, in Washington's *Writings.*

The army in Bedford. William Gould gives his impression of Bedford. Fennell describes the review of troops and cites the *Gazette of the United States,* 10/18/1794, on the transparency.

Hamilton, Lee, and Washington on the suppression. For Washington's orders to Lee, see Hamilton to Lee, 10/20/1794, *American State Papers,* misc., volume 1. For Washington on troop discipline, see Washington to Hamilton, 10/26/94 and 10/31/94, Washington's *Writings.* Slaughter describes Hamilton's legalizing pillage and cites one of the impressment officers on the obvious consequences for poor families; Findley describes the officers' references to Hannibal's crossing the Alps. For Hamilton's and Washington's shared and divergent understandings, both tacit and explicit, of the purpose of the military presence, see letters from Hamilton to Washington of 10/25/94, 10/31/94, 11/8/94, and 11/15/94, in Hamilton's *Papers*; and for Washington's worries about the consequences of Husband's early arrest, 10/19/94, in the diary cited above.

Husband's arrest. Jones describes Husband's arrest; Fennell suggests that ten or more men waited at Husband's home for their captors; she cites the *Pennsylvania General Advertiser,* 10/24/1794. In a letter of 10/31/94, in *Writings,* Washington informs Hamilton of Husband's arrival in Philadelphia. Given how operations developed at the Forks, it seems clear that while Peters and Rawle managed the arrest, they were following Hamilton's orders.

The flight of suspects. Brackenridge's *Incidents* gives two thousand as the number of suspects who fled the Forks. David Bradford's escape is described in a letter of 11/15/1794 from a Captain D'Hebecourt to Henry Lee, *Pennsylvania Archives.*

The arrests. See Lee's orders to General Irvine, 11/9/1794, *Pennsylvania Archives.* H. M. Brackenridge suggests that the army carried out the operation as must have been expected and joins Findley in decrying the abrogation of civil rights, blaming it solely on Hamilton, holding Washington ultimately blameless. Both Findley and H. H. Brackenridge's *Incidents* tell the story of General Morgan. The claim of Judge Peters that he held men on little evidence out of fear of troop revolt is cited secondhand by H. M. Brackenridge, who also describes the prisoner escort, quoting the eyewitness James Carnahan. Hamilton's reassurances to Washington are in his letter of 10/25/94, in his *Papers.* For Hamilton's attitude about prosecution, compare his enthusiastic presuppression letter to Washington of 9/2/94, with its long list of prominent suspects and predictions of prosecuting them, with the desultoriness regarding prosecution in his letters of 11/11/94 and 11/15/94; the latter focuses on the need to maintain a military force at the Forks. The Powers interrogation is related by H. M. Brackenridge, the John Hamilton arrest by Findley. Holt is the source of the idea that many of the detainees' names might appear only on militia lists.

Brackenridge's suspense and interrogation. Brackenridge's *Incidents.* David Bradford's letter to Craig appears in H. M. Brackenridge. I've inserted in

Brackenridge's thoughts about flying to the Indians the reference to Mamachtaga. Ross's reviewing Brackenridge's handwriting is told secondhand by Brackenridge, whose dialogue I repeat, breaking it up—and I've added Ross's emphasis on William Bradford's first name.

The rebels in Philadelphia. Henry Marie Brackenridge includes excerpts from the diary of Robert Porter, one of the detainees sent to Philadelphia, who describes the journey and arrival. Slaughter and Holt, citing the *Philadelphia Gazette,* describe the president as viewing the prisoners on Christmas Day, but Baldwin gives 12/17/1794 as the date of the same *Gazette* article; apparently the president was actually observing the return of a horse regiment to the city and did not review the prisoners on Christmas.

CHAPTER ELEVEN: THAT SO-CALLED WHISKEY REBELLION

"That so-called whiskey rebellion." Adapted from Ewing's title.

The trials. Many writers in the rebellion cover the trial phase; Holt is the major source on legal issues involved.

Occupation and tax collection in the west. Many sources describe the occupation in greater detail than I do; Fennell discusses continued tax recalcitrance.

Hamilton on the Whiskey Rebellion. Hamilton wrote two letters to his sister-in-law Angelica Church regarding the rebellion, important because his flirtatious relationship with Church, reviving the exuberance of youth, inspired unusual freedom. In the letter of 10/23/1794, he reassures her that "the insurrection will do us a great deal of good and add to the solidity of everything in this country." In the letter of 12/8/94—which, I follow Bouton in noting, contains the first known use of "whiskey insurrection," a phrase that determined the place of the rebellion in the public mind—he says, "Our insurrection is most happily terminated. Government has gained from it reputation and strength," and goes on to refer with pride and satisfaction to the "flourishing" condition of the nation's finances. Both letters are in his *Papers.* "Put Virginia to the test": Hamilton to Sedgwick, 2/2/99, also in *Papers.* Some biographers write off this letter as mere venting; Ellis, in Chapter Five of *Founding Brothers,* takes it seriously, as the letter's tone seems to warrant; Hamilton makes a direct connection between his new military ambitions and his suppression of the whiskey rebels. For Hamilton's role in the quasi-war with France, see Kohn and Elkins and McKitrick.

Washington's lands and still. "George Washington's Distillery" has a wealth of archaeological and other information. Slaughter cites Washington's letter to Ross of 3/14/1794 on the improvement in western Pennsylvania real estate holdings and estimates the increase in value at about 50 percent.

Randolph's resignation. In "Vindication," Randolph tells the story. Elkins and McKitrick have illuminating detail.

Findley as proto-Jacksonian. Wood discusses Findley as a new kind of professional politician in the context of post-revolutionary American ideas about social mobility.

Brackenridge's later career. See Marder and Newlin, as well as Ellis in *After the Revolution.* For Neville's hiring Brackenridge to prosecute excise cases: deposition of John Wells, 12/29/1815, in the Benjamin Wells Claims, HR 21A–G3.1.

Husband's death. Jones and Lazenby tell the story; Lazenby's notes describe Emmy's and John's presence at the tavern, based on Husband-family accounts. I follow Fennell in calling prophecy Husband's profession. The letter to Emmy is quoted by Lazenby; according to *The History of Bedford and Somerset Counties,* in 1906 the original letter had recently been in existence.

SOURCES

ARCHIVES

Tench Coxe Letters, RG 58 NC 151–57, Series II, Reel 61; National Archives.
Tench Coxe Papers, Historical Society of Pennsylvania.
Isaac Craig Papers, Carnegie Library of Pittsburgh.
Craig-Neville Papers, Historical Society of Western Pennsylvania.
Mary Elinor Lazenby Papers, Darlington Library, University of Pittsburgh.
Rawle Papers, Historical Society of Pennsylvania.
John Irwin Scull Archive, Historical Society of Western Pennsylvania.
Wallace Papers, Historical Society of Pennsylvania.
Benjamin Wells Claims, HR 17A–F7.1, HR 21A–G3.1, HR 22A–G3.1; National Archives.
Whiskey Rebellion Collection, Library of Congress.
Oliver Wolcott, Jr., Papers, Connecticut Historical Society.
Yeates Papers, Historical Society of Pennsylvania.

PUBLICATIONS

Achenbach, Joel. *The Grand Idea: George Washington's Potomac and the Race to the West.* Simon & Schuster, 2004.
American State Papers, Library of Congress, http://memory.loc.gov/ammem/amlaw/lwsp.html.
Annals of Congress, Library of Congress, http://memory.loc.gov/ammem/amlaw/lwac.html.
"Another Revolutionary Hero Gone," *The Souvenir,* April 23, 1828, Vol. 1, No. 43; USGenWeb Project, Pennsylvania pages for Philadelphia, http://ftp.rootsweb.com/pub/usgenweb/pa/philadelphia/newspapers/souv0001.txt.
Bailyn, Bernard. *The Ideological Origins of the American Revolution.* Belknap Press of Harvard University Press, 1967.
Baldwin, Leland D. *Whiskey Rebels: The Story of a Frontier Uprising.* University of Pittsburgh Press, 1939 (revised 1968).

Barksdale, Kevin T., and Henry Lee. "Our Rebellious Neighbors: Virginia's Border Counties during Pennsylvania's Whiskey Rebellion," *The Virginia Magazine of History and Biography*, Vol. 111, Issue 1, 2003.

Beers Commemorative Biographical Record of Washington County, Pennsylvania, J. H. Beers & Co., 1893; USGenWeb Project, Pennsylvania pages for Washington County, http://www.chartiers.com.

Black, Jeremy. *Robert Walpole and the Nature of Politics in Early Eighteenth-Century Britain*. Macmillan, 1990.

Bouton, Terry. "A Road Closed: Rural Insurgency in Post-Independence Philadelphia," *Journal of American History*, Vol. 87, Issue 3.

———. *Tying Up the Revolution: Money, Power, and the Regulation in Pennsylvania*. Ph.D. dissertation, Duke University, 1996.

Boyd, Julian P. "'Herman Husband: A Story of His Life' by Mary Elinor Lazenby," *Pennsylvania Magazine of History and Biography*, Vol. 65, April 1941.

Boyd, Stephen, ed. *The Whiskey Rebellion: Past and Present Perspectives*. Greenwood Press, 1985.

Brackenridge, Henry Marie. *History of the Western Insurrection in Western Pennsylvania, Commonly Called the Whiskey Insurrection, 1794*. W. S. Haven, 1859.

Brackenridge, Hugh Henry. *Incidents of the Insurrection in the Western Parts of Pennsylvania, in the Year 1794*. John McCulloch, 1795.

———. *Narrative of a Late Expedition against the Indians; with an Account of the Barbarous Execution of Col. Crawford; and the Wonderful Escape of Dr. Knight & John Slover from Captivity in 1782. To Which is Added, A Narrative of the Captivity & Escape of Mrs. Frances Scott, an Inhabitant of Washington County, Virginia*. Ames & Parker, 1799.

———. *Gazette Publications*. Alexander and Phillips, 1806.

———. *Modern Chivalry*. Ed. Claude M. Newlin. Hafner Publishing Company, 1968.

———. *Incidents of the Insurrection*. Ed. Daniel Marder. College and University Press, 1972.

Brock, Leslie V. *The Currency of the American Colonies, 1700–1764: A Study in Colonial Finance and Imperial Relations*. Arno Press, 1975.

Brookhiser, Richard. *Alexander Hamilton, American*. Touchstone, 1999.

Brunhouse, Robert L. *The Counter-Revolution in Pennsylvania, 1776–1790*. Octagon Books, 1971.

Buck, Solon J., and Elizabeth Hawthorn Buck. *The Planting of Civilization in Western Pennsylvania*. University of Pittsburgh Press, 1939.

Chernow, Ron. *Alexander Hamilton*. Penguin Press, 2004.

Clouse, Jerry A. *The Whiskey Rebellion: Southwestern Pennsylvania's Frontier People Test the American Constitution*. Pennsylvania Historical and Museum Commission, 1994.

SOURCES

"Commemorative Souvenir Program of the Bicentennial of the Battle of Alamance," 1971, Sons of Dewitt Colony, Texas, http://www.tamu.edu/ccbn/dewitt/mckstmerreg1.htm.

"The Constitution of Pennsylvania, September 28, 1776," Avalon Project at Yale Law School, http://www.yale.edu/lawweb/avalon/states/pa08.htm.

Cook, Roy Bird. *Washington's Western Lands*. Shenandoah Publishing House, 1930.

Countryman, Edward. *The American Revolution*. Hill & Wang, 1985.

Craig, Neville B. *The History of Pittsburgh: With a Brief Notice of Its Facilities of Communication, and Other Advantages for Commercial and Manufacturing Purposes*. J. H. Mellor, 1851.

———. *Exposure of a Few of the Many Misstatements in H. M. Brackenridge's History of the Whiskey Insurrection*. J. S. Davison, 1859.

Crist, Robert G. *Robert Whitehill and the Struggle for Civil Rights*. Lemoyne Trust Co., 1958.

Crumrine, Boyd, ed. *History of Washington County, Pennsylvania: With Biographical Sketches of Many of Its Pioneers and Prominent Men*. L. H. Everts, 1882.

"Davis-Lenox House," *Seven Walking Tours Through Historic Philadelphia*. Independence Hall Association, http://www.ushistory.org/districts/societyhill/davis.htm.

Decatur, Stephen. *Private Affairs of George Washington, from the Records and Accounts of Tobias Lear, Esquire, His Secretary*. Houghton Mifflin, 1933.

Edwards, Jonathan. *A Faithful Narrative of the Surprising Work of God: In the Conversion of Many Hundred Souls in Northampton, and the Neighboring Towns and Villages of New-Hampshire, in New-England, in a Letter to the Rev. Dr. Benjamin Colman, of Boston*. Holden and Dowson, 1808.

Elkins, Stanley, and Eric McKitrick. *The Age of Federalism: The Early American Republic, 1788–1800*. Oxford University Press, 1993.

Ellis, Joseph J. *After the Revolution: Profiles in Early American Culture*. Norton, 1979.

———. *Founding Brothers*. Vintage, 2002.

"English Dissenters," http://www.exlibris.org.

Ewing, Charles M. *The Causes of That So Called Whiskey Insurrection of 1794*. 1930; excerpts at http://www.whiskeyrebellion.org.

Farrand, Max, ed. *The Records of the Federal Convention of 1787*. Library of Congress, http://memory.loc.gov/ammem/amlaw/lwfr.html.

Felton, Margaret Moore. "Paper on General John Neville." Abstract of M.A. thesis, 1932, Historical Society of Western Pennsylvania.

Fennell, Dorothy E. *From Rebelliousness to Insurrection: A Social History of the Whiskey Rebellion, 1765–1802.* Ph.D. dissertation, University of Pittsburgh, 1981.

Ferguson, E. James. *The Power of the Purse: A History of American Public Finance, 1776–1790.* University of North Carolina Press, 1961.

Ferguson, Russell J. *Early Western Pennsylvania Politics.* University of Pittsburgh Press, 1938.

Findley, William. *History of the Insurrection in the Four Western Counties of Pennsylvania, in the Year MDCCXCIV: With a Recital of the Circumstances Specially Connected Therewith: And an Historical Review of the Previous Situation of the Country.* Samuel Harrison Smith, 1796.

Fischer, David Hackett. *Albion's Seed: Four British Folkways in America.* Oxford University Press, 1989.

Flexner, James Thomas. *George Washington.* Little, Brown, 1965–72.

Foner, Eric. *Tom Paine and Revolutionary America.* Oxford University Press, 1976.

Ford, David. "Journal of an Expedition Made in the Autumn of 1794, with a Detachment of New Jersey Troops, into Western Pennsylvania, to Aid in Suppressing the 'Whiskey Rebellion,'" *Proceedings of the New Jersey Historical Society,* Series 1, Vol. 8, 1859.

Ford, Paul Leicester. *The True George Washington.* J. B. Lippincott, 1896.

Freeman, Douglas Southall. *George Washington: A Biography.* Scribner, 1948–1957.

"George Washington's Distillery," *George Washington's Mount Vernon,* http://www.mountvernon.org.

Gideon, Richard. "The Whiskey Flags: An Intoxicating Look into a Sobering Subject," American Vexillum, http://www.americanvexillum.com.

Gould, Roger. "Patron-Client Ties, State Centralization, and the Whiskey Rebellion," *American Journal of Sociology,* September 1996.

Gould, William. "Journal of Major William Gould of the New Jersey Infantry, During an Expedition into Pennsylvania in 1794," *Proceedings of the New Jersey Historical Society,* Series 1, Vol. 3.

Grubb, Farley. "Creating the U.S.-Dollar Currency Union, 1748–1811: A Quest for Monetary Stability or a Usurpation of State Sovereignty for Personal Gain?" *American Economic Review,* December 2003.

Ha-Joon Chang. "Kicking Away the Ladder: How the Economic and Intellectual Histories of Capitalism Have Been Re-Written to Justify Neo-Liberal Capitalism," *Post-Autistic Economics Review,* No. 14, September 2002, http://www.btinternet.com/~pae_news/review/issue15.htm.

Hamilton, Alexander. *The Papers of Alexander Hamilton.* Ed. Harold C. Syrett, assoc. ed. Jacob E. Cooke. Columbia University Press, 1961–87.

Harper, Robert Eugene. *The Class Structure of Western Pennsylvania.* Ph.D. dissertation, University of Pittsburgh, 1969.

Hartman, Norma W. "Which Oliver Miller?" *Pittsburgh History Magazine,* Winter 1992–93.

Hassler, Edgar W. *Old Westmoreland: A History of Western Pennsylvania During the Revolution,* J. R. Weldin, 1900, http://www.geocities.com/lydick_1999/History/o2w.html.

Hawke, David Freeman. *In the Midst of a Revolution.* University of Pennsylvania Press, 1961.

———. *The Colonial Experience.* Bobbs-Merrill, 1966.

Heimert, Alan. *Religion and the American Mind.* Harvard University Press, 1966.

Hildreth, Richard. *The History of the United States of America.* Harper, 1849–1852.

The History of Bedford and Somerset Counties, 1906; USGenWeb Project, Pennsylvania pages for Somerset County, http://www.rootsweb.com/~pasomers/hbs/chapter10.htm.

Holt, Wythe. "The Whiskey Rebellion of 1794: a Democratic Working-Class Insurrection," http://www.uga.edu/colonialseminar/pastevents.htm.

House Journal, Library of Congress, http://memory.loc.gov/ammem/amlaw/lwhj.html.

Husband, Herman. *A Fan for Fanning, and a Touch-stone to Tryon, Containing an Impartial Account of the Rise and Progress of the So Much Talked of Regulation in North-Carolina, by Regulus.* Boston, 1771.

———. *Proposals to Amend and Perfect the Policy of the Government of the United States of America: Or, The Fulfilling of the Prophecies in the Latter Days, Commenced by the Independence of America. Containing, a New Mode of Elections; with a Method of Supporting Government without Taxing or Fining the People.* M. K. Goddard, 1782.

———. *Dialogue between an Assembly-Man and a Convention-Man.* William Spotswood, c. 1788.

———. *Sermon to the Bucks and Hinds of America.* William Spotswood, 1788.

———. *XIV Sermons on the Characters of Jacob's Fourteen Sons.* William Spotswood, 1789.

Jones, Mark H. *Herman Husband: Millenarian, Carolina Regulator, and Whiskey Rebel.* Ph.D. dissertation, Northern Illinois University, 1982.

Journals of the American Congress from 1774–1788, Way and Gideon, 1823.

Kars, Marjoleine. *Breaking Loose Together: The Regulator Rebellion in Pre-Revolutionary North Carolina.* University of North Carolina Press, 2002.

Kellner, Esther. *Moonshine, Its History and Folklore.* Bobbs-Merrill, 1971.

Klein, Philip S., and Ari Hoogenboom. *A History of Pennsylvania.* McGraw-Hill, 1973.

Knollenberg, Bernhard. *George Washington: The Virginia Period, 1732–1775.* Duke University Press, 1964.

Kohn, Richard H. "The Inside Story of the Newburgh Conspiracy: America and the Coup d'Etat," *William and Mary Quarterly* 27, April 1970.

———. *Eagle and Sword: The Federalists and the Creation of the Military Establishment in America, 1783–1802.* Free Press, 1975.

Kramnick, Isaac. *Bolingbroke and His Circle.* Harvard University Press, 1968.

Langford, Paul. *The Excise Crisis: Society and Politics in the Age of Walpole.* Clarendon Press, Oxford, 1975.

Lazenby, Mary Elinor. *Herman Husband: A Story of His Life.* Old Neighborhoods Press, 1940.

Lincoln, Charles H. *The Revolutionary Movement in Pennsylvania, 1760–1776.* University of Pennsylvania, 1901.

Lowman, Moses. *Paraphrase and Notes on the Revelation of St. John.* W. Baynes, 1807.

Maclay, William. *The Journal of William Maclay, United States Senator from Pennsylvania, 1789–1791.* A. & C. Boni, 1927.

Marder, Daniel. *Hugh Henry Brackenridge.* Twayne Publishers, 1967.

Marshall, John. *The Life of George Washington.* J. Crissy and Thomas Copperthwaite, 1843.

McClure, James Patrick. *The Ends of the American Earth: Pittsburgh and the Upper Ohio Valley to 1795.* Ph.D. dissertation, University of Michigan, 1983.

McCook, Henry Christopher. *The Latimers: A Tale of the Western Insurrection of 1794.* George W. Jacobs, 1897.

Miller, John C. *Alexander Hamilton: Portrait in Paradox.* Harper and Brothers, 1959.

Mitchell, Broadus. *Alexander Hamilton.* Macmillan, 1957–62.

Morris, Robert. *The Papers of Robert Morris.* Ed. Edward J. Ferguson. University of Pittsburgh Press, 1973.

Nash, Gary B. *The Urban Crucible: Social Change, Political Consciousness, and the Origins of the American Revolution.* Harvard University Press, 1979.

———. *Race, Class, and Politics: Essays on American Colonial and Revolutionary Society.* University of Illinois Press, 1986.

Nelson, Paul David. "Horatio Gates at Newburgh, 1783: A Misunderstood Role," *William and Mary Quarterly* 29, January 1975.

"New Light on the Whiskey Insurrection," *The Magazine of Western History,* Vol. 6, September 1887.

Newlin, Claude Milton. *The Life and Writings of Hugh Henry Brackenridge.* Princeton University Press, 1932.

Newton, Isaac. *Observations on the Prophecies of Daniel and the Apocalypse.* Ed. S. J. Barnett. E. Mellen Press, 1999.

Niebuhr, H. Richard. *The Kingdom of God in America.* Harper and Brothers, 1937.

Nixon, Michael, and Michael McCaw. *The Compleat Distiller.* Amphora Society, 2002.

Noll, Mark A. *A History of Christianity in the United States and Canada.* William B. Eerdmans, 1992.

Page, Elizabeth. *Tree of Liberty.* Rhinehart, 1939.

Paine, Thomas. *Common Sense.* Rimington & Hooper, 1928.

Pencak, William, Matthew Dennis, and Simon P. Newman, eds. *Riot and Revelry in Early America.* Pennsylvania State University Press, 2002.

Pennsylvania Archives, Series 2, Vol. 4, 1896.

Plumb, J. H. *Sir Robert Walpole, The King's Minister.* Houghton Mifflin, 1961.

Randolph, Edmund. *A Vindication of Edmund Randolph, Written by Himself, and Published in 1795.* C. H. Wynne, 1855.

Rexroth, Kenneth. *Communalism: From Its Origins to the Twentieth Century.* Seabury Press, 1974.

Rorabaugh, W. J. *The Alcoholic Republic: An American Tradition.* Oxford University Press, 1979.

Ryerson, Richard Alan. *"The Revolution Is Now Begun": The Radical Committees of Philadelphia, 1765–1776.* University of Pennsylvania Press, 1978.

Sakolski, A. M. *The Great American Land Bubble: The Amazing Story of Land-Grabbing, Speculations, and Booms from Colonial Days to the Present Time.* Harper and Brothers, 1932.

Schama, Simon. *A History of Britain.* BBC Press, 2001–02.

Schoepf, Johann. *Travels in the Confederation, 1783–1784.* Ed. Alfred J. Morrison. Campbell, 1911.

Selsam, J. Paul. *The Pennsylvania Constitution of 1776: A Study in Revolutionary Democracy.* University of Pennsylvania Press, 1936.

Shaw, Peter. *American Patriots and the Rituals of Revolution.* Harvard University Press, 1981.

Slaughter, Thomas P. *The Whiskey Rebellion: Frontier Epilogue to the American Revolution.* Oxford University Press, 1986.

Smiley, Ian. *Making Pure Corn Whiskey: A Professional Guide for Amateur and Micro Distillers.* Amphora Society, 2003.

Smith, Helene. *The Great Whisky Rebellion: Rebels with a Cause.* MacDonald/Sward, 1994.

Smith, Richard Norton. *Patriarch: George Washington and the New American Nation.* Houghton Mifflin, 1993.

Statutes at Large of the United States, Library of Congress, http://memory.loc.gov/ammem/amlaw/lwsl.html.

Swanger, Mary Pat. "Insurrection! a Short History of the Whiskey Rebellion of 1794," Oliver Miller Homestead Associates, Pittsburgh, Pennsylvania.

Tachau, Mary K. Bonsteel. "The Whiskey Rebellion in Kentucky," *Journal of the Early Republic* II, 1982.

Thompson, E. P. *Whigs and Hunters: The Origin of the Black Act.* Allen Lane, 1975.

———. *Customs in Common.* Merlin Press, 1991.

Tinkcom, Harry Marlin. *The Republicans and Federalists in Pennsylvania, 1790–1801: A Study in National Stimulus and Local Response.* Pennsylvania Historical and Museum Commission, 1950.

Tracy, Joseph. *The Great Awakening: A History of the Revival of Religion in the Time of Edwards and Whitefield.* Dayton & Newman, 1842.

Wallace, Paul A. *Indians in Pennsylvania.* Pennsylvania Historical and Museum Commission, 1981.

Washington, George. *Papers.* Library of Congress, http://memory.loc.gov/ammem/gwhtml/gwhome.html.

———. *The Writings of George Washington from the Original Manuscript Sources.* Ed. John C. Fitzpatrick. Washington Resources at the University of Virginia Library, http://etext.lib.virginia.edu/washington/fitzpatrick/.

Williams, Roger. *Experiments of Spiritual Life & Health, and Their Preservatives in Which the Weakest Child of God May Get Assurance of His Spiritual Life and Blessedness, and the Strongest May Find Discoveries of His Christian Growth, and the Means of It.* S. S. Rider, 1863.

Wills, Garry. *Explaining America.* Penguin, 1981.

———. *Cincinattus: George Washington and the Enlightenment.* Doubleday, 1984.

———. *A Necessary Evil: A History of American Distrust of Government.* Simon & Schuster, 1999.

Wood, Gordon S. *The Radicalism of the American Revolution.* Knopf, 1992.

Young, Alfred P. *The Shoemaker and the Tea Party: Memory and the American Revolution.* Beacon Press, 1999.

Zobel, Hiller B. *The Boston Massacre.* Norton, 1970.

ACKNOWLEDGMENTS

When this book was nothing but an idea, Suzanne Gluck's embracing and representing it made all the difference. I'm forever grateful to Suzanne for helping refine my thoughts, ushering me into a process that's been even more satisfying than I'd hoped, and advising me with such pragmatism and insight along the way.

I feel enormously lucky to have had as my editor Lisa Drew, whose expertise and intelligence blessed my struggles—and whose spot-on understanding of what I'm trying to do has been a source of great comfort and optimism. Thanks also to Samantha Martin and everyone else at Scribner whose diligence, taste, and creativity helped turn a manuscript into a book.

I'm deeply grateful for the contributions of Daniel Bergner and Carol Rawlings Miller, who gave generous critical attention to the manuscript. To put it too briefly, each of these indispensable friends has taken the best kind of care of my work for many years. For more than I can say here, thanks also to Marilyn Sande, and to Ed Finnegan, Kyle Gann, John Gulla, Marc Haefele, Henrietta Hallenborg, Mary Ann Hallenborg, Neil Hallenborg, Bruce Makous, Paul O'Rourke, Steve Plumlee, Sam Sifton, Emily Stone, and Eric Zicklin, who have given a damn for a long time about the ups and downs of getting here. Thanks to Pamela Keogh for advice at a tough early moment; Eric Price for business acumen; Bob Swacker for authorial comradeship; and the whole staff, past and present, of Atelier 06 in Brooklyn.

It's hard to imagine how I could have told this story without the Humanities Research Library of the New York Public Library, especially the seemingly inexhaustible collection and helpful staff of the Irma and Paul Millstein Division of United States History. Other libraries, archives, and online resources on whose collections and staffs I've happily relied: the Library and Archives of the Historical Society of Western Pennsylvania; the National Archives; the Library of Congress, as well as its "American Memory" Website; the Historical Society of Pennsylvania; the Historical Society of Connecticut; the Historical Society of Bedford County, Pennsylvania; the Historical Society of Washington County, Pennsylvania; the U. Grant Miller Library of Washington and Jefferson College; the

Carnegie Library of Pittsburgh (main and Braddock branches); the Darlington Library of the University of Pittsburgh; the Saint Ann's School Library; the New Jersey Historical Society; the University of Virginia Library's online George Washington Resources.

Jack Ryan, all-around pen-and-ink man, approached my sometimes vague and oddball ideas for maps with creativity and patience, bringing skill, verve, and wit to the world I'm writing about. Thanks to Jack for jumping on a moving train with characteristic fearlessness. (Any errors and fancifulness in the maps are mine, not his.)

In Pittsburgh, the Oliver Miller Homestead Associates are living-history keepers of the Whiskey Rebellion flame. Correspondence with the ever-informative and trenchant Barbara Bockrath, the recording secretary and an OMHA director, was of particular help in orienting me to some lively eighteenth-century realities. Phil Haines kindly welcomed my unannounced appearance at an OMHA event and has been generous with his interest. Lynette Sell informed me of the association's resources; Bob Barton gave me an impromptu tour of the Oliver Miller home; Charles McCormick was informative on a number of other matters; and Kelly Thakur's directions got me at last to whiskey cave.

In Uniontown, Nancy and Bill Ross, proprietors of The Inne at Watson's Choice, kindly offered help and introductions in tracking down Whiskey Rebellion sites. The Coal Baron restaurant happens to be in Uniontown; no matter where it might be located, it would be the right place for bedraggled researchers to have dinner. Sites overseen by the Western Pennsylvania Conservancy, including the Laurel Highlands hiking trail and Frank Lloyd Wright's Fallingwater, enhanced my feeling for the region's landscape and topography, as did the falls at Ohiopyle State Park. Presentations at Fort Necessity and Jumonville's Glen in western Pennsylvania, and at the Chesapeake and Ohio Canal near Washington, D.C., brought home the importance of the National Parks Service to preservation and interpretation.

And without the roadside historical marker at a suburban McDonald's, shaken by truck and commuter traffic, where the rebel fallback at Couch's Fort once stood, certain ironies of the story would have been fuzzier in my imagination.

I began looking for historical markers—and for narrative history—long ago, from the sometimes turbulent backseats of family cars. Thanks to my brothers: David loaned some research materials, as well as much supportive interest; and I benefited mightily from discussion of themes and context with Webster, as well as from his astute and encouraging comments on the manuscript. Throughout my research and writing I was keenly aware of the absence (and sometimes also the presence) of my late father, whose namesake I am; thanks also to my stepmother, Brigid Hogeland. My mother, Elizabeth Hogeland, died while I was writing this book. She took pride in and gave essential support to the endeavor until the end.

Above all: Thanks to my wife, Gail, and my stepdaughter, Barbara, for—among other things!—many years of smart, loving reading.

WH

INDEX

Page numbers in italics refer to maps.

"Act Repealing . . ." (1791), 27, 258*n*

Adams, John, on Pennsylvania's constitution, 36

Addison, Alexander, 127, 170, 187, 224,
239, 251*n*, 269*n*

Alamance, Battle of, 84, 182, 260*n*

Allegheny County, Pa., 23, 97, 103, 106,
119, 145

Allegheny River, 12

Allegheny Valley, 74

American Revolution, 22, 132
debts of, 8, 29, 32, 40, 53, 55
Forks area in, 15
McFarlanes in, 151–52, 154
R. Morris's financial dealings in, 32
R. Morris's view of, 36
Washington's land speculations legit-
imized by, 139
see also Newburgh crisis

Ames, Fisher, 62

Anglicans, 71, 72, 73, 75, 77–78, 79,
80

Anti-federalists, 107, 108, 110, 137

Apocalypse, 75–76

Army, British:
at Fort Pitt, 13–14
forts in U.S. territory maintained by,
1

Army, Continental, 28

Army, U.S., 139
A. Hamilton's command of, 239
Bower Hill defended by, 150, 151,
152

Articles of Confederation, 37, 39

bank, central:
A. Hamilton's plan for, 111, 133
R. Morris's plans for, 36–37

Baptists, 74, 80

Bear Inn, 127

Bedford, Pa., 94, 97, 118, 165, 191,
216–17, 274*n*

Bill of Rights, 219

bills of exchange, 35

Black, John, 156–58

Black Act, 34

blackfaced gangs, 14, 20–23, 27, 34, 106,
117, 132, 143–44, 180, 203

Black Horse Tavern, 235–36

bonds, federal, 8, 30–31, 56, 59, 61, 62,
63

bonds, state, 38, 56
Pennsylvania, 55
speculators' investments in, 61

Bower Hill, 97, 99–100, 132, 146, 151,
262*n*
first rebel attack on, 147–48, 150,
267*n*–68*n*
second rebel attack on, 152–56, 161,
163, 165, 166, 167, 185, 197, 221,
226, 246*n*, 268*n*–69*n*

Brackenridge, Hugh Henry, 11–12,
17–18, 110, 113, 122, 144–46,
149–50, 152, 154–55, 157–59,
171, 175, 176, 177, 197, 198, 204,
205, 214, 229, 233, 242–43, 267*n*,
269*n*
A. Hamilton's questioning of,
233–35
appeal to Congress of, 106
as army chaplain, 17
article on French Revolution by, 138,
169
as author of Modern Chivalry, 109,
115, 170, 243
at Braddock's Field, 173–77
childhood of, 16–17
eastern speculators as viewed by, 19

Brackenridge, Hugh Henry (*cont.*)
  election to the Pennsylvania legisla-
    ture of, 106
  federal troops' hatred of, 207–8
  Federalists in Pittsburgh disparaged
    by, 108, 109
  at first anti-excise convention, 23–25,
    105
  in first meeting with Husband,
    25–26, 71, 252*n*
  and Gallatin, 197, 272*n*
  humanity as viewed by, 11, 20
  and Indians, 18–19, 109, 229, 276*n*
  letter to Coxe by, 181–82, 194–95,
    198
  memoir of rebellion by, 246*n*
  at Mingo Creek church meeting,
    161–65
  National Gazette articles of, 110–12,
    115, 228
  Nevilles' campaign against, 227–33,
    238, 274*n*
  Parkinson's Ferry congress and,
    181–82, 201–2
  Pennsylvania's revised constitution
    opposed by, 110
  Presley Neville and, 100, 148–50,
    180–81, 191, 233–34
  R. Morris's finance policy favored by,
    107, 108
  on rebel negotiating committee, 193,
    197, 198, 200
  second marriage of, 108–9
  squatters defended by, 19
  views on western development of,
    18
  vision for America of, 17, 71
  Westsylvanian secession opposed by,
    16
Brackenridge, Sabina Wolfe, 108–9,
    262*n*
Braddock, General Edward, 14, 98
Braddock's Field, 168, 169, 171, 172–76,
    176–177, 180, 185, 190, 205, 220,
    226, 227, 234, 235, 238, 269*n*
Bradford, David, 151, 167–68, 170, 171,
    178, 180, 197, 224, 227, 231–32,
    238, 242, 259*n*, 268*n*
  at anti-excise conventions, 24, 123
  at Braddock's Field, 174–76
  Brownsville speech of, 201
  escape of, 220, 227

  at Mingo Church meeting, 163, 165
  on rebel negotiation committee, 193,
    197, 205
  Ross and, 171
  secessionist views of, 168
  support for Faulkner attack of, 124
  submission vote and, 202
  in Washington County democratic
    society, 137, 138, 151
  Washington courthouse speech of,
    169
Bradford, William, 141, 142, 144,
    193–94, 237, 266*n*, 267*n*, 273*n*
  as A. Hamilton's cabinet ally, 136,
    199–200
  and Brackenridge 197, 232
  Findley correspondence with, 208
  military intelligence gathered by,
    194
  negotiation urged by, 189
  on presidential negotiating commis-
    sion, 190–94, 198, 202–3, 204
Brison, James, 171, 172, 177
Brison family, 101
Brownsville, Pa., 23, 122, 200–202,
    252*n*, 273*n*
Brush Creek, 12
Bunker Hill, Battle of, 17
Butler, Major, 171, 176

Canada, British troops in, 15
canals, 5, 139, 140, 209–10
Canonsburg, Pa., 167–68
Carlisle, Pa., 206, 209, 210, 213, 240
Catholics, 76
Cervantes, Miguel de, 17
Charleston, S.C., 99
Chartiers Creek, 147
Cherokees, 140
Chesapeake Bay, 71, 72
Chickasaws, 6
Clymer, George, 126–28, 129, 187,
    252*n*, 264*n*, 265*n*
Common Sense (Paine), 36
Concord, Battle of, 98
congress, grand western, *see* Parkinson's
    Ferry congress
Congress, U.S., 57, 238
  A. Hamilton investigated by, 112,
    133–136
  A. Hamilton's reports to, 60–61,
    62–64, 67

Brackenridge's anti-excise appeal to, 106, 110–11
excise-enforcement law passed by, 185
excise seen as betrayal by some in, 27–28
excise trial rules reformed by, 142
first taxes imposed by, 58
Gallatin in, 170
impost passed by, 52, 58
Indian attacks and, 57
militia act of, 112
presidential war council kept secret from, 195
rebel demands and, 195
1791 whiskey tax passed by, 68, 70
1792 whiskey tax passed by, 115
Wells's claims on, 245n
whiskey tax petition received by, 105
Congress, confederation:
impost and, 37, 39, 47
IOUs of, 38–39
Newburgh crisis and, 44, 45–47
R. Morris's control of, 33
war bonds of, 30–31
Connor, John, 103–4, 117, 262n
Constitution, English, 82
Constitution, Pennsylvania, 36, 54, 59, 87, 94, 110, 122, 126, 186, 254n
Constitution, U.S.:
Brackenridge's support for, 11, 108, 109, 110
Husband's views of, 93, 261n
impact on populists of, 58
Pennsylvania's ratification of, 11, 108
ratification of, 57, 109, 117, 126
taxing power in, 58
Constitutional Convention, 107, 188, 189
Continental Army, Morris's control of, 33
Continental Congress, 98
Continental paper currency, 31–32
Couch's Fort, 148, 149–50, 152, 155, 166, 268n
Coxe, Tench, 181–82, 194, 198, 258n, 259n, 266n, 268n, 270n
Craig, Isaac, 100, 101, 114, 156, 161, 163, 170, 175, 178, 185, 190, 197–98, 227–28, 245n, 262n, 275n

creditors, 37, 186, 253n–54n
A. Hamilton's congressional report and, 60
concerns regarding bonds' stability of, 56
Congress's payments to, 33
Constitutional ratification and, 107–8
debtors' conflict with, 33–34
in Pennsylvania assembly, 54–55, 59, 109–10
Washington's suspicions of, 48
Creeks, 140
Cromwell, Oliver, 34
Cumberland, Fort, 128–29, 206, 210, 216, 219
Cumberland, Pa., 54
Cumberland County, Va., 203
currency, paper, 30–32, 35–36, 38
gold standard and, 88
taxes and, 53

Daniel, Book of, 26, 71, 76, 77, 80, 81, 89, 90–91, 94, 259n, 260n–61n
"Dash to the Mountains, Jersey Blue" (song), 212
Day, Edward, 171, 172, 177
Day family, 101
debt, federal, 60, 61, 135–36
A. Hamilton's plan for, 59, 256n; see also Hamilton, Alexander, whiskey tax and
Morris's plan for, 38, 40, 62, 254n
in war effort, 8, 29, 32, 40, 53, 55
debtors, 52, 253n—54n
creditors' conflicts with, 33–34
Pennsylvania politics and, 53–56
violence of, 52–53
debts, state, 60, 61, 62
Deep River, 79
Delaware Indians, 13
democratic societies, 137, 138, 141, 204, 213, 254n
Democratic Society of the County of Washington in Pennsylvania, 137–38, 141, 151, 266n
Detroit, 140
diggers, 80, 88
Dreadful Night, 220–21, 222
Duer, William, 111
duties, import, 52, 62–63

Edwards, Jonathan, 74, 78
Eighth Pennsylvania Regiment, 151
England, 30
excises, 27–28, 37, 39, 52, 62–63, 105
    see also whiskey tax
Ezekiel, Book of, 26, 71, 76, 89, 90–91,
    197

Fairfax, Lord, 98
farms, farmers:
    Congressional IOUs to, 38
    federal bonds and, 8
    Pennsylvania bank and, 54
    Whiskey Rebellion perpetrators and,
        8
    whiskey tax and, 68
Farrago, Captain, 109
Faulkner, Mrs., 121–22
Faulkner, William, 119–21, 123–24,
    128, 151, 264n
Fayette, Fort, 101, 114, 119, 127, 149,
    171, 191, 262n
    arms stored at, 194
    D. Bradford's threat against, 168
    fortification of, 169–7
    militias' threat to, 174
    Powers held at, 226
    prisoners held at, 223
Fayette, Pa., 23, 97, 122, 128, 170
Federalist, The, 107
Federalists, 57–58, 108, 141, 231
Finance Department, confederation
    Congress, 33
Findley, William, 122, 170, 201, 223–24,
    262n, 263n, 273n, 274n, 277n
    as A. Hamilton's enemy, 115, 170,
        208, 214, 225, 242
    A. Hamilton's investigation of,
        225–26, 230, 233, 238
    and Brackenridge, 106, 109, 229
    excise tax reduction promoted by, 115
    excise trial reform promoted by,
        142–43
    on Gallatin, 272n
    Gazette letter of, 107
    history of rebellion by, 245n
    moderation of, 170
    Nevilles' statement against, 227
    in Pennsylvania assembly, 54, 55, 106
    U.S. Constitution opposed by, 108
    W. Bradford's correspondence with,
        208

Washington's and Hamilton's meeting
    with, 207, 209, 214–16, 274n
First Pennsylvania Regiment, 151
Florida, A. Hamilton's invasion plan for,
    239
Foreign Affairs Department of confed-
    eration Congress, 33
Forks of the Ohio, viii, 13, 40, 105, 115,
    142, 251n
    A. Hamilton's plans for military
        action against, 124–25
    A. Hamilton's views on people of, 238
    American Revolution and, 15
    first excise office in, 120
    gathering unity of, 129
    Mingo Creek Association and, 115
    Neville's popularity in, 97
    regional independence movement in,
        16
    squatters at, 19
    Washington's impressions of, 138–40
    Westsylvania and, 57
    whiskey in, 66, 70
    whiskey tax and, 28
Fox, Joseph, 103
France, 31
    decapitation of king in, 130, 138, 169
    possible war with, 239
    in Seven Years' War, 13–14, 98
Franklin (state), 16, 57
Frederick's Town, Md., 203
French and Indian War, see Seven Years'
    War
French Revolution, 130, 137, 138
Friendship Hill, 122
Fulton, Alexander, 165–68, 220, 225,
    245n, 269n

Gallatin, Albert, 242, 262n, 269n, 270n
    A. Hamilton's investigation of,
        225–26, 230, 233, 238
    Brackenridge's understanding with,
        197, 272n
    as moderate, 170
    Neville campaign against, 227
    Parkinson's Ferry committee speech
        of, 201
    Parkinson's Ferry congress and, 181
    on rebel negotiating committee, 193,
        197
    at second Pittsburgh convention,
        122–23

Gates, Horatio, 41, 42, 44, 45, 46, 48, 255*n*
Gazette, *see* Pittsburgh Gazette
Germantown, Pa., 99, 209
Gibson, John, 171, 172, 177
Glades, 25, 85–86, 89
gold standard, 88
grand western congress, *see* Parkinson's Ferry congress
Granville, Lord, 79
Great Awakening, 34, 73–77, 80, 260*n*
Great Britain, 68, 73, 80, 130, 198, 229, 240
militias' proposed alliance with, 169
Great Columbian Federal City, construction of, 3
Green Mountain Boys, 168
Greensburg, Pa., 191
Green Tree Tavern, *see* Sign of the Green Tree Tavern
Grindletonians, 80

Hamilton, Alexander, 2, 29, 31, 32, 35, 37, 40, 44, 51, 133–35, 136–37, 220–21
appointment to Treasury of, 57
and army-supply reform, 113–14
Brackenridge's criticism of, 110, 113
central bank and, 111, 133
childhood and background of, 28–29
in conflict with Jefferson, 1
congressional investigations of, 112, 133–34
domestic debt and, 59, 256*n*
Dutch debt and, 135–36
Findley as enemy of, 115, 170, 208, 214
on governmental force, 271*n*
Militia Act supported by, 112, 196–97
modern biographies of, 247
national finance and, 94, 110
Newburgh crisis and, 42, 44–46, 47–49, 124, 255*n*
R. Morris's finance plans and, 36–37, 39, 253*n*
reports to Congress of, 60–61, 62–64, 67, 105, 136
retirement of, 239
Shays Rebellion as viewed by, 53, 257*n*
taxes and, 58–59
vision for America of, 71, 91
W. Bradford's letter to, 199–200
Walpole's influence on, 252*n*
as Washington's staff officer, 42–44
yellow fever contracted by, 130, 135
Hamilton, Alexander, Whiskey Rebellion and, 7, 9, 185, 206, 209, 211, 223, 237, 239, 276*n*
admonition to Lee to postdate orders of, 195
as acting secretary of war, 192, 210
arrests made under the direction of, 219–21
Brackenridge and, 227–28, 231–35, 238
civilian deaths and, 213
Findley's and Redick's meeting with, 207, 214–16
Husband as prime suspect of, 259*n*
investigative tactics of, 223–25
J. Hamilton and, 226–27
Lee's general orders conveyed by, 217
letter to Mifflin by, 218
letter to Washington by, 218
Mifflin disputed by, 196
military action urged by, 189, 190, 192
military expedition against rebels considered by, 115, 117, 124–26, 129, 130, 141, 188–89, 206, 263*n*, 264*n*–65*n*
report on insurrection by, 187–88, 245*n*–46*n*, 265*n*, 267*n*
reports to Washington by, 225
role in cabinet war council of, 195, 271*n*
supply-impressment order issued by, 218
"Tully" articles by, 195–96, 203, 210
on usefulness to nation of Rebellion, 240
Washington's relationship to tactics of, 217–18, 223–24
Hamilton, Alexander, whiskey tax and, 8, 28, 29, 33, 40, 51, 52
Brackenridge on, 110
congressional reports on, 60–64, 67
large-scale distillers and, 69–70, 131
manual for collection of, 102
petitions on, 111, 112–13, 114
as wealth redistribution, 68–70

Hamilton, Daniel, 21–23, 24, 28, 33, 70, 103, 104–5, 165, 167, 220
Hamilton, David, 121, 155–56, 157, 158–59, 162, 177, 268*n*, 269*n*
Hamilton, John, 21, 24, 118–19, 121, 122, 151, 169, 175, 226–27, 235, 268*n*, 275*n*
Harrisburg, Pa., 209
Hillsborough, N.C., 82
History of the Insurrection (Findley), 245*n*
Holcroft, John, 131, 147–48, 150, 205, 225
House of Representatives, U.S., 24
    securities funded by, 61–62
    see also Congress, U.S.
Howell, Governor, 212
Hume, David, 33
Husband, Emmy, 84–85, 86, 243–44, 259*n*, 261*n*
Husband, Herman, 86, 172, 203, 236, 237, 248*n*, 259*n*–61*n*
    administration's desire for arrest of, 217
    aliases of, 85–86
    Alleghenies explored by, 87
    arrest of, 219–20, 225
    as assemblyman, 83
    childhood of, 71–72
    Constitution as viewed by, 93, 261*n*
    death of, 243, 277*n*
    early political views of, 80–81
    federal government envisioned by, 91–93, 94–95
    first marriage of, 79
    Hillsborough riot and, 82
    as "Hutrim Hutrim," 91
    indictment of, 243
    militia plans of, 117
    North Carolina move of, 79
    in Parkinson's Ferry congress, 182
    in Pennsylvania assembly, 87–88
    as "the Philosopher of the Allegheny," 91
    in Quaker meeting, 78–80
    on rebel negotiating committee, 193, 197
    as Regulator, 82–84
    religious reflections and struggles of, 25–26, 71, 77–78, 252*n*
    revelation of, 89–91
    third marriage of, 84

    Wells's evidence against, 179
    Whitefield heard by, 73–75
Husband, Isaac Tuscape, 86
Husband, John, 86, 90, 243
Husband, William, 90
"Hutrim Hutrim," 91

impost, 37, 39–40, 47, 52, 58, 59
impressment, 218
Incidents of the Insurrection (Brackenridge), 246*n*, 259*n*, 268*n*, 269*n*, 270*n*, 272*n*, 273*n*, 275*n*
Indian Queen, 127
Indians, 198, 229
    in American Revolution, 15
    attacks on western settlers by, 56–57, 89
    Brackenridge's disdain for, 18–19
    British arms sales to, 14
    Forks lands sold by, 15
    Husband family and, 86
    Husband's proposed government and, 92, 93
    McFarlane's trade with, 151
    royal proclamations regarding, 13, 14, 139
    wars against, 1, 101, 120, 146, 147, 168, 240, 262*n*
Iroquois, Six Nations of, 12

Jacobs Creek, 12
Jay, John, 124, 125
Jefferson, Thomas, 1, 2, 134, 135, 136, 242
Johnson, Robert, 20–21, 24, 28, 103, 117, 118, 143, 144, 151, 158–59, 178, 251*n*–52*n*, 263*n*, 271*n*
Justice Department, U.S., Wells's testimony to, 129

Kentucky, 137, 164
    military spending in, 113
    Mingo Creek Association and, 117
    new-state movements and, 57
    rebels' escape to, 209
    whiskey tax and, 124, 141
Kirkpatrick, Abraham, 100, 101, 114, 146, 162, 228, 268*n*
    Andrew McFarlane's threat against, 177
    defense of Bower Hill by, 150, 152–54, 167

eviction from Pittsburgh of, 171,
172, 175, 178, 180
letters to Washington from, 190
as prisoner of rebels, 155–56
threats to property of, 177
Knox, Henry, 101, 126, 136, 262n
Brackenridge's mimicry of, 164
call to militias of, 190
Craig's letter to, 156, 185
Maine visit of, 192, 272n
military expedition urged by, 189,
271n
in the Newburgh crisis, 41, 42, 48

Lafayette, Marquis de, 43
Le Beouf, Fort, 194
Lee, Charles, 42
Lee, Henry:
arrests ordered by, 219–21
and "Blackbeard" White, 222
and Brackenridge, 230, 234
postdating orders of, 195
and prisoners, 223
Rebellion suppressed by, 210–11,
216, 217–18, 219, 224, 225, 238,
275n
Virginia militia called out by, 192
Lee, Thomas, 192
Lenox, David, 150, 157, 190, 259n,
268n–69n
at Bower Hill attack, 153
Brackenridge's meeting with,
144–46, 267n
escape from Pittsburgh of, 159,
161
as prisoner of rebels, 155
summonses served by, 144–46, 148,
185
W. Bradford's meeting with, 191
levelers, 80, 88
Lexington, Battle of, 98
liberty poles, 132, 145, 182, 203, 208,
213, 221, 265n, 270n
Lives (Plutarch), 230–31
Long, Jacob, 132
"Louis Capet has Lost His Caput"
(Brackenridge), 138
Louisiana, Spanish, 56
Louisiana territory, 242
Loyalists, 87
Lucian, 17
Lynn, John, 143–44, 267n

McFarlane, Andrew, 151–52, 156, 162,
165, 174, 177, 205
McFarlane, James, 151–54, 155, 162,
166–67
Madison, James, 17, 20, 107, 242, 258n,
270n–71n
on A. Hamilton's investigation by
Congress, 135
on congressional tax debate, 45
on insurgencies, 188
on Newburgh crisis, 255n
whiskey tax and, 62
Mamachtaga, 18–19, 109, 229, 276n
manufacture, excises on, 27
Marshall, James, 137, 138, 151, 163,
167–68, 169, 177, 193, 197, 268n
Maryland, 85
Anglican church in, 79
insurgency in, 203
militia call in, 190, 192
troops from, 206, 216
Massachusetts:
constitution of, 36
Shays Rebellion in, 53
merchants, 35, 63
Mexico, 30
Mifflin, Thomas, 172, 186–87, 190, 192,
207, 261n
A. Hamilton's letter to, 219
cabinet war council kept secret from,
195
drunken order of, 213
as enemy of Washington administration, 186, 189
on militia law, 196
proclamation of, 191
Militia Act, 164, 185, 262n
Miller, Oliver, 148, 268n
Miller, William, 145–46, 148, 185,
267n, 268n
mills, 5, 12, 22
Mingo Creek, 12, 21, 205, 222
Mingo Creek Association, 117, 132,
138, 144, 151, 263n–64n
attacks on Bower Hill by, 147–48,
150, 152–56
constitution of, 121
as court, 119, 147
demands of, 150–51
Faulkner and, 121
government file on, 141
J. McFarlane's association with, 152

Mingo Creek Association (*cont.*)
at second Pittsburgh convention,
122–23
takeover of Forks militias of, 118–19
Mingo Creek church meeting, 161–65,
167, 234, 269*n*
Mitchell, John, 238
Modern Chivalry (Brackenridge), 109,
115, 170, 243
Monongahela River, 12, 23, 131, 155,
159, 172, 182, 200, 225
Monongahela rye, 66
Morris, Gouverneur, 42, 45, 47, 48
Morris, Robert, 32, 34, 35, 51, 106, 107,
141, 253*n*, 254*n*, 256*n*, 257*n*
A. Hamilton recommended to cabinet by, 51
A. Hamilton's defense of, 48
A. Hamilton's finance-policy advice
to, 51
Brackenridge's support for, 107, 108
and central banking, 36–37
and the impost, 37, 39–40
J. Wilson and, 186
Newburgh crisis and, 41, 42, 45, 47,
48, 255*n*
on paper money, 35–36
in Pennsylvania assembly, 54–55
Pennsylvania bank of, 54–55
plan for federal IOU's of, 38–40
revolution as viewed by, 36
state bonds purchased by, 61
state debt assumption and, 62
taxes as viewed by, 33, 37, 38, 52,
256*n*
war bonds and, 31
Morrison, Robert, 120–21
Mount Vernon, 139, 250*n*
distilling at, 240
Washington's trip to, 1–6, 185

National Gazette, 110–12, 228
Netherlands, 135–36
Neville, Amelia, 100
Neville, John, ix, 91, 119–20, 129, 130,
131–132, 142, 143, 144, 157, 165,
190–91, 214, 220, 252*n*, 259*n*,
265*n*, 267*n*
in American Revolution, 98–99
background of, 98–99
Bower Hill attacks and, 147–48,
152–54, 163, 186

Brackenridge and, 108, 227–28, 230,
231–33, 274*n*
campaign against Brackenridge of,
208
Clymer and, 128
demands for resignation of, 123, 151,
157
as distiller, 97, 102
escape from Pittsburgh of, 159, 161
Faulkner and, 119–21
letters of, 245*n*
military enforcement urged by, 112,
128, 129–30
popularity of, 97
role in Connor attack of, 103–4, 262*n*
salary of, 102
tax collection by, 145–46, 239
tax collector attacks reported by, 137,
138
tax survey of, 97, 118
witnesses threatened by, 227
Neville, Mrs., 99, 100, 131, 147–48
Neville, Presley, 100, 131, 140, 157, 168,
170, 171, 178, 191, 214, 252*n*
at Bower Hill attack, 153
Brackenridge and, 100, 148–49,
180–81, 191, 208, 227–28, 230,
233–34
eviction from Pittsburgh of, 172,
175, 180, 181, 221
Mingo Church meeting and, 162,
163
as prisoner of rebels, 155
threats to property of, 177
as Washington's land agent, 240
Neville Connection, 100, 103, 145, 156,
161, 171, 180, 200, 227, 239,
262*n*
Brackenridge's disparagement of,
109, 149, 163, 228
expulsion from Pittsburgh of, 173,
180, 185, 197–98, 209
federal help requested by, 167–68
Ross as member of, 170
Woods as spy for, 101
New Bern, N.C., 83
Newburgh crisis, 40–42, 44–49, 115,
124, 255*n*
Newburyport, N.H., 77
New Jersey, 38, 74, 190, 192,
troops from, 206, 207, 212, 214, 216
New Jerusalem, 71, 90, 172

Newton, Isaac, 90
New York, 37, 38, 52, 61, 62, 74
New York, N.Y., U.S. Congress in, 57
Northampton, Mass., 53
North Carolina, 16, 79, 87, 124
North East, Md., 73
Northwest Territory, 141
notes, war debt, 29–30

Ohio County, Va., in Parkinson's Ferry
    congress, 180, 182
Ohio River, 4, 13, 209
Oldham, Winifred, 99–100
Old Testament, 75
O'Regan, Teague, 109
Ormsby, John, 150
Ormsby family, 101

Paine, Thomas, 36
Parkinson, Benjamin, 264n
    at Bower Hill attack, 155, 166, 268n
    Brackenridge and, 176
    Faulkner's meeting with, 120–21
    in hiding, 225
    at McFarlane's funeral, 156
    at Mingo Creek church meeting,
        161–65
    Neville Connection and, 167–68
    at second Pittsburgh convention, 122
    submission recommended by, 205
Parkinson's Ferry, 182, 185, 192, 197,
    239, 243
Parkinson's Ferry congress, 165, 180,
    181–82, 185, 200, 217, 221, 259n,
    270n, 273n
    first meeting of, 182–83
    submission resolution of, 207
    submission vote of, 201–2
    tension at, 192–93
    Washington's proposed pardons and,
        199
Parliament, British, 68
Pennsylvania, ix, x, 38, 74, 186, 190, 192,
    206, 207
    bank of, 54–55
    bonds of, 106
    Brackenridge in legislature of, 106
    constitutions of, 36, 54, 59, 87, 94,
        110, 122, 126, 186, 254n
    military spending in, 113
    militia of, 186–87
    troops from, 214, 216

Pennsylvania, assembly of:
    Brackenridge in, 11
    creditors and, 54–55, 59, 109–10
    Morris's bank and, 54–55
    state constitution and, 94
    U.S. Constitution ratification con-
        vention of, 11, 107–8
    Whiskey tax petition and, 105
Pennsylvania, University of, 100
Pennsylvania province:
    counties erected in, 15
    Forks lands purchased by, 15
    settlement rules of, 13
    Virginia's skirmishes with, 15, 16, 98
Peters, Richard, 219, 222–23, 226–27,
    235, 237, 275n
Philadelphia, Pa., 62, 66, 73, 112, 195
Philadelphia College of Physicians, 63,
    66
Philadelphia Light Horse, 213, 223, 227
"Philosopher of the Allegheny, the,"
    Husband as, 91
Pickering, Timothy, 240–41
Pigeon Creek, 12, 20, 120
Pitt, Fort, 13–14, 15, 34, 98–99
Pittsburgh, Pa., 11, 106, 140, 155, 156
    Clymer's trip to, 126
    demographics of, 11–12
    end of rebellion declared in, 209
    first anti-excise convention in, 23–25,
        187
    founding and early growth of, 13–14
    as Indian war staging area, 101
    militia of, 173–74
    second anti-excise convention in,
        122–23, 125, 187
    threats against, 156–57, 169, 190
Pittsburgh Gazette, 107, 110, 124, 129,
    132, 159, 171
    Brackenridge's Federalist articles in,
        108
    excise convention advertised in, 122
    Neville's ads in, 119–20, 143
    radicalism in, 138
    Tom the Tinker's letters to, 130, 204
    Washington, P.A., radical resolutions
        in, 20
Plutarch, 230–31
Potomac Company, 5
Potomac River, 4–5
Powers, John, 225–26
Presbyterians, 77–78, 99

presidential commission, 190–94
    Craig's testimony to, 197–98
    submission form of, 204–5
Presque Isle, 186
Price, Richard, 91
Princeton, N.J., 99
Puritans, 77, 80

Quakers, 76, 78, 79–80, 99
Quebec, 152

Randolph, Edmund, 194, 195, 270n
    A. Hamilton investigation and, 134,
        135–36
    in cabinet war council, 195, 271n
    at Constitutional Convention, 58
    negotiation with rebels urged by, 9,
        189, 190
    resignation of, 240–42, 277n
    on right to assemble, 124–25
    W. Bradford's reports to, 191–92
    on Washington, 250
Ranters, 80
Rawle, William, 141, 142, 143, 219,
    220, 221, 226, 237, 266n, 268n,
    275n
Reagan, Philip, 178–79, 143, 243, 259n,
    261n, 269n–70n
Redick, David, 207, 209, 214–16,
    228–29
Redstone, 200
Regulators, 82–84, 87
religion:
    Great Awakening and, 73–77
    Husband and, 25–26, 71–72, 89–91,
        252n
"Report on Opposition to Internal
    Duties," 245n–46n, 265n, 267n
"Report on Public Credit," 60–61,
    253n
Revelation, book of, 75–76, 89, 90, 92
Rhode Island, impost rejected by, 39
roads, 139, 140
Robespierre, Maximilien, 163
Ross, James, 140, 170, 171, 197, 198,
    205, 210
    as Brackenridge's advocate, 231
    at Braddock's Field, 175, 176
    oath signing and, 203
    Parkinson' Ferry congress and, 181
    on presidential negotiating commis-
        sion, 190, 192, 193, 205–6, 209

Washington courthouse speech of,
    169
    as Washington's land agent, 240
Rousseau, Jean-Jacques, 18
Royal Navy, U.S. ships seized by, 1

St. Clair, Arthur, 45
Sandy Creek, 79
Schuyler, Philip, 37, 39, 42, 43
Schuyler family, 29
Scots-Irish, immigration of, 15
Senate, U.S., 61, 93
    see also Congress, U.S.
Seven Years' War, 13–14, 22, 148, 216
    attacks by Indians in, 18
Sewickley tributary, 12
Shawnees, 13
    attack by, 18
    in Seven Years' War, 14, 98
Shays, Daniel, 53, 257n
Shays Rebellion, 53, 56, 57, 58, 131,
    256n, 257n
Sign of the Green Tree tavern, 23–25,
    27, 101, 103, 105, 112–13, 117,
    122, 123, 252n
slaves, slavery:
    at Bower Hill, 99, 132, 147
    Husband family's ownership of, 72
    Husband's proposed abolition of,
        93
    Quaker opposition to, 78
Society of Friends, see Quakers
Society of the Cincinnati, 47
Solon, 231
South America, Hamilton's invasion
    plan for, 240
South Carolina, whiskey tax and, 124
Spain, 30, 56, 140, 198, 229
    Franklin state and, 16, 57
speculators:
    Brackenridge's view of, 19
    landed classes scorn of, 61
    Pennsylvania Bank and, 55
    state bonds purchased by, 61
squatters, 15–16, 117
    Brackenridge's defense of, 19, 24,
        109
    in North Carolina, 79
    Washington's position on, 139
Stamp Act (1765), 27, 80, 260n
state-sovereigntists, 57–58, 61
Supreme Court, Pennsylvania, 190

Supreme Court, U.S., 185, 186
Susquehanna River, 209
Swift, Jonathan, 17

tarring and feathering, 35
    of Johnson, 20–23, 158
    of Lynn, 143–44
taxes, 38–39, 44, 53, 60, 82, 87, 141
    Husband's plan for, 93
    impact on backcountry of, 81–82
    land and poll, 37, 39
    Newburgh crisis and, 41, 42
    Pittsburgh anti-excise convention's
        proposal for, 123
    R. Morris on, 33, 37, 38, 52, 256n
    see also excises; impost
Ticonderoga, Fort, 168
Tom the Tinker, 130–31, 132, 147, 161,
    178, 179, 189, 192, 204, 208,
    265n
Tories, 17
Traddle the Weaver, 115, 170
Treasury Department, U.S., 51–52, 58,
    64, 102, 103, 104, 105, 135, 136
    A. Hamilton's military role and,
        210
    suspicion among Fork's residents of,
        126
    Neville's letters to, 130
    Wells's testimony to, 129
Trenton, N.J., 99
Tryon, Lord, 83–84
"Tully," 195, 203, 210
Turtle Creek, 12
"Tuscape Death," 85–86

Uniontown, Pa., 129, 218

Valley Forge, Pa., 99, 151
Vermont, early statehood of, 16
Virginia, 38, 206, 190, 192, 216
    constitution of, 36
    Hamilton's invasion plan for, 240
    impost rejected by, 39
    insurgency in, 203
    Mingo Creek Association and, 117
Virginia province:
    Forks claimed by, 15
    Pennsylvania's skirmishes with, 15,
        16, 98
    settlement rules of, 13
Voltaire, 90, 122

War Department, U.S., supply issues in,
    210
War of Independence, see American
    Revolution
Washington, D.C., see Great Columbian
    Federal City
Washington, George, 6, 77, 93, 123,
    133–136, 151, 186, 192, 207
    and A. Hamilton, 29, 42–44, 48,
        124–25, 133–136, 210–11
    accusation of Randolph by 240–41
    Brackenridge as chaplain under, 17
    on democratic societies, 137, 141
    as farmer, 2–3
    financial difficulties of, 41
    and Great Columbian Federal City,
        3–4
    infirmities of, 1, 6–7, 185, 250n, 274n
    as land speculator, 56, 248n,
        250n–51n
    Mount Vernon trip of, 1–2
    Newburgh crisis and, 40, 41, 42, 44,
        45–46, 48–49, 115, 255n
    notebooks of, 209–10
    Potomac and, 4–5
    press criticism of, 130
    R. Morris's plan for war debt and, 40,
        254n
    in Seven Years' War, 13–14, 98
    in Society of the Cincinnati, 47
    squatters as viewed by, 139
    views on Forks of, 138–40
    western land of, 4, 5
Washington, George, Whiskey Rebellion
    and, 7–8, 9, 206, 209, 214, 217–18,
        240, 245n, 264n–65n, 269n
    A. Hamilton's leadership approved
        by, 223–24
    A. Hamilton's official report and,
        187–88
    at cabinet war council, 195
    civilian deaths and, 213
    emergency cabinet meeting of, 185
    Findley's and Redick's meeting with,
        207, 214–16, 274n
    Husband as prime suspect of, 259n
    Mifflin's meeting with, 186–87
    in negotiation with rebels, 183, 190,
        193–94
    pardons offered by, 199
    proclamation of, 190
    on success of suppression, 240

Washington, Martha, 2, 43
Washington, Pa., 23, 97, 119, 128, 208, 218, 222
  armed militias in, 169
  democratic society in, 137–38, 141, 151, 266n
  new-state movement in, 57
  occupying force near, 239
  radical resolves of, 20, 104, 117, 121, 269n
  Watauga, 16
Webster, John, 179, 192, 270n
Wells, Benjamin, 128–29, 143, 238, 269n–70n
  attacks on, 179, 238, 270n
  congressional claims of, 245n, 265n, 267n
  deposition of, 243, 259n, 261n
  as informant, 129–30, 141–42
Wells, John, 129, 143, 178–79
Westmoreland, Pa., 23, 54, 97, 128, 143, 178
Westsylvania, 16, 57
Wheeling, Virginia, 190
Whig Literary Club, 17
Whigs, 81
whiskey, 64–67
  distillation of, 64–66, 258n
  at Mount Vernon, 240
  role in rural economies of, 66–67
Whiskey Rebellion, 7–9, 202–3, 211–14
  A. Hamilton's naming of, 239
  historiography of, 245n–50n
  see also Hamilton, Alexander, Whiskey Rebellion and; Washington, George, Whiskey Rebellion and
Whiskey Rebellion perpetrators, 7–8, 235
  convictions of, 238
  costumes of, 7, 173
  dreams of, 8–9
  in Philadelphia, 237–39
  see also blackfaced gangs; Mingo Creek Association; specific individuals
whiskey tax, 7, 8, 20–21, 62, 140–41
  in A. Hamilton's national finance plan, 60–64, 67

"Act Repealing . . ." (1791), 27, 258n
  Brackenridge on, 106, 110–11, 228
  collection methods for, 68, 102–3, 239
  convention to protest, at Sign of the Green Tree, 23–25, 27, 101, 105, 112–13, 117, 122, 123, 252n
  enforcement law for, 185
  Findley's and Gallatin's opposition to, 225
  impact on distillers of, 114
  large-scale distillers and, 69–70, 131
  Parkinson's Ferry committee's demands regarding, 200
  passage of, 64, 68, 70, 115
  petitions against, 105–6, 110–11, 112, 114, 262n
  radical demand for repeal of, 193
  reform of trial rules for, 142–43
  repeal of, 242
  as symbol, 183
  as wealth redistribution, 68–70
  see also Hamilton, Alexander, whiskey tax and
White, Anthony "Blackbeard," 221–22, 235–36
Whitefield, George, 73, 75, 76, 77, 260n
Whitehill, Robert, 54–55, 106
Wigle, James, 129
Wigle, Phillip, 129, 238
Wilkins, John, Jr., 170, 171, 177, 181
Wilkins, John, Sr., 170, 172, 181, 269n
Wilson, James, 54–55, 59, 106, 185–86, 189, 196, 270n
Wilson, Robert, 104–5, 117
Winchester, Va., 179
Witherspoon, Dr., 17
Wolcott, Oliver, 240–41
Wolfe, Sabina, see Brackenridge, Sabina Wolfe
Woods, John, 24, 100–101, 105, 106, 230, 232

Yeates, Jasper, 190, 191–92, 203, 204, 205
yellow fever, 130
Yohogania, Pa., 98
Yorktown, battle of, 7, 44, 99
Youghiogheny River, 12, 131, 216, 225